Wildlife Wars ❖

✕✕✕✕✕✕✕✕✕✕✕✕✕✕✕

ALSO BY RICHARD LEAKEY ❖

The Sixth Extinction:
Patterns of Life and the Future of Humankind

The Origin of Humankind

Origins Reconsidered: In Search of What Makes Us Human

One Life

Human Origins

The Making of Mankind

Origins

ALSO BY VIRGINIA MORELL ❖

Ancestral Passions: The Leakey Family and the Quest for
Humankind's Beginnings

Blue Nile: Ethiopia's River of Magic
and Mystery

WILDLIFE WARS ❖

*My Fight to Save Africa's
Natural Treasures*

RICHARD LEAKEY

and VIRGINIA MORELL

ST. MARTIN'S PRESS

NEW YORK

www.stmartins.com

Design by Kathryn Parise

LIBRARY OF CONGRESS CATALOGING-IN-PUBLICATION DATA

Leakey, Richard E.
    Wildlife wars : my fight to save Africa's natural treasures / Richard Leakey and Virginia Morell.—1st ed.
      p. cm.
    ISBN 0-312-20626-7
     1. Leakey, Richard E.   2. Wildlife conservationists—Kenya—Biography.   3. Kenya Wildlife Service—Officials and employees—Biography.   4. African elephant—Kenya.   I. Morell, Virginia.
II. Title.

QL31.L42 A3 2001
333.95'416'096762—dc21
[B]

2001019677

First Edition: September 2001

10 9 8 7 6 5 4 3 2 1

ACKNOWLEDGMENTS

I am grateful to Kenya's president Daniel arap Moi for having given me the opportunity to establish the Kenya Wildlife Service in 1990.

Many people played critical roles in the events that are narrated in the pages that follow, but special thanks are due Carol Wainaina, Abdi Bashir, David Mwiraria, Lynette Anyonge, Joe Kioko, Joyce Poole, Robert Bensted Smith, and Phil Mathews. Tom Allen and Agi Kiss of the World Bank offered special support; and without the generosity of Margo Walker and George Bronfman, the first year of the battle for the elephants would not have been the success that it was. My thanks go to all of them, as well as to all those who are not specifically mentioned here.

Virginia Morell took on the task of putting the story on paper, using my extensive notes, diaries, and many discussions. To her I am indeed indebted and grateful.

My wife Meave's forbearance and support through every crisis deserves the ultimate credit and special tributes for which words alone cannot suffice.

FOREWORD

In this book I have attempted to give the flavor of a period in my life at a time in Kenya when poaching of elephants for their ivory was a matter of great concern to relatively few people, either in Africa or elsewhere. Incidents and events are described from my own perspective. Many people—friends, colleagues, and adversaries—have struggled and will continue to struggle with the challenges facing conservation in Kenya and in other countries. There is surely no simple prescription. I hope that I have not trivialized the problems. African elephants continue to be threatened and probably will be for many years to come.

Managing public institutions in countries that suffer from underdevelopment and poverty is never easy. I often hear people say that they simply cannot understand why a particluar solution to a particular problem is not adopted. In most cases the problems are more complex than they realize, and this applies not only to conservation but to other fields as well. Poverty is the most insidious threat to our planet. We must address the fact that a growing number of people live with far less than the bare minimum of resources.

Conservation of biodiversity may be a global imperative, but eating one cooked meal a day and drinking clean water are more basic to the survival of most of the world's population. Protecting elephants and conserving natural ecosystems remain my personal priorities. But I am not so sure this would be so were I ill, hungry, and living in despair. I enjoy fresh air, sunshine, and crisp starlit nights. I do so, however, knowing full well that when I need it I can find shelter. We must somehow find a way to provide for our own species if we are also to preserve others.

In Kenya, as in any number of African countries, poverty is real. Famine, drought, and floods are constant. Malaria and other tropical diseases continue to devastate the population. HIV/AIDS threatens too many to contemplate. Felling forests, turning parks into cattle ranches, and draining wetlands are short-term political responses to immediate problems. Giving up natural spaces and killing animal species will not bring prosperity. The way toward eradicating poverty cannot be through environmental degradation. The greater challenge is to create jobs, generate modest affluence, and encourage people to live away from lands that are critical for our planet's health.

Generating the political will to maintain systems for protected areas or to rigorously defend national parks and national forests from encroachment is not as difficult as providing adequate funds to sustain them once they are protected. One of the lessons I learned from my years as a director of a wildlife agency is the importance of long-term, guaranteed operating costs for wildlife conservation.

Today the Kenya Wildlife Service is operating successfully, and the revenues generated from tourism in the national parks are substantial. However, Kenya, while peaceful and civilized, lies in a region of great volatility, and the flow of tourists can be cut off or dramatically reduced because of activities and events beyond our boundaries. For that reason the country's great national parks will remain very vulnerable. Their loss would be the world's loss.

In this book's last chapter, I summarize some of my activities since leaving the Kenya Wildlife Service. Although I am no longer working in Kenya's public sector I have had to excercise some restraint about divulging the identities of some colleagues and details of certain events. I do not think, however, that this restraint compromises the essence of my story.

Clean air, clean water, plentiful forests, and a human population that is well fed, educated, and reasonably affluent is our goal in Kenya. Saving the elephants is symbolic—a means to achieve these greater objectives.

Area of
Detail

N

ETHIOPIA

SUDAN

RIFT VALLEY

Lake
Turkana

Koobi Fora

Sibiloi
National Park

Marsabit
National Reserve

UGANDA

RIFT VALLEY

South Turkana
National Reserve

KENYA

SOMALIA

Mt. Elgon
National Park

Kitale

Lake
Baringo

Maralal

Lake Nakuru
National Park

Aberdares
National
Park

MT. KENYA

Meru
National Park

Kisumu

Nyeri

Kora National Reserve

Lake
Victoria

Kanjera

Naivasha

Lake Naivasha

Mt. Kenya
National Park

Masai Mara
National Reserve

Nairobi

Nairobi
National Park

Tana River
Primate National
Reserve

Peninj

Lake Magadi

Amboseli
National Park

Tsavo East
National Park

Lamu

Serengeti
National Park

Lake Natron

MT. KILAMANJARO

Tsavo West
National Park

Malindi

Gedi

Lake Eyasi

Lake Manyara

Mombasa

Shimba Hills
National Reserve

Indian
Ocean

TANZANIA

Miles
0   200
0   200
Kms.

Map by James Sinclair

WILDLIFE
WARS ❖

❖❖❖❖❖❖❖❖❖❖❖❖❖❖❖❖❖❖

CHAPTER 1

It was late one afternoon in May 1989, only ten days after President Daniel arap Moi had appointed me director of Kenya's Wildlife Department, when I first saw the elephant tusks. Rangers and policemen from the Kenyan government had confiscated the ivory from poachers and stacked it in neat piles in a stone warehouse with steel doors (it had been built to store weapons and ammunition) on Museum Hill in Nairobi. It was all to be sold to the highest bidder. Rangers armed with assault rifles stood guard—and with good reason. On the open market, raw ivory like this was then going for about a hundred dollars a pound. The approximately two thousand tusks stored here were therefore worth a considerable sum of money. The money to be earned from the ivory auction was earmarked for the Wildlife Department, which was in desperate financial straits and rife with corruption and inefficiency. Were I to straighten it out and stop the poaching that was destroying our elephant population, those funds would certainly help.

I had never really paid much attention to elephant tusks. In fact, before that day, I had almost never had occasion to handle one. Prior to my appointment to Wildlife, I had been director of the National Kenya Museums—and best known as a paleontologist and discoverer of early human fossils. Moi's announcement that I would take over

Wildlife had come out of the blue, and I was scrambling hard trying to figure out how to proceed. I knew that elephant poaching was a major problem, potentially a national disaster, and I had been revolted by photos I had seen of gruesomely mangled animals, their faces and tusks hacked away. I was also familiar with the numbers that indicated the seriousness of their decline: eighty-five thousand elephants lived in Kenya in 1979, only twenty-two thousand a decade later. But nothing conveyed the horror of the slaughter—or the enormity of the task that I had been given—than what I saw in that storeroom on that afternoon.

It was windowless and airless; a slightly acrid, musty odor hung in the air. The only light came from a bare bulb suspended from the ceiling by a long black cord. Stacks of elephant tusks rose to the ceiling along the entire length of the cement floor. I walked among the piles, stopping occasionally to lift a tusk and feel its weight. The kind of elephant ivory I knew best came from ancient, extinct species, some of them several million years old. Those tusks often crumbled at the slightest touch, and I had spent hours in the desert sun painting a lacquer over their breaks and fissures to harden them so that they could be transported. In contrast, these tusks, which came from recently slaughtered elephants, were smooth and solid. Ranging in hue from pure white to a yellowish brown, they seemed sensuously warm to the touch. Some of the largest ones swept out in arcs over six feet long; they were from males, I guessed. Others were shorter, more delicate in shape, and I assumed that they came from females and younger males. But it was the small tusks, some no longer than the length of my hand, that were the most disturbing—not just because they came from very young elephants, but because they indicated that whoever was behind the poaching was willing to kill every last animal in a herd. These poachers and their backers were ruthless. And now it was my job to stop them.

I wandered from the main hall into an adjacent room, only to find another depressing sight: piles of zebra skins and pelts of leopards, cheetahs, and other wild cats, most of them rotting. These, too, had been confiscated from poachers, as had been about a hundred rhino horns that were stacked on some wooden shelves. And there were the trophies confiscated from curio shops: elephant feet that had been made into stools or umbrella stands, and belts, wallets, and purses made of elephant and zebra hide. The storehouse was damp and smelled of decomposing skins. I was anxious to get out. I had seen enough. The pelts, especially those from leopards and cheetahs, haunted me. I remembered Brigitte Bardot's "burn the coats" campaign in the 1970s. By setting fire to her fur coats in a street demonstration in Paris, Bardot had launched a campaign against using baby-seal skins and wild-cat pelts in the fashion world, and by doing so had changed an entire industry.

That evening, while showering at home, I had a sudden flash of inspiration. My wife, Meave, was getting ready for dinner. I leaned out of the shower and shouted, "I'm not selling that ivory. I'm going to burn it."

"But it's worth a lot of money, Richard," she replied. "Are you sure the government will let you do that?"

"I don't know yet. But I do know we need to be bold," I said, turning off the water. "We've got to show the world we're serious about putting an end to this poaching and the ivory trade."

"But," Meave asked, "does ivory burn?"

Her words brought me back to earth. I didn't know whether you could burn ivory. I didn't even know whether the government would let me burn the entire stock of tusks—except perhaps for some exceptionally large examples that might be of interest to museums—but I would find out.

Finding things out was the nature of my new job at Wildlife. There were lots of things I didn't know: how to wear the official Wildlife uniform or salute the rangers on my staff, for starters. More important, I really knew nothing about elephants or their behavior; and if I was to save these animals, both for Kenya's sake and for their own, I would have to learn fast.

I was aware of the enormous irony this presented. I had spent hours, as I've mentioned, preserving old tusks. Now here I was trying to figure out the best way to destroy two thousand or so modern tusks, objects that many cultures of the world valued and cherished. It was all a long way from the cloistered world of fossils and museums, and I found myself reflecting upon the events that had led me to this job—and to this crusade.

About a year earlier, in the spring of 1988, Fiona Alexander, a friend who was a lobbyist for animal causes, had stopped me at Nairobi's Wilson Airport. She and I are both pilots, and I had just returned from a trip to Kenya's Lake Turkana, where I had been leading a fossil-hunting expedition. Fiona told me that she had become a spokeswoman for a group that wanted something done about the elephant poaching. They hoped that as chairman of the board of the East African Wildlife Society, a conservation organization, I would join them in speaking out against it. At the time, like many other Kenyans, I assumed the government was doing everything it could to contain the problem. Fiona told me that the opposite was true. I suggested that we meet again, and that she bring something to back up what she had told me.

A few days later Fiona stopped by my office at the National Museums with a report she had compiled from her discussions with wardens working in the parks. These wardens had quietly been gathering information, supported by photographs, about the elephant slaughter. The animals were not being killed with spears and arrows by poor, hungry tribesmen; they were being killed with automatic weapons by well-organized bands. It was nothing less than orchestrated economic sabotage.

Some of the wardens had told Fiona confidentially that the poaching had gotten completely out of control: elephants were being gunned down in full view of tourist lodges and along roads, and nothing was being done to stop it. It was widely believed that certain park rangers and wardens were colluding with the poachers. Fiona also told me that a secret report had been prepared for Dr. Perez Olindo, who at the time was director of the Wildlife Department (its full name was Department of Wildlife and Conservation Management), and his boss, George Muhoho, minister of Tourism and Wildlife. This secret report allegedly contained a list of senior government employees thought to be behind the poaching. I asked Fiona whether there wasn't some way to see that report. She told me that that would be impossible. The government kept it tightly under wraps, and no one was leaking any copies.

Others in the conservation community backed up what Fiona had told me. Several said that they, too, were deeply concerned about both the scale of the poaching and the corruption within the Wildlife Department and didn't know what to do. Some feared that if I spoke up, someone in the government might retaliate.

Something needed to be done. I agreed to Fiona's request to speak out. I found the pictures of the bullet-riddled elephants appalling and the thought that armed gangs were freely wandering around our national parks terrifying. I was even more outraged that some of Kenya's own government officials apparently had a hand in the slaughter. Fiona was right. These things needed to be made public—particularly since it seemed unlikely that the secret report would ever see the light of day. I also knew that any action was politically dangerous. As director of the National Museums of Kenya, I was, technically speaking, a Kenyan public servant. Were I to speak out, reprisals would surely follow.

As my family and others can attest, I'm known for speaking my mind, a trait I probably inherited from my parents, Louis and Mary Leakey— neither of whom was renowned for tact. Yet, twenty-five years of public service had taught me patience. I realized that I couldn't suddenly make a rushed announcement about corruption and incompetence. Moreover, elephant poaching needed to be raised in a way that would bring to it a maximum amount of press attention. An opportunity presented itself in late August 1989. I took full advantage of it.

An ornithological conference was to be held at the Museum, and Dr. Olindo, Minister Muhoho, and I were to convene it. The day before the conference, poachers shot and killed two Wildlife rangers in Tsavo National Park; the newspapers carried a brief mention of their deaths. When reporters arrived at the Museum to cover the conference, I asked them whether they also wanted to meet with the Wildlife director and the Tourism minister, to ask them about the murders. They replied that they were very keen to do so. I promised that there would be a press conference in the Museum's board room immediately after the opening ceremonies.

At those ceremonies, I took a seat next to Muhoho and whispered to him that the press was eager to meet with him to talk about the importance of birding to Kenya's tourism industry. I suggested that he might use the occasion to offer some reassuring statements about government action following the loss of the two rangers. Muhoho nodded his head; he'd be happy to do this. The trap was set.

Muhoho and Olindo sat together at the press conference; I kept to the back of the room. After a few remarks about Kenya's wonderful bird life, Muhoho announced that every effort was being made to apprehend the elephant poachers. He pledged that the families of the murdered rangers would be fully compensated. A reporter asked him what the government was doing to stop the poaching. Muhoho replied that everything possible was being done, and that the situation wasn't as bad as had been suggested. The press conference then broke up. While they were leaving, several reporters asked me whether I had anything to say in response. I replied that I certainly did, and that I would be holding my own press conference at two o'clock that very afternoon. That, of course, piqued their interest.

In the late 1980s, Kenya was still a one-party state with a tightly controlled media. People—whether private citizens or government employees—seldom criticized anything the government said or did. Doing so could land you in prison, or worse. Thus, when I announced that what Muhoho had told them that morning was frankly untrue, a ripple of surprise moved through the room. Pens started flying across notebooks. I told the reporters that Muhoho had done no more than pay lip service to a national crisis that was clearly out of control, and that I, for one, wondered why the government was doing nothing. I likened the slaughter of our elephants to economic sabotage: elephants were the flagship species of our wildlife and the basis for Kenya's biggest industry, tourism. The decimation of elephants and other wildlife therefore posed a direct economic threat to our country. Its being allowed to continue,

I suggested, made it appear that powerful government figures must be involved. Indeed, I added, a secret report existed that named names, and I hinted that I had seen this report. I called on Minister Muhoho to tell the citizens of Kenya the truth once and for all.

Needless to say, the press loved it: here was Richard Leakey, well-known personality and government employee, speaking out on the record. This was a new experience for them. For a week, newspaper headlines trumpeted LEAKEY TELLS ALL ABOUT POACHING, NAMES OF POACHERS WITH MINISTER, SAYS LEAKEY. I had never been involved in such a bare-knuckled public fight. Muhoho didn't waste time in counterattacking—MUHOHO ACCUSES LEAKEY ran one headline. He resented what he perceived as my meddling and tried to frame it in racist terms, telling the press that I had revealed a "cheeky white mentality" in believing that only whites were concerned about preserving wildlife. He said that he had already dismissed several high-ranking government officials for colluding with the poachers, and that the list of culprits in the secret report I had mentioned contained "nothing new." But Muhoho's broadside found few sympathizers; most of the letters to the editor chastised him for trying to turn elephant poaching into a racial issue instead of a matter of national concern. I clearly wasn't the only one to see how closely our economic fate was tied to our wildlife. Tourism employed more Kenyans than any other industry. No one expected the government to stand idly by while the animals were being slaughtered. My statements to the press sparked a small national debate and put the elephants squarely where they should have been—on page one.

A short while later, I went to talk to President Moi about another matter; and while I was in his office, he asked me about the elephant poaching. Was it really as bad as what I had told the press? I assured him that it was and said that more should be done to stop it.

President Moi's response was to announce, the next day, that Wildlife rangers and other security officers should retaliate forcefully and put a stop to poaching once and for all. For some time after that, Moi's exhortation that poachers should be "shot on sight" was misconstrued as an order simply to execute any and all apprehended poachers. This is not what was said, nor, as far as I know, was this ever done. Nonetheless, Moi's directive acknowledged that these poachers weren't simply poor tribesmen trying to catch something for dinner, but well-armed criminals who not only killed elephants but rangers as well. The problem with this new approach was that Kenya's rangers were vastly outgunned by the poachers—it seemed more likely that the rangers and not the poachers would suffer most from the president's directive. But Moi's strong words kept Kenya's elephant troubles in the international spotlight, which I thought was a good thing.

For the next few months, I had little time to think about the elephants. High-level government officials were working behind the scenes, lobbying hard to make my life at the National Museums so miserable that I would quit. And, in fact, I did resign at one point. But others in the government's higher circles persuaded me to come back. Then the plotting suddenly ceased. Whether or not the president was aware of these machinations or had had a hand in shutting them down, I'll never know.

During that time, the elephants' plight didn't improve, despite the government's get-tough policy. Between late 1988 and early 1989, the papers were full of reports of elephants being killed and of shoot-outs between poachers and rangers. Muhoho did rid the Wildlife Department of a few corrupt wardens; he and Dr. Olindo were often quoted as saying that Kenya was winning the battle with the poachers. But when a gang succeeded in killing five white rhinos—essentially tame animals that were supposedly kept under heavy ranger guard in Meru National Park in Central Kenya—it was clear to everyone that nothing had really changed. A few weeks later, another gang of bandits attacked and robbed tourists visiting Tsavo National Park, killing one.

Something needed to be done, and done quickly, but as director of National Museums I didn't exactly have the best platform. I thought about again using my position as chairman of the board of the East African Wildlife Society to rally the support of other international conservation organizations based in Nairobi. We might have been able to offer the government some constructive advice. However, I met with only a lukewarm response from the other conservationists, who did not want to interfere in Kenya's internal affairs. Though disappointed, I felt that I had done everything I could.

No one was more surprised than I when, on the afternoon of April 20, 1989, a member of my museum staff came bursting into my office, thrust his hand into mine, and began shaking it vigorously. "Congratulations!" he exclaimed. "Congratulations! Everyone will be so happy." I could not imagine why congratulations were in order and demanded an explanation. Hadn't I heard? the fellow asked. There'd just been a news flash on the radio. President Moi had issued an announcement appointing me as director of Kenya's Department of Wildlife and Conservation Management.

I thought there must have been a mistake. Perhaps the radio report had been misheard. My brother Philip was an assistant minister at the Environment and Natural Resources Department at the time, and it seemed more likely that he would be the Leakey the president would appoint to run the Wildlife Department. I called the newsroom of Kenya's national radio service. The manager confirmed the report: the announcement had referred to me. I sat back in my chair, feeling slightly nauseous and light-headed, trying to absorb the news. Then I grabbed my briefcase and left. A few minutes later, I was in my car heading to my home on the edge of the Rift Valley. My wife, Meave, would help me sort out my thoughts.

Meave was head of the Department of Palaeontology at the National Museums. She had earned her Ph.D. from the University of Wales, and although I was usually referred to as the paleoanthropologist, my formal education had not gone beyond high school. Meave and I had worked as a team for almost twenty-five years, much as my parents, Louis and Mary, had. We had tramped together with our band of hominid fossil hunters across the deserts of Kenya, gathering and identifying the bones of ancient human ancestors. We had knelt side-by-side in dusty excavations carefully removing the soil around the fossils, and we had sat together far into the night under the stars debating the bones' significance. We had built a home and raised two daughters. Meave has always been my chief sounding board, and we had weathered many storms together, particularly my nearly dying following a kidney transplant in 1979. She knew that since my resignation and reinstatement at the Museum I had not been happy in my job, and that I was looking for a new and bigger challenge.

Being named Kenya's Wildlife director, however, was not the challenge she had expected, and when I told her my news I could see that Meave was not entirely pleased. She anticipated the many adjustments my new position would require. I would be highly stressed and, she feared, in constant personal danger. Our professional life together—working at the Museum or at our field site at Lake Turkana—would change. We did not talk at length about my new job that first evening, but it was enough for me to realize that if I accepted it, things would not be easy for Meave.

But how could I possibly turn down President Moi's appointment? Moi had been president since 1978 and ruled the country on a very direct, hands-on basis. No Kenyan, so far as I knew, had ever said "no" to a presidential appointment; and were I to do so there might be repercussions, beginning most likely with my dismissal from the National Museums. Moreover, in all honesty, the appointment was an exciting opportunity. My job at the Museum had left me increasingly weary and bored. Here was a chance to do something of great importance for my country: turn a completely corrupt government department around. Before we went to sleep, I had made up my mind.

"I know you're worried about this," I said to Meave, "but I've got to do it. If the president gives me his full backing, I'll tell him I'll do it. I'll accept his appointment."

Meave sighed and nodded her head. She knew that once I was set on a certain course of action, trying to deter me was useless.

With the support of the president and his government, I told her, I could do something good for Kenya that desperately needed doing— stop the killing of the elephants.

CHAPTER 2

It is at least an hour's drive from our home to Nairobi, the first part over a long stretch of dirt road with ruts and loose stones—a very rough track at the best of times. But it also affords grand views. On some mornings, after a night's rain, you can see the snowy peaks of Mount Kenya to the north and Mount Kilimanjaro to the south, their white caps rising high above the green and red of the land. I'm an early riser and usually leave at 5 A.M. I find the drive an excellent time to think— the cool air, spectacular vistas, and deliberate pace help me plan my day.

On the day following my appointment, however, I wasn't sure what to do next. Should I go to the Wildlife Department or check in with my staff at the Museum and tell them I was leaving? I needed to talk to the president and clarify what he expected of me, yet I couldn't just drop in on him. It seemed easiest to follow my old routine, and once I reached Nairobi I drove to Museum Hill.

By 6:30 A.M. I was at my desk, shuffling through the latest pile of correspondence and penning a few replies. My mind, though, was else-where. It felt odd, knowing this was probably the last day I would be seated like this in my office and in this building, which I had raised money for and built as a memorial to my father, who'd died in 1972. He'd also been the director of this Museum, then the Coryndon Memorial Museum, now the National Museums of Kenya, and at a time when it consisted of little more than a few rough stone-and-wooden buildings. Every day, as I walked down the flight of steps leading to my office, I would pass a statue of my father and always make a point of acknowledging him. I would miss the museum to which we'd both given much of our lives.

I actually spent the first few years of my life growing up on the Coryndon Museum grounds in a small wooden home the museum's board of trustees built for my father in 1944. World War II was drawing to a close when I was born in December of that year, and my father had recently been appointed to run the museum. He and my mother were already well known for their pioneering work on East African prehistory, but they were far from being either famous or wealthy. The museum could offer only a small salary, but at least the little house they gave our family was rent free. Louis and Mary Leakey were devoted to their research, spending whatever extra money and time they had on it. Whenever my father took a leave from the museum, they would pack their old truck and head off to one of their field sites. Our parents almost always took my older brother, Jonathan, and me into the field with them.

My father was born near the Kikuyu region of Kabete, north of Nairobi. His parents were missionaries with the Church Missionary Society, and they started some of the first schools for the Kikuyu, a farming people who live in Kenya's fertile, central highlands. One, the Mary Leakey School for Girls, which was named for my grandmother (who coincidentally had the same first name as my mother), is still educating young Kenyan girls today. Louis grew up with Kikuyu children as his playmates and was initiated into the tribe when he was thirteen. Sometimes, on our expeditions, he would tell us over dinner, in the glow of a kerosene lantern, about his hunting forays with Joshua Muhia, an elder in the tribe. Joshua taught him how to make a bow and arrows, to bend a few sticks into traps for wild birds, and to catch small antelopes barehanded. I loved going for walks with my father. He showed us the same things Joshua had shown him, and told us the names of the birds, and how to make a blind so that we could watch animals while not being seen by them.

My father's primary interest on these expeditions, however, was not living animals but fossilized ones. Since his college days at Cambridge, Louis had argued that humankind's earliest ancestors would be found in Africa. He was one of only a handful of people who believed this. Almost every other anthropologist believed China to be the cradle of humanity (although Charles Darwin, my father liked to note, favored Africa, since our closest relatives, the chimpanzee and gorilla, are also found here). Indeed, most prehistorians then did not think that Africa had any history to speak of. My parents filled in large portions of that void, finding sites with early pottery as well as metal and rock artifacts that few believed ancient Africans would have been capable of making. But they were most interested in human origins, and the majority of the expeditions I went on as a child were to search for the fossilized bones of an ancestor that would prove my parents—and Darwin—right.

There were few things as wonderful to me as the preparations for one of our journeys. Our small house would be filled with tents, lanterns, cases of canned goods and flour, rice, and tins of cigarettes. My parents arranged a place for my brother and me (and later our other brother, Philip, who was born in 1949) to sleep on top of the stacked cartons in the rear of their old Dodge. We'd be on our way just before dawn, climbing up the Kikuyu escarpment north of Nairobi, then heading down into the open expanse of the Rift Valley. I loved those early morning journeys, watching the sky change from black to a soft blue, while the rich smells of Africa—the smoke of cedar-wood fires, mixed with the odors of cattle and goats—wafted over us from small homesteads along the way.

I wasn't as enamored of my parents' work, which struck me as boring. They were usually on their hands and knees, digging in the rock-hard earth in some shadeless, barren spot with flies buzzing about. I decided early on that I would never have anything to do with such a life. My parents kept at it year after year until several major fossil discoveries put them on the front pages of newspapers the world over. Their most dramatic find of all occurred after I had grown old enough to stay behind, so I wasn't there when it happened. My mother actually made the discovery. In the summer of 1959, at Olduvai Gorge in Tanzania, she found the partially buried skull of a humanlike creature called *Australopithecus boisei*. My parents had been excavating at Olduvai for nearly thirty years hoping to find fossilized remains like these. They'd set their eyes on the gorge because, like the Grand Canyon, it reveals layer after layer of the geological past. In those layers, they had found numerous fossilized animal bones, mostly of extinct species, and stone hand axes, the tools that early humans (or "hominids," as scientists call them) used. The actual bones of these early human ancestors had, however, largely eluded them—until that summer.

The fragments of skull she unearthed turned out to be a truly monumental find. The molar teeth were huge (in comparison to ours). It had wide cheek bones, a bony crest along the top of the skull, and generally a very apelike appearance. It was also remarkable because of its age. Scientists were able to estimate that it was almost 1.75 million years old. This more than doubled the span it was then believed that our early ancestors had been around. (Since then the earliest stages of the human story have been pushed back to over 4 million years.)

I was almost fifteen when Louis and Mary made their big find. I have to confess that I remember little about the event. I was too busy watching and trapping small wild animals, such as bush babies and mongooses (which I sold to a wildlife photographer) and riding my horse among the zebras, giraffes, and antelopes near our home. My parents had moved to a house on the edge of the Athi Plains when I was about five. A few years later, they bought me my first pony, and after that I was seldom without a horse. At that time, there were few houses between ours and the knobby Ngong Hills, where the Masai lived, and I loved nothing more than galloping at top speed over the plains, chasing zebras or coming up fast behind a thundering rhino and smacking it on the rump.

My interests were in the out-of-doors, and I'm afraid I wasn't much of a student. After leaving school when I was sixteen, I spent time trapping small animals for researchers and collecting animals and birds that I sold to museums that were looking for skeletons of African species for their research collections. On turning eighteen, I started a safari-guiding business with a friend. My father lent me $500 to launch my business. I don't think he fully approved of me abandoning my education, but he never tried to stop me.

Many of my safari clients signed up with me because of the Leakey name. After the discovery of "Dear Boy"—the nickname of the skull my mother found—my parents' work was featured in *National Geographic* and on television, and my father traveled every year to the United States giving lectures. People knew about his research and admired his ideas, tenacity, and enthusiasm. I'm sure many of my clients thought that the famous Louis Leakey would be guiding them into the wilds of Africa. It must have been a shock when this tall, skinny youth showed up instead. But by then, it didn't matter.

I took my customers on some wonderful safaris, but the glamour of being a guide wore off after a few years. I disliked having to wait on people and worry about their needs and wishes. In October 1963, just a few months before my nineteenth birthday, I obtained a pilot's license. I had learned to fly in order to overcome my fear of flying and made my first solo flight to Olduvai Gorge. On my way there, I happened to fly over Lake Natron, an alkaline lake located in Tanzania, and was struck by the sight of the barren, eroded sediments along its western shores. They reminded me of the fossil beds at Olduvai. I immediately decided to organize an expedition and explore them.

I don't think I had really decided to change careers; I simply wanted a little diversion from my safari work. Nevertheless, that Lake Natron expedition profoundly altered my life. One member of my team, Kamoya Kimeu, discovered the fossilized lower jawbone of an ancient hominid, a robust australopithecine much like "Dear Boy" (whose lower jaw was never found). It wasn't just that discovery that was exciting. I found that I enjoyed looking for fossils, even excavating them, and discussing them with the scientists. Of course, I didn't consider myself an equal of any of the researchers, all of whom had their Ph.D.s; I had gone no further than my high-school studies.

Elsewhere, I've described myself at that time as an angry young man. I was impatient, driven, hotheaded, and full of ambition. I wanted success in a hurry, and I pushed hard to get it. I made a few concessions, stopping long enough to attend a school in England to get that wretched high-school diploma. I even made a stab at applying to a university, but my heart wasn't in it. I could think of few things more dreary than sitting in a classroom all day. My parents, of course, thought I was going about my fossil-hunting career in the wrong way, but I was helpful to them and they never really confronted me about it. I think my father secretly hoped that once I was "hooked" on anthropology I would get a university education.

In early 1967, I was sent off by my father to represent his interests in an international expedition heading off to the Omo River in southeastern Ethiopia where there were known to be rich fossil deposits. Through assisting my parents, I had by then become increasingly involved in archaeology, and I was thrilled by an opportunity to go to an area where there was every chance of both making some exciting finds and having exciting adventures.

In August 1967, an event occurred that ranks as one of the most serendipitous of my life. I was being flown in a light aircraft from Nairobi to rejoin the Omo River expedition, and the pilot was forced to fly offtrack to avoid some bad weather. Because we were flying over an area that I had never flown over before, I was studying the landscape and noticed that there were miles and miles of what seemed to be very promising, and unexplored, fossil beds. That was how my fossil-hunting career at Lake Turkana got launched. By the summer of 1968, I had been given some support from the National Geographic Society to lead my own expedition to the northeastern shore of Lake Turkana. Within a few weeks it was clear that we had chosen a fantastic site. My mind was made up: I would make my career in fossils.

Coincidentally, I had also negotiated a position for myself at Kenya's

National Museums and began working there on October 1, 1968. By then I had completed the first of what were to be more than twenty field seasons. By the time I was twenty-five years old, I had become the director of the Museum and the leader of a team of young scientists studying human origins.

I was young for such a position. But Kenya was young then, too. Our country had become independent five years earlier, in 1963, and every government department and office was busy replacing the formerly British staff with Kenyans. Many British residents of Kenya had doubts about taking on Kenyan citizenship. I had absolutely no doubts. Kenya was my home, and I was eager for the chance to help rebuild it. It was what my family had fought for since coming to Kenya: the right of the native peoples to build and lead their own country. My grandparents and my father had devoted most of their lives to this cause, even petitioning the British government to restore to the Kikuyus the land the British farmers had taken from them. They did not win those fights, but their battles became part of our family legacy—a legacy that connected us more closely to black Kenyans than to whites. (Let me say that I dislike using the terms "black" and "white," and use them as seldom as possible in this book, and where possible will use "indigenous" to refer to black Kenyans.)

As a child I was always painfully aware of the differences between my life and that of the indigenous Kenyan children around me, though I did not grow up in a Kenyan village as my father had. I apparently wore my sympathies on my sleeve, since at the private school I attended I was bullied for being a "nigger lover." Young though I was, I wanted to live in a society where the color of one's skin wasn't the sole basis for determining one's worth, where there was equal opportunity for all, and where people joined together to work for the betterment of their country.

At the time of independence, few other young Europeans shared my views (although my brothers did), but my patriotism and enthusiasm were shared by young Africans. Some served on the Museum's board, including Perez Olindo, who had recently been appointed the first indigenous director of Kenya's National Parks (a position he held until 1976). Olindo wanted to see a native-born Kenyan in charge of the National Museums, too, and they teamed up to support my bid for the directorship. They never said anything about my relative youth; and though I was inexperienced and unskilled, I like to believe that they thought my family legacy and my potential were qualifications.

My goal was to develop a museum along the lines of the Smithsonian Institute. The hominid fossils my team and I were finding at Turkana brought me the same kind of international attention my parents had received. I was able to use that to build a bigger and better museum in Nairobi, as well as a chain of smaller museums throughout Kenya. My reputation grew when I published (with Roger Lewin) two best-selling books, *Origins* and *People of the Lake*, in the 1970s, and made a television series about human origins.

Ironically, while I was working so hard to build a life around museums and fossils, I was also dying from a kidney disease—about which I'll say more later. Suffice it to say that I survived thanks only to a kidney transplant from my younger brother, Philip, in 1979. The transplant marked the beginning of a new life for me. When I was in the hospital I made a vow that if I lived through this I would spend more time with my family, more time sailing and enjoying good food and wine, and less time engaging in the petty quarrels that all too often dominate the science of human origins. I hadn't abandoned my desire to contribute to Kenya (that would have gone against what my mother described as my "missionary genes"). In fact, I had begun drawing up plans for a pan-African museum that would be built in Nairobi. I had met with several people about the idea and was busy organizing the project when President Moi made his announcement about my appointment to Wildlife.

I was once again embarking on an entirely different career. And on a new life.

❖   ❖   ❖

Usually one leaves a job because one's been promoted or become fed up or been fired. In all of these cases, there's a structure and logic to guide one's reactions. To a greater or lesser extent, one is prepared. My appointment, as I've said, had come out of the blue. It was a promotion—and certainly an incredible opportunity—but it was, most of all, a complete surprise. It seemed less like a job than an impossibility. The politics, corruption, and inertia in the Wildlife Department—and in the government at large—were all so entrenched that failure almost seemed inevitable. And because I was so out of my element, I had no one to ask for advice.

My previous meetings with Kenya's president had all been arranged through "people with access," and it always took a little time to get a slot in his busy schedule. I doubted if anyone would be at the State House, the presidential offices, before eight o'clock, and although it was only seven o'clock on the day after my appointment, I decided to call. Someone answered the phone. "This is Richard Leakey calling," I said simply. "I would like to speak with the president." I was asked to hold for a moment and then was put straight through to him. This I hadn't anticipated, and for a brief moment I was at a loss for words. Recovering as quickly as I could, I explained to Moi that I couldn't really accept the new job, flattered though I was, unless we had a chance to discuss some of my concerns. He told me I should come to see him immediately.

The State House is about a fifteen-minute drive from the Museum. Formerly the colonial governor's mansion, the white stone structure sits on a grassy knoll behind guarded iron gates. It is a rather large colonial building with cavernous halls, long, carpeted corridors, and a number of spacious offices on the ground floor. Before our country's independence, the building had housed the official office of the colonial governor. In 1963, our first president, Jomo Kenyatta, moved in. Neither President Kenyatta, who died in 1978, nor his successor, President Moi, have lived in the State House, preferring instead to live in their own homes.

Though grand, the State House is not grandiose, and the furnishings are simple. Paintings of Kenyans in traditional dress adorn the walls, painted by the late Joy Adamson, later so well known for *Born Free*, her book about Elsa the lioness. The State House conveys stability and national purpose without being overstated. A doorman met me at the entrance and ushered me into a small antechamber outside Moi's office. I wasn't kept waiting long. The president himself appeared in his office doorway. He gave me a slight smile.

"Richard. It's good to see you," he greeted me, then turned and led me inside.

I sat in an armchair, he across from me on an overstuffed sofa. He seemed a little ill-at-ease, as if unsure of what I would say. Speaking in Swahili, Kenya's national language, we exchanged a few pleasantries; and then I asked him point-blank whether he was certain he wanted to appoint me as director of Wildlife, given that we might have strong differences of opinion on key issues. I emphasized how stubborn I could be, and that I couldn't be expected to compromise myself or my new office in any way.

President Moi listened closely, occasionally nodding his head. When I had finished, he replied that he absolutely wanted me in this job. He knew that I was strong-willed and determined. Those were the very reasons he'd chosen me, he said. He wanted someone who could actually get something done.

"Fine," I replied. "But hard decisions have to be made, and I'll need your firm backing on all of them."

"You have my full support," Moi said, looking me straight in the eye.

I then raised the issue of George Muhoho with whom I had publicly crossed swords over the elephant poaching. He was still the minister of Wildlife and Tourism, and therefore my immediate superior, but I didn't see how I could work with him. We needed a new team. Moi nodded in agreement.

"We'll find him another position," he said. (A few weeks later, Moi gave Muhoho a new ministry to oversee; Katana Ngala was appointed the new minister of Wildlife and Tourism.) In the meantime, Moi told me he wanted me to report to him directly. He assured me I would have access to him at anytime, and we agreed to meet and talk frequently.

We spoke about a number of issues, but the discussion was brief and businesslike. When I rose to take my leave, President Moi shook my hand warmly. "You have my full support to do what has to be done," he repeated.

As I drove to the Museum I knew that not only did I have a new job, I was also beginning a new journey. All my doubts and worries had vanished. Now there was only one thing to do: get on with that job.

When I got back to my office at the Museum, I phoned the Wildlife offices and asked if Dr. Olindo was in. His secretary said no, he wasn't expected. Her tone was understandably cool. She connected me to the deputy director, Colonel Cheboi. "I'll be there at nine-thirty," I told him. "Have the entire staff assembled in a meeting room by ten. I want to speak to them." I then called in a couple of my senior staff members at the Museum and confirmed that I had accepted the new appointment. I assured them that a worthy replacement would be found. Then I headed out the door.

I had inherited a large staff at the Wildlife Department—three hundred employees at headquarters, and about four thousand others in the numerous parks and reserves spread out across the country. I had heard enough from Fiona Alexander and others to know that they were a demoralized and not entirely honest lot. My first job would be to mold them into a team ready to fight to preserve Kenya's wildlife. And the first step in building that team was to follow through on my own promises.

The Wildlife Department was then housed in several musty, rundown buildings located on the edge of Nairobi National Park, which borders the city. They looked particularly dismal on this cold, drizzly morning. Most of the expressions I saw on the people I passed in the hallways were equally dour; no one appeared either happy or motivated. The corridors were messy, dirty streaks covered the walls and floors, and the stench of a plugged-up toilet hung in the air. Shaking my head, I opened the door to the director's waiting room and came face-to-face with Perez Olindo's secretary. She greeted me with a frown. I smiled anyway, spoke to her in Swahili (which did bring a slight smile), and asked to be shown my office.

She pushed open the door to a small, dark room. I was flabbergasted by what I saw: files, files, and more files. They covered the huge desk (which nearly took up the entire room), the chairs, every surface available. Stacks of files, maps, and bundles of papers were even piled along the window ledges; more papers were bursting from the desk drawers.

"What are all these?" I asked the secretary, pointing to one pile.

"Those are marked 'For the Director's Action,'" she replied. "You must read them and make decisions."

I sighed audibly then sank into the chair—at least it was free of papers. I liked Olindo, and in the past we'd supported each other's careers in public service. Still, looking at the piles of dusty files, I couldn't help wondering what he had been doing. Judging from the height of the stacks—and the dust covering them—some of these "action" files had been sitting there for months, maybe years. Wearily, I pushed them aside and asked the secretary to call Joseph Mburugu, one of the assistant directors. Joseph was an old friend, and right then I needed one. Moreover, Joseph had worked at the Wildlife Department—and at its previous incarnation, the now-defunct National Parks organization—for almost thirty years, both in the field and at headquarters. There was little he didn't know about how things really worked.

Joseph is a short, stout man, fairly bursting with energy. He came rushing into my office, eyes alight, a wide smile on his face, his hand stretched out in greeting.

"Welcome! Welcome, Richard!" he exclaimed, pumping my arm. "Congratulations to you—and to us. We need someone like you here."

I blushed in response, but laughed, too. At last someone was happy to see me. There were only a few minutes before the ten o'clock staff meeting, so I came right to the point. I told Joseph I needed a quick rundown on the Wildlife employees and the general problems in the department. My outside sources had told me that Wildlife was rife with corruption, and that a number of rangers and staff were involved in the poaching and other schemes, but I wanted to hear this confirmed by an insider. How bad was the corruption? I asked him, as we left my office and headed down the corridor to the assembly hall.

"It's everywhere, and it affects everything," Joseph replied, shrugging. In addition to corruption, there was rampant theft, absenteeism, and what he described as a general "don't care" attitude at Wildlife. People came late to work, left early, and did little while they were there. Joseph also sadly affirmed what I had been told: many rangers and some wardens were working closely with the illegal ivory trade. "I believe the corruption is even worse than what you have heard," he concluded.

At precisely ten o'clock, most of the Wildlife employees had crowded into the department's main meeting hall. I had to squeeze through to reach the podium at the front. The room was dark because only one light was working (no one had bothered to replace the burned-out bulbs), so that it felt about as bleak inside as it was outside. I could see row after row of scowling faces. Some were glaring hatefully at me. They knew I had been appointed to clean up the department, which meant that some of them were probably going to be fired. Though I had done my share of public speaking, I knew at once it would be next to impossible to win over this crowd. I decided right then always to address them in Swahili; it was the language they were most comfortable with, and it would make me seem less foreign to them.

I started out by saying that I hadn't asked to be appointed director and I didn't want the job; but having got it, I would do it. I told them that I had seen the president earlier that morning, and that he had given me a very free hand to sort things out. I then issued a strong warning, drawing on what Joseph, Fiona, and others had told me.

"I want to make it absolutely clear that things are going to change around here. Many of you are corrupt, all of you are lazy, and before long the worst of you will be gone." Tough words, I knew. But all I could think about was that there were people in that audience who'd stolen from the department and abetted the poachers. So I wanted them to understand there was a new sheriff in town.

To lighten the atmosphere, I tried telling a couple of jokes. Unsurprisingly, no one laughed. It didn't seem wise to take any questions. I did, however, invite to my office anyone wishing to brief me about particular matters.

I went back to my file-strewn cubicle, feeling rather despondent. What was I to do next? How was I going to come to grips with everything—these "action files," all these unhappy people—and avoid being overwhelmed by the mess that surrounded me? I stayed awhile longer then fled back to my sunny, well-ordered museum office. It felt so much more like home—how could I ever have thought of leaving it?

I spent a few pleasant hours at the Museum, sorting out my affairs, talking to my staff, and generally relaxing in the friendly, cheerful atmosphere. Somehow I had to find a way to inspire the same feelings of trust I enjoyed here in the Wildlife Department. I puzzled awhile over this, then headed for home. I wanted to sit on our verandah overlooking the Rift Valley and watch the sunset.

My family and I have fifty acres on the edge of the Rift Valley, a great geological feature that runs from the shores of the Red Sea in Eritrea all the way to the plains of Mozambique. From our porch, we look westward across the valley, which drops away some fifteen hundred feet and stretches across forty miles. The view is nothing less than magnificent. Looking southwest along the valley on a clear day, you can see for more than a hundred miles. The highlands of Tanzania's famous Ngorongoro Crater and the last active volcano in this area, Oldonyo Lengai, are both clearly visible. The changing patterns of light on the mountains, the cloud formations, distant thunderstorms, the electrical storms some nights, and the full moon on others are some of the wonders afforded by this very special spot. Here is the Africa of unlimited space, of tranquility and great beauty. Most of all, here is our home.

A small cluster of Maasai homes are arrayed on the ridge across a small river valley from ours. Every evening at dusk, young boys guide their cattle home from watering and grazing in the valley. Watching them wind their way back up the hillside and past the whistling thorn-trees in the last, slanting rays of the sun always gives me a feeling of peace. Sometimes, a gentle evening breeze blows from the west, bringing with it the smells and the sounds of village life across the valley: the lowing of cattle being milked, the clanking of cow bells, and the laughter of children mix with the aroma of acacia smoke from the fires. By the time the sun sets on the far side of the Rift Valley, I am usually in an excellent mood.

That night I needed a little more cheering up. I like to cook and usu-ally prepare our dinners at home, so I roasted a leg of lamb, seasoned with fresh rosemary from our garden, and uncorked a bottle of wine. Meave and I were alone that evening, as our daughters, Louise and Sa-mira, were away in England finishing their education. Meave was cu-rious about how my first day at Wildlife had gone. I w'as reluctant to paint too dark a picture, so I merely said that there were problems, of course, but that in time I believed these could be solved. I told her that Moi had given me his full support and that that would help me enormously. But beyond that, I said little. She didn't press me. In the nearly twenty years Meave and I had worked together at the Museum, I had made it a point not to involve her in all the political intrigues and scandals. I didn't want any charges of favoritism leveled at either of us. Still, the Museum and its affairs had always been central to our life together, and that night both of us realized that we were going to miss that professional bond.

Meave and I had first met in 1968, twenty-one years before. She had just completed her Ph.D. on the anatomy of primates and had taken a job working with my father at a primate research center affil-iated with the Museum. I was then twenty-four and married—but un-happily so. My first wife, Margaret, had studied archaeology. We'd joined forces, much as my parents had—with me looking after the fossils, she the stone tools. Our marriage also mirrored other, less happy, aspects of my parents' marriage. Like them, we were prone to quarrels, which both frightened and depressed me. Perhaps because I had grown up listening to heated exchanges between my parents, I had—and still have—an absolute horror of domestic disputes. I realized far too late that I had serious personal problems, and that Margaret and I were simply not getting along. We were expecting a baby and I felt that if we were going to separate, it would be better to do so before our child was damaged by the bickering and arguing. Separation and divorce are never easy. I will never feel certain whether I did the right thing at the right time.

I had also met Meave and liked her instantly. She was, and is, full of energy, humor, with a tomboyish sense of adventure. She also seemed to be impressed by—rather than critical of, as Margaret had been—my grand plans for the Museum and fossil-hunting expeditions. At the time I had just completed that 1968 expedition to the eastern shores of Lake Turkana in northern Kenya. The National Geographic Society had given me a grant—choosing my project over one my father had recommended—to return to Ethiopia for a second season but I had used the money to explore Turkana instead. I know now that I hadn't gone about achieving my goal in the best way. But in the end, I was proved right: we found several hominid fossils during that first season (it had taken my parents nearly thirty years to make their first big discovery), turning me almost overnight into a celebrity in the fiercely competitive field of human origins.

Margaret had been a member of my 1968 team. In 1969, I asked Meave to join me instead. Margaret soon afterward filed divorce proceedings, which I did not contest. And two years later, Meave and I were married.

Almost every year since our first expedition together, Meave and I had spent our summers in the field, hunting for fossils. Now, for nearly the first time in twenty years, I knew I would not be going to Turkana with Meave. I simply wouldn't have the time. We both knew this, although little was said. Those wonderful times at Turkana, our halcyon days together, were over. Meave would continue the Turkana expeditions without me.

She cared deeply about wildlife and fully supported the idea that something had to be done to stop the elephant slaughter as well as the general deterioration of Kenya's national parks. President Moi had given me an incredible opportunity. But we both knew it was going to be full-time, stressful, and probably dangerous.

CHAPTER 3

With an area of 270,000 square miles, Kenya is roughly the size of Texas. Only about 20 percent of this land is arable, however, and most farms are small scale, designed for feeding single families. Moreover, unfortunately, Kenya is not rich in minerals. No significant oil deposits have been found, although new exploration is currently underway. In addition to a range of horticultural products, including cut flowers, the country's main exports are coffee and tea. Tourism is Kenya's most vital industry. The natural scenery, the wildlife, and our coastline offer world-class opportunities for ecopositive recreation. This is one of the reasons conservation work is so critical.

Kenya's wildlife abundance was apparent to the first European settlers in the early twentieth century. Herds of game literally stretched across the coasts (where elephants slid down sandy embankments and swam in the Indian Ocean) to the bamboo-covered slopes of Mount Kenya. This was the Kenya my father knew. He traveled everywhere and from his descriptions, what he saw must have been quite incredible. The open plains were covered with large herds of gazelle, zebras, wildebeests, giraffes, and ostriches. Lions were common, as were rhinos. Early travelers wrote volumes about the spectacle, but sadly their written records are all that remain. European settlers in East Africa embarked upon a killing spree that greatly reduced both the herds and many of the predators.

Kenya became particularly famous as a big-game hunting destination after Theodore Roosevelt's safari there in 1909. With five hundred porters to support him and his retinue, Roosevelt spent nearly a year shooting lions, rhinos, antelopes, and elephants—some for the Smithsonian Institute's collection and some for mere sport. Other hunters from the privileged classes, including two future British kings (the Duke of York, later King George VI, and the Prince of Wales, later King Edward VIII), followed in Roosevelt's tracks.

At the same time, European settlers were creating large farms and cattle ranches in the country. They, too, killed large numbers of wild animals to clear the land and to protect their livestock, and with the support of the colonial government's Game Department, established in 1906. One of the department's functions was to kill animals living in agriculturally desirable areas. One professional hunter, commissioned to clear game from an area that was to become a sisal plantation, had killed 163 rhinos in less than a year. The plantation was probably no more than a few square miles in extent.

With this kind of unmanaged slaughter going on, it wasn't long before the vast numbers of wild animals began to decline sharply. Fortunately, as early as 1899, the colonial government had also taken some steps to preserve some of Kenya's wild beauty and wildlife. Two large game reserves—the Northern and the Southern, each protecting about thirteen thousand square miles—were set aside. Two years later, the first game ranger was appointed; and in 1906, the Game Department was formed. Besides clearing agricultural areas of animals, the department issued hunting licenses and enforced game laws. By 1930, it had grown into a far more substantial agency with a dozen wardens responsible for monitoring wildlife throughout the country. The two biggest jobs were controlling dangerous animals, such as man-killing elephants, lions, and buffaloes, and crop-raiding animals.

Many of Kenya's predators, particularly lions, leopards, and wild dogs, were regularly gunned down or poisoned by white farmers because they were regarded as vermin. White farmers were the only ones allowed by the government to have guns. Native Kenyans took a much smaller share of game with their bows and arrows, spears, and traps. The government tended to regard this kind of killing as "poaching."

Finally, by 1938, the settler and ardent conservationist Mervyn Cowie had had enough of the killing. Cowie had traveled in the United States and visited Yellowstone and Yosemite National Parks, some of the world's first natural preserves, and had been so impressed by the idea of setting aside wildlands for the enjoyment and needs of future generations that he suggested such areas be developed in Kenya. His idea was initially opposed by the government, which argued that the land was needed for farming and for settling the growing African population. Cowie and his supporters (including my father) persisted; and in 1945, legislation was enacted establishing Kenya's national park system.

Nairobi National Park became the first of our parks in 1946, followed by Tsavo in 1948 (split into Tsavo East and West the following year). Over the next two years, Kenya's prime mountain parks, Mount Kenya and Aberdares National Parks, were created. Although some feared that the park system would be dismantled after Kenya gained its independence in 1963, in fact even more land was set aside by the new government. Meru, Mount Elgon, and Ol Donyo Sabuk were declared national parks within five years, as were the marine parks of Malindi and Watamu. Marsabit and Shimba Hills were made national reserves—protected areas that the National Parks would oversee with the assistance of the local county councils.

During this time, and indeed during its first thirty years of existence, National Parks operated independently of the Game Department. Two separate legislative acts had created them, and each had a different responsibility. The Game Department continued to manage wildlife outside of the parks, while National Parks cared for animals inside the boundaries of the parks and reserves. This closely resembles the system in the United States, where the U.S. Fish and Wildlife Service has certain responsibilities for animals throughout the country, while the National Parks Service concerns itself with matters inside its parks.

I have always thought that this was a good system, particularly since Kenya's Game Department's staff managed animals principally by killing them. National Parks rangers are guided by a different perception of wildlife and management issues, one centered on conservation.

As I've mentioned, the government brought in the first Kenyan to head its National Parks, Dr. Perez Olindo, in 1967. Olindo was responsible for creating many of our finest parks. Ten years later, when the government decided to merge the Game Department and National Parks, Olindo, to his credit, resigned. He could see that the merger would not be a success. But advisers from the World Bank and many within Kenya, including Dr. David Western, argued that money could be saved by having one agency rather than two manage the parks and animals. The new agency was renamed the Department of Wildlife and Conservation Management.

To help get the Wildlife Department on its feet, the World Bank approved a loan for $26 million dollars. That money spelled the end of our national parks. Until 1976, National Parks had not been a government agency; it had been separate from the country's civil service. Now it was to be controlled by the Game Department, which was infamous for its bureaucracy (one reason Dr. Olindo resigned). Park wardens who had spent their lives protecting animals were transferred to areas where they were expected to shoot animals. And people who had spent their lives in the Game Department shooting animals were transferred to the parks where, naturally, they went on shooting animals. It was no coincidence that many of the rangers implicated in the poaching were former Game Department employees.

Sitting in the Wildlife director's chair, it was clear to me that the mess I had inherited had been created when National Parks lost its independence. When it was forced to turn over its revenue to the government treasury—from which it received substantially reduced operating funds—serious elephant poaching got underway. Unable to fight back against the poachers, many within Wildlife either watched helplessly or joined in the lucrative ivory trade business.

By my second day as head of Wildlife, I had already made one decision: I would somehow resurrect the old National Parks organization. It had worked and worked well, and with effort and determination it would work again.

Directing a museum for twenty years had taught me a thing or two about managing people and handling administrative tasks. One was that if you arrived at your office early in the morning, before any of your staff, you could have a good uninterrupted hour or so to yourself. I used the time for answering correspondence, writing memos or action plans, or reviewing accounts; it gave me a chance to clean my desk of any pending business. At Wildlife, it would take me awhile to catch up on the many pending matters and answer all the unanswered correspondence. Nonetheless, as unpleasant as that task was, it was the first order of business. To get it out of the way even sooner, I decided to arrive at the office at precisely 6 A.M. every day. My early arrival would have the added benefit of sending a message to the staff that I was serious about my job and maybe also inspire in them a similar sense of urgency.

I was back in my dark, cluttered cubbyhole at six the next morning. There was no point in dwelling on how many files required my attention. I simply needed to dive in. I pulled a stack toward me and flipped open the top folder. Inside was a memo from the Office of the Permanent Secretary. (His position is similar to the assistant secretary of the Interior in the United States government; he reports to the minister of Tourism and Wildlife.) The memo asked whether the director would be attending a meeting the next day to review the bids for a sale of tusks, most of which had been confiscated either from poachers or illegal shipments. The sale had been arranged as a means of getting a quick infusion of money into the cash-strapped department. The bids for the tusks were to be opened at this meeting. I instantly had the feeling that something about this sale wasn't on the up-and-up. It all seemed too bureaucratic. *Something stinks here,* I thought, fingering the memo. I quickly jotted a reply, asking the permanent secretary's office to delay the meeting for a few days as I had just been appointed and was still finding my way. That would give me time to find out what was really going on.

Over the course of the next few days, I worked my way through most of the files (including those blocking the light from the windows) and met with the senior staff, including several of the National Parks wardens. Many were good men. Joe Kioko, for instance. A tall, mild-mannered man, Joe had worked at Wildlife for twenty years and was then head warden of Tsavo National Park, Kenya's biggest reserve. Tsavo had once been home to some of the largest elephant herds in our country. By the late 1960s, in fact, so many herds roamed its savannas that Wildlife biologists had debated reducing their size. They feared that the elephants were eating their way through the park's ecosystem and would turn it into a dustbowl. But a severe drought had taken many of the animals, and the poachers had then started in on the rest. Some forty thousand elephants had lived in Tsavo in 1970; in 1989, there were barely five thousand. Yet the poachers hadn't put down their guns. Almost weekly came reports that they were slaughtering more of Tsavo's elephants. And just before my appointment, they had taken to robbing and killing tourists, too.

"What is going on in Tsavo?" I asked Joe, who had the same slump-shouldered, beaten-down appearance as so many on my staff. He sighed audibly at the question. Like several other park wardens, Joe was a pilot and had tried to make daily surveillance flights to keep track of the elephants and to spot any poachers. He replied that there were often days when there wasn't enough fuel for the planes nor for the rangers' Land Rovers, most of which were wrecks with missing parts and flat tires. Given that there was no money for spare parts, tires, or fuel, most of the vehicles were sitting idle. The headquarters and parks were graveyards of equipment. I had seen them for myself, and I knew what Joe was talking about. Wildlife supposedly had eleven airplanes, but only one was capable of daily flights. I spotted one of the other planes in the hanger at Wilson Airport. It looked fine—except that its engine was missing. "What happened to the engine?" I asked an attendant. He replied with a shrug, "It got lost." I stared at the man. "You can't lose engines from airplanes." "Well, sir, it's lost." The engine never did turn up.

Olindo had struggled with the same problem. Among his papers, I found a report indicating that out of 574 cars, trucks, vans, tractors, and other vehicles owned by the department, barely 5 percent were "battle-worthy." And none were considered "road-worthy"—they wouldn't have passed the police department's road test. How could the rangers be expected to stop the poachers without the tools for the job?

Joe's wasn't the only such lament. I heard the same story from all the wardens, including those stationed at headquarters in Nairobi. They wanted to do their jobs but were hamstrung by the lack of money and equipment. They also seemed ashamed of their poor performance. Kenya's newspapers consistently reported how many elephants or rangers or policemen the poachers had killed. Very seldom was there ever a story about a poacher meeting a similar fate. Our rangers knew that they looked like the Keystone Kops to their countrymen.

That had to change. On my third day in office, I met with the directors of all the major oil companies in Nairobi—Shell, Esso, Caltex, Agip, and Mobil. I didn't waste words.

"We have a terrible problem with poaching in our country, as you know," I began, "and we've got to stop it and get out parks working or it will be the end of our economy. My men can't get into the field without fuel." I then asked for an immediate supply of 250,000 liters of gasoline and diesel, and a grace period of two months' time to pay the bill.

The gentlemen were polite but shook their heads. The government departments, including Wildlife, already owed their companies so much money that I could not expect to get one liter of fuel on credit.

I tried another tactic. Would they give me, personally, two months' credit for the 250,000 liters of fuel? It was an audacious, even desperate, request, and to my surprise they agreed that this could be arranged. I signed the papers for what amounted to a bill of $100,000, for which I alone was responsible.

I used the same approach with Cooper Motors, the supplier of Land Rovers in Kenya. Its CEO, Martin Forster, also said he could not make a credit arrangement with the Wildlife Department, but that he was willing to give me $500,000 in credit, payable over twelve months. I immediately signed papers exchanging the $500,000 for eighteen new vehicles. (To Martin's credit, the loan was interest free.)

Within a week, the Wildlife Department was mobile again. Rangers were out patrolling the parks in their shiny Land Rovers. Already I saw fewer slumped shoulders and more smiles. Of course, I had also amassed a debt larger than any I had ever had in my life. I also had friends who would help me out. Margo Walker, an American friend for many years, came to my aid, as did Nehemiah Rotich, who headed the East African Wildlife Society. Both put out appeals for help. Before the end of the first month, I had paid the oil companies back in full, putting me (and my department, I hoped) in good standing for future loans.

The fuel and new vehicles signaled a change. Kenya's Wildlife Department was no longer just going to sit back and let the poachers have the run of the parks. If they wanted a battle, fine. We'd fight them. I would have to build a fighting force first, of course. I would also have to learn more about the poachers. Who were they? Who financed their operations? To what extent were rangers and government officials involved?

I thought back to that memo about the ivory sale. Perhaps it contained clues. I contacted the permanent secretary again. "I'm ready for your meeting," I told him. "Let's open the bids."

CHAPTER 4

Kenya was not the only African country suffering from elephant poaching. By the late 1980s, it had become nearly a continent-wide plague. Ivory-hunting poachers, many armed with Kalishnikova AK-47 assault rifles, were slaughtering elephants from Kenya and Tanzania to the Central African Republic and Angola. In some countries, such as Uganda and Sudan, where more than a hundred thousand elephants had roamed in the 1970s, you would have been hard-pressed, ten years later, to find ten thousand. In Tanzania, a hundred thousand elephants alone had lived in the Selous Game Reserve in 1976; a decade later, that figure had dropped to fifty-five thousand. And now, only three years further on, it stood at a mere twenty-seven thousand. In Kenya, we were down to fewer than twenty thousand elephants—and still losing on average three elephants a day.

It didn't take a genius to figure out that such a high rate of killing couldn't go on indefinitely. The African elephant was clearly headed for extinction throughout much of its range. That thought struck me forcefully one morning as I read through a stack of background reports in preparation for the ivory-sale meeting.

I had studied the bones of extinct animals for many years. About 2 million years ago, five species of elephants—one with huge, downward-pointing tusks—lived on the vast savanna of eastern Africa. They'd lived alongside some equally fabulous creatures such as antlered giraffes and massively horned antelopes; one species of the latter had horns that spanned more than ten feet. Most of these animals had died out, apparently because of climate change. But two lineages of elephants survived, giving rise to the two species of elephants we know today: the African elephant, *Loxodonta africana,* and its Asian cousin, *Elephas maximus.*

Extinctions are part of the evolutionary process. However, they are also relatively rare events—or, more properly, *should be* rare, according to conservationists who compute the rates at which species disappear. In the last century, the number of plant and animal species faced with extinction has shot up dramatically, largely because of the spread and indifference of humankind. I understood these things intellectually, as I expect most people do who care about the natural world around them. Now I was faced with the very real fact that one of the remaining species of elephants—the African elephant—was facing a serious threat of extinction throughout most of its range during the course of my lifetime. When the elephant disappeared from the habitats, other species would surely disappear, too, and the biodiversity that we know would be irrevocably reduced.

I am not much given to reflection. I am a practical-minded person, someone who likes making decisions and acting on them. I can't even sit still for very long, something about which my friends and family tease me. But when I realized what the figures I was reading meant, I thought long and hard. Perhaps because of my fossil-hunting background, I always associated the word "extinction" with things that happened long ago not something I would watch happen. Nonetheless, I was seeing it happen. And largely because of the illegal ivory trade.

I needed to know more about how the trade operated. I found that it was fairly easy to do so. Nairobi was buzzing with rumors about who was involved and where and how the ivory was moved. There were stories of huge numbers of tusks being hidden inside specially built, secret compartments of trucks then shipped across borders into Somalia. Military officers in South Africa were openly engaged in the killing of elephants in Mozambique, Angola, and elsewhere. The ivory was considered part of the "spoils of war." Other reports told of ivory being moved out of Africa in the luggage of embassy officials, who could claim diplomatic privilege and seldom had their baggage searched by customs. Only a few months before, in January 1989, customs officers in Tanzania had found dozens of ivory carvings inside the bags of the Indonesian ambassador. He and his wife were on their way to Singapore, where they'd apparently intended to sell their smuggled goods. And in Kenya itself, there were persistent (and by now, as far as I was concerned, believable) rumors that high-ranking government officials were behind the poaching. Such rumors had been around since the 1970s, when many alleged that President Kenyatta's own family had been engaged in the illegal ivory trade. These allegations always remained that; no one was ever charged let alone convicted of the crime. In the current crisis, it was difficult to tell how far up the government ladder the ivory trade led, although I never suspected that President Moi was involved. His hard-line policy on poachers, and his support for me, spoke against it.

The rumors and reports I read convinced me that poaching was only part of the problem. The legal trade in ivory, regulated through international trade agreements, was a bigger problem. Smuggling and the use of forged or "purchased" documents was common throughout Africa, and a huge volume of the ivory leaving Africa "legally" was in fact from illegally killed elephants.

Ivory has long been a staple of African trade. Since Roman times, and probably before, ivory has been a commodity, something to be bought and sold. The Roman hunger for ivory led to the elimination of elephants from the northern half of the continent by the end of the Roman Empire. Starting at least as early as the eleventh century, Arab traders began traveling into the interior of East Africa seeking ivory and slaves. Tusks and people were shipped by sea on *dhows* to the Far East and to the Arabian peninsula and the Persian Gulf. Some slaves were kept to work on coastal plantations.

When the British colonized East Africa in the late 1800s, they put an end to slavery but continued the ivory trade, shipping out most of the tusks through Mombassa, Kenya's port city. Ivory helped make that city into the thriving metropolis it is today. Most of these tusks—some 1 million pounds a year—went to Britain, where the ivory was turned into billiard balls, combs, and handles for cutlery. Another half-million pounds were shipped to America, which had become a major producer of pianos; elephant ivory provided the keys.

So many elephants were being killed that a few early conservationists began to worry that elephants might be wiped out entirely—just as we were worrying now. Their concern led lawmakers in England in 1890 to pass the first laws protecting elephants in East Africa. There was to be no further shooting of female elephants or any elephant with tusks weighing less than ten pounds each. Over the years, other laws were enacted to regulate the trade but not to stop it, since it brought in badly needed revenue to the colonial governments. Ironically, ivory even financed colonial Kenya's first Wildlife Department. Conservationists and government officials believed they were managing ivory in a sustainable way—killing just enough elephants to supply the ivory market and fill their coffers but not so many that the species was put at risk. And maybe it was sustainable.

Then, about thirty years ago, things began to change. At that time more than 150,000 elephants lived in Kenya, a large proportion of them outside national parks and other protected areas. They roamed freely throughout the country, traversing migration paths that went back centuries. About 12 million people also lived in Kenya then, many of them farmers in the highlands, where small farm communities raised corn, vegetables, and other produce. Though it might have seemed that people and elephants coexisted happily, they in fact gave each other a wide berth. Elephants trampled crops and sometimes people, and consequently people did not wish to farm in areas where elephants lived. And elephants, having been hunted for centuries, rightly viewed humans with suspicion. The elephant population hovered around 200,000. Kenya's human population, on the other hand, grew exponentially. In 1989, nearly 20 million people lived in Kenya, a growing number in areas where elephants and other wild game had roamed as recently as the

1970s. Kenya's rapidly growing human population (30 million people in the year 2000) put pressure on the land and consequently on elephants and other wildlife.

The 1970s also saw explosive growth in international tourism and travel. There was a staggering increase in the numbers of people, from Western nations particularly, wanting to visit exotic destinations like Kenya. And everyone wanted to take home souvenirs, creating a market for curios. Ivory carvings were big business not only in Africa but throughout the Middle East and the Far East. The traditional sources of raw ivory could not possibly meet this growing demand, and, consequently, prices rose rapidly. Ivory traders and conservationists alike began to realize that elephants weren't sustainable after all. As with many other natural resources, there was only a limited supply, and their numbers were plunging.

Some have suggested that the oil crisis of the 1970s and coinciding financial instability around the world helped push the price of ivory higher because people were searching for commodities that would retain their value. Whatever the cause, the numbers speak for themselves. In 1970, ivory was trading at a mere $2.50 a pound. Ten years later, that figure had shot up to $60 a pound. In 1989, a pound of raw, unworked ivory fetched nearly $100 per pound. Today, after the ivory ban, a pound of ivory is worth $20 (that is the amount paid to the first seller—the poacher, in other words; it increases along the chain).

Not surprisingly, elephants began to look like meal tickets to a lot of people. In 1973, 1,000 elephants were being poached each month. In four years, Kenya's elephant population fell from 167,000 to 59,000. Partly this was because of the drought, but poaching played an even bigger role.

Ivory trading was legal in Kenya in the early 1970s. Every curio shop and street corner kiosk in Nairobi sold ivory: you could buy little animal carvings, necklaces, even an entire tusk. You could also buy such grisly souvenirs as ashtrays made from a gorilla's hand or footstools supported on zebra legs or an elephant's foot. While, thankfully, the Kenyan government put an end to the local trade in wildlife products in 1977, it continued to permit the sale of unworked ivory. Every year large numbers of tusks were sold in auction to ivory traders from the Eastern nations as well as from the Persian Gulf.

Most of the auctioned ivory was shipped to Japan and Hong Kong, where the bulk of the tusks were carved into seals (called *hankos*) for validating checks and business documents. In Japan, a seal rather than a signature is required, and everyone in its growing middle class wanted a seal of his own. In 1983 alone, Japan imported 1 million pounds of ivory. Someone once calculated that it took fifty elephants to produce one thousand pounds of ivory (assuming that each tusk weighed ten pounds). Thus, an astonishing five thousand elephants were killed to supply the Japanese market in that one year alone. And when I took over Wildlife, Japan was still importing ivory—and if the department went ahead with the scheduled sale, we would be selling the Japanese, or someone, even more.

Another aspect of the ivory trade I studied up on before the sale was the role of the Convention on International Trade in Endangered Species (or CITES), a treaty the United Nations helped establish in 1973. CITES regulates the enormous worldwide trade in furs, skins, horns, ivory, and other products made from wild animals.

CITES employs three main lists to govern this trade. Animals regarded as "threatened with extinction"—or endangered—are listed on the so-called Appendix I. Trading in these species is absolutely prohibited. Over the years, Appendix I has included gorillas, rhinoceroses, leopards, snow leopards, California condors, blue and fin whales, and hundreds of plant species. Species that are not yet endangered but might become so were their trade not regulated are listed on Appendix II. Those CITES still allows to be traded are on Appendix III. The elephant was placed on Appendix II in 1977. Ten years later a growing number of conservationists and conservation groups were asking that the elephant be moved to Appendix I. Such an upgrade would have banned any sale or purchase of ivory between countries signatory to the CITES treaty.

As I read and talked to people about CITES, I quickly began to understand why conservationists thought the elephant needed Appendix I protection. The basic problem was that the rules CITES had developed for governing the ivory trade didn't have much bite. For starters, the organization had no way of enforcing them or of imposing fines. A further complication was that only those countries that had signed the CITES agreement were bound by it (in 1989, 117 countries were signatories). That meant that any country that hadn't signed the agreement could act as a warehouse, storing and selling illegally obtained ivory. For instance, Belgium imported five hundred tons of ivory in the early 1980s, then sold it; only after unloading the ivory did it join CITES. Similarly, Burundi, a tiny country in the middle of Africa, has no elephants of its own. Yet between 1979 and 1987 it exported nearly fifteen hundred tons of tusks. I suspect that some of that tonnage came from Kenya's elephants.

In 1985, the CITES board had tried to tighten things up with a quota system. Each country wanting to sell ivory had to inform the CITES secretariat annually how many tusks they planned to market. As far as I could tell, this only led to more abuses. Somalia, for example, set its quota at seventeen thousand tusks in 1986. But Somalia had only six thousand elephants, if that. Nevertheless, they filled their quota—and with our elephants, I'm sure.

This was how illegally obtained ivory—poached ivory—became legal. Wherever the tusks came from, they had only to be shipped to a country that belonged to CITES and was authorized to sell ivory. They were then put on the market under these so-called quotas.

The more I found out about CITES and the ivory trade, the less sure I became that there was any way to manage it legally. As long as ivory was considered a valuable commodity, there would be a black market for it. Despite CITES and its well-intentioned rules, the ivory trade was clearly corrupt, and no matter who regulated it or what system they put in place, it would always be corrupt. The high price assured that. Even if a poacher's cut was only $50 per tusk, a few tusks could add up to more than a year's income in a poor country like Kenya, where, in 1989, the average annual income was a mere $450. Poorly paid public servants made ends meet by using their influence to help out friends and family members, who paid them for these favors. The ivory trade in Kenya (and throughout Africa) was riddled with bribery and kickbacks. Elephants were dying in such high numbers because officials were being paid to look the other way. As long as the legal ivory trade continued, we were going to lose elephants to poachers.

That didn't mean that I had yet planned to stop the scheduled sale. On the contrary, much as I was beginning to dislike the trade, I thought—and so did many conservationists in Zimbabwe and South Africa at the time—that the money the tusks would bring could be put to good use. As I've noted, the Wildlife Department that I had just taken over sorely needed the cash. Indeed, this was the first time that the department would benefit directly from an ivory sale. The proceeds of all previous auctions had gone straight into the government's treasury. It was because the poaching was so out of control, and the Wildlife Department in such a state of disrepair, that Perez Olindo had persuaded the authorities to make an exception this time.

Initially, I for one was glad Dr. Olindo had been so persuasive. I also decided, however, that this would be the last such sale and said as much to several reporters. After it was over, I told them in an interview, I would be joining with other conservationists and calling for a worldwide ban on the ivory trade.

During the week before the sale, I spoke to a number of people connected in various ways to the ivory trade. One in particular, Ian Parker, enlightened me about the nature of these auctions. Parker, a blunt-talking, intelligent fellow now in his sixties, has worked all sides of the trade. At one point he was a professional elephant hunter. After that he became a game-management specialist and carried out research on elephant populations in Uganda. He has also sometimes acted as an adviser on big ivory sales (such as the one we were planning), providing estimations of the tusks' value to the seller. At the time, Parker was an outspoken opponent of efforts to give the elephant total protection and was generally regarded with suspicion by strict conservationists because he believed that commercial use should be a fundamental part of any policy on elephant management.

I thought that Parker might be of some help. When I asked him point-blank about what I could expect from a sale like this, his answer was blunt.

"Well, you're being a bit naive if you think this is an auction like you'd see at Sotheby's," Parker said.

I asked him to be more specific.

"It's already been decided. All of it. The price for the ivory and the buyer. Someone has accepted the price, and the buyer is just here waiting for the formalities to be concluded. He's probably already lined up a shipper for the ivory."

Actually I was not the least surprised, and I had a few sources of my own whose identity I cannot reveal. Before the sale even took place, I knew who the buyer would be and how much he planned to pay for the ivory.

The permanent secretary apparently got wind of my little investigation into the ivory business, for a few days before we were scheduled to meet, I received a call from his secretary.

"The permanent secretary knows how very busy you are there at Wildlife," she said, "so really, there is no need for you to attend this meeting." It would all be just routine government business, she said, involving the kind of bureaucratic detail that was best left to "lesser people." I assured her that I nonetheless wanted to attend. I needed to know as much about every aspect of my new position as possible.

Her call only intrigued me all the more about this sale. I showed up at the permanent secretary's office a few minutes ahead of time. I was shown at once into his office, and we exchanged a few pleasantries. A large man with an open, friendly manner, he said again how unusual it was for the Wildlife director to trouble himself over an ivory sale. Then he smiled affably and told me he was glad I was so interested in even the minor details of my new job. I smiled back then followed him into an adjoining conference room, where some officials from the Ministry of Tourism and Wildlife were waiting.

It didn't take long to realize that nothing about this meeting was as it appeared. One of the officials read out the bids, which ranged from $2.2 million to $3.1 million, while another one dutifully recorded them in a logbook. Like everyone else there, I knew that a businessman from East Asia had made the highest offer. Parker had told me that the man already knew about his good fortune and was simply waiting for us to sign the papers approving his purchase. He had a ship waiting at Mombassa to transport the tusks home.

Fortunately, from my point of view, the East Asian businessman had made some errors on his offer form, and while the bureaucrats puzzled over what to do about them, I spoke up.

I said that it didn't look to me as if everything about the sale contract was in order, and that because our president had given me a firm directive to straighten out the Wildlife Department, I couldn't approve this sale unless it were done properly.

"If we're going to have a sale, we need to reweigh and remeasure the ivory and then advertise it again," I announced. "I don't want there to be any suspicions about how we've handled this business."

You could have heard a pin drop in that room. The permanent secretary stared at me, incredulous. Then he recovered his friendly smile. "Of course, of course, Richard. Let's reschedule the sale and see that it's done properly next time."

We shook hands. I said I would have someone from my department contact them as soon as we were ready. (In retrospect, I probably had no authority to question, let alone stop, the sale. The permanent secretary was two large steps above me in the government hierarchy. There was a key difference between me and previous holders of my position, however. President Moi, and not the minister of Tourism and Wildlife nor the permanent secretary, had appointed me to my job. And I had direct access to the president.)

The instant I was back in my office, I phoned Iain Douglas-Hamilton. A trim scientist of Scottish origin, Iain began studying elephants and their behavior in the wild in the early 1970s. He'd made his home in Kenya, married, and had two children, while continuing to study and count elephant populations throughout eastern and Central Africa. We'd been friends for many years and had already met a few times after I had become director. He'd provided me with background about the illegal ivory trade and about CITES. In addition, he was a leading proponent of a ban on elephant hunting.

I told Iain about my decision and asked him if he would examine the tusks. He agreed willingly, since it would afford him a chance to get additional information about the size and age of the elephants the poachers were killing. He was certain they'd taken most of the mature adults and males, and now were hunting primarily young adult females and juveniles.

Over the next few days, Iain and a graduate student worked in the government's ivory warehouse, measuring and weighing all the tusks. Their conclusions didn't surprise me: there were more tusks, and of a greater weight and higher grade, than what the department had reported. The businessman from East Asia would have bought, at a greatly reduced price, nearly thirteen tons of high-quality ivory. And someone, or several people, in some government office would have received a handsome payoff at my department's expense, although I never found out who they were.

About this same time, Hilary N'gweno, the publisher and editor-in-chief of the *Weekly Review,* a magazine that advocated for a free press in Kenya, took me to task in one of his editorials. He criticized my plans to go ahead with the auction, particularly at a time when I was also lobbying for an international ban on the ivory trade. This was the first criticism I had received from the press since taking office, and it hurt—especially since it was justified.

I liked being the good guy, and Hilary was right; this time I was not. But the department desperately needed the money the sale would bring. I read Hilary's opinion piece one morning shortly after arriving at my office. An hour later I headed into Nairobi and paid my second and final visit to the ivory warehouse. I knew then I could not in good conscience sell these tusks.

It was that night that I made up my mind to burn the ivory.

Only two questions remained: would the ivory burn, as Meave had wondered? And what would President Moi think?

CHAPTER 5

Each day of the first three weeks I had been in office, I discovered more problems; seldom did I have immediate solutions. At one point, I had written in my diary: *No money, no morale, no vehicles, planes are grounded, inadequate senior staff, no fuel, no ideas.*

I told no one—not even Meave—about how desperate I felt things were, how worried I was about the lack of money. I found myself waking in the middle of the night, a knot in my stomach from the stress. I had signed on to fight a battle, but how could I fight it without the means to do so? And given the high commercial value of ivory, I knew this battle was going to be part of a costly, drawn-out war, one fought on many fronts: poachers, middlemen, and corrupt officials. Waging war wasn't my department's only concern. Roads needed to be repaired, airfields regraded, buildings and roofs fixed, new uniforms ordered—an endless list.

Among the parks I oversaw were three mountain parks—Mount Kenya, Mount Elgon, and Aberdare—that attracted large numbers of hikers and climbers. Mountaineers were especially keen to summit the 17,089-foot, rock-and-ice peak of Mount Kenya, but the trails leading to it were not well marked, and the mountain's weather could be temperamental. Without a good guide, it was easy to get lost, as several foreign visitors did shortly after I took office. Unfortunately, the Wildlife Department no longer had the funds to mount an effective rescue operation. In the early days, National Parks rangers were trained in Austria, and the department boasted an excellent guide and rescue service. By the time I took over from Olindo, the service had been dismantled and equipment lost. We would have to start over again. Indeed, a number of climbing accidents did happen during my first few months. This only added to my feelings of desperation.

The Marine National Parks were also underfunded. Each year, thousands of tourists visited the coral reefs off our seashore, usually by sailing out to them on small boats with local guides, then diving and swimming from these. Were anyone to get into trouble, we could not help: we had no reliable boats and most of the marine rangers and wardens, who came from Central Kenya, could not swim. Safety wasn't the only issue. The fragile reefs were being destroyed because the rangers could not police them. Indeed, they were looking after a park they themselves had never seen. Not one of the staff had been trained to use scuba gear, nor did they even have the most basic equipment for supervising an underwater environment, such as snorkeling masks and flippers.

These problems would not have been that difficult to solve. All that was really required was money and training. However, almost all our funds were earmarked for waging the poaching "war"; there was very little left over for these other needs. Where and how was I going to get the money we needed—and as fast as we needed it?

I don't think anyone knew how deeply worried I was about all this, but I was determined not to let my doubts show. I felt I had to project a sense of confidence even when I had none.

The idea of burning the ivory gave me a boost. For weeks I had been searching for something that would fire up my staff and shake them out of their inertia and despondency. I was also now certain that burning the ivory would be worth more to us than selling it. Last, I believed it would help bring the poaching war to an end once and for all. The more I thought about it, the more eager I became to put the ivory to the torch.

When I laid out my plan to President Moi the next morning, he looked at me as if I were slightly crazed. "Burn the ivory?" he asked, aghast. "It is worth at least 3 *million* dollars." He thought about how angry Kenya's citizens would be with him for permitting this wasteful display.

"I know it sounds mad," I admitted. "But we need to take bold action. Most of the world doesn't believe we're committed to saving our elephants. Burning the ivory will show them that we are. We'll get a huge amount of publicity and good will from doing this. I'm certain of it."

"It would also help us in our battle with the poachers," I continued, leaning forward to press my point. About 40 percent of Africa's ivory went to the West for trinkets and baubles. I told Moi that were we to make the very idea of buying and wearing ivory abhorrent to Europeans and Americans, we would eliminate almost half the market for it. And without a market, there would be no poaching.

Moi sat back in his chair, shaking his head. He pressed his lips together, took a deep breath, and shook his head again. He and I had been meeting regularly—two and three times a week—and he'd supported me on every decision I had taken so far, just as he'd promised. I could see he didn't want to let me down, but he was also far from convinced that my latest request made any sense.

I emphasized again the enormous public relations value involved, not only to Kenya's image in the eyes of conservationists, but to the government itself. If the burning was part of a formal ceremony in which he—Kenya's president—were to light the fire and then address the press, the government would gain credibility at a time when it was facing increasing criticism from the West on human rights issues. (The criticism was in my mind fully justified, but I decided that this was neither the time nor place to make this observation.) Animal rights and human rights activists were generally closely linked, I pointed out, and they often supported each other on issues. Thus, pleasing the animal lobby would surely help appease his human rights critics.

President Moi mulled this over. Then he asked me the very question Meave had. "Will the ivory burn? You must be sure of that." I was not to make a fool of him or the country, he warned.

I had as yet no idea how we would get the tusks to burn, but I was certain it could be done. I nodded my head vigorously. "Yes, it will burn."

Moi still looked uncomfortable, as if my idea were causing him indigestion. He let out an audible sigh. Finally he turned to me. "All right then," he said, without much enthusiasm. "We will burn the ivory."

"Good," I replied firmly. I had a great urge to smile broadly but suppressed it. This was a time for seriousness.

President Moi then summoned his secretary. We had to pick a date for the event when the president was free. We settled on July 18, 1989. That gave me five weeks to get things ready—and to find a way to burn that ivory.

Elephant tusks are actually incisor teeth that have evolved into tools and weapons. They use them for digging, feeding, fighting, playing, carrying, and marking. Like the teeth of every mammal, tusks are a mass of hard dentine (a kind of calcium). Only the tips have any enamel, and this is usually worn away early in the elephant's life. The oldest bulls generally have the largest tusks, which can weigh as much as sixty pounds or more each. Tusks have a warmth, luminescence, and resilience that make them ideal for carving. Ivory feels good in the hand; it is smooth to the touch, yet hard and durable.

It was these latter two qualities that concerned me. The very properties that made ivory wonderful to carve and sculpt might also make it difficult to burn. Dentine is astonishingly long-lasting; I knew this from my fossil research. You might come across a fragment of a hominid's jaw, broken and crumbling in the desert air, but the teeth would be perfectly intact. Similarly, human teeth often turn up in the ashes at crematoria, barely marred by the heat and flames. Elephant ivory has that same indestructibility.

I needed to burn some ivory just to see what would happen. A few days after my meeting with the president I got my chance. I had been invited with Meave to spend the weekend on Kuki Gallman's ranch on the Laikipia Plateau, north of Nairobi. She and a number of other ranchers of European origin maintain large tracts of land where wildlife coexist with the cattle and sheep they raise. Elephants, rhinos, giraffes, and buffalo are plentiful on these ranches, and several have facilities for tourists. But poachers had recently been active in the area; some had even killed elephants on their farms. The owners wanted to know what I was going to do to protect them and their guests. In turn, I wanted to enlist them as allies. Many of the ranchers were wealthy and had connections overseas. I thought they could help me in pressing for an international ban against the ivory trade.

Kuki is a Kenyan citizen of Italian origin, and exuberant and colorful. She had lost both her husband and son in tragic accidents some years before, but because she had fallen in love with Kenya's wildlife and open spaces, she'd stayed on. We had been friends for a number of years.

Iain Douglas-Hamilton and his wife, Oria, were also staying at Kuki's. Before dinner that night, I brought up my plan to burn the tusks being kept in the government's storeroom. Kuki gasped at the idea, while Iain and Oria vigorously nodded their approval.

"Brilliant," said Oria. "That will make people think."

"But, Richard," Kuki said, "it is worth so much. Is it the best plan?"

"I think so," I replied. "But it may be no plan at all if it won't burn. What do you think, Iain?"

Iain shook his head. "I'm not sure, Richard. That's a difficult question."

"We can make a test," Kuki volunteered. She had some broken tusks from elephants that had died on her ranch, and placed a small one on the fire in her sitting room. The flames licked tenuously at the ivory. It didn't catch. Kuki stoked the fire beneath it.

We watched awhile then moved on to eat dinner in her dinning room. Two hours later, after a fine meal and good conversation, we trooped back in to examine the results. They weren't promising. One of Kuki's house staff had added more wood—actually a good deal more wood—and the tusk now looked like a piece of coal. But it was still intact.

"I'm afraid you're going to have to burn down a forest to burn your ivory," Meave said.

"Well, it does burn," I countered. "It just doesn't burn very well."

It was not the kind of bonfire I imagined. Our test sparked Kuki's interest. She had a friend, Robin Hollister, who happened to work on special effects with Hollywood filmmakers. After we left, Kuki discussed my dilemma with Robin, and a few days later he came to see me.

"I can get your ivory to burn," he announced.

"Oh?" I asked, at once curious and doubtful.

"Sure," he said. "Paint some highly flammable liquid glue on it, build up a good, hot fire—one that's got some gasoline behind it—and it'll burn. I guarantee you."

"Well, I don't want to burn up the audience," I replied. "Just the ivory."

Robin laughed. "No, no. There are ways to contain these things. It won't get out of control. You won't lose your president. But it will be a spectacular fire."

I liked the sound of that. I wanted something spectacular, something that would stay in peoples' minds so that when they thought about buying ivory they also thought about burning ivory.

I didn't hesitate. Robin wouldn't be there in July, but Kuki's ranch manager, Colin Francombe, agreed to take on the task of building and supervising the ivory bonfire. It seemed to me that we risked setting off a mighty explosion when we ignited a pyre richly garnished with petroleum and oil, but the experts reassured me this wouldn't happen. I finally slept that night without a knot in my stomach.

❖ ❖ ❖

The morning after our dinner at Kuki's I was up at the crack of dawn and airborne again, flying north to Sibiloi, one of Kenya's most remote national parks, located on the shores of Lake Turkana. Enroute, we stopped at Koobi Fora, where Meave and I had spent so many good times. I wanted to visit the park headquarters at Sibiloi National Park and introduce myself to the rangers, who I knew to be living in pretty poor conditions. I left Meave at the camp and flew on to Sibiloi. None of the previous directors had ever gone there. They might visit Tsavo, or the bigger national parks, but seldom traveled to those farther afield. I'm sure that contributed to the suspicion among many rangers that their superiors in Nairobi cared little about them or their work. I also wanted the rangers to see me, to put a face to my name. In the days ahead, I was going to be asking a lot from these men, and I wanted them to feel that they knew me.

Park rangers come from tribes located throughout Kenya, some living in very isolated parts of the country. Many attend a wildlife-training college in western Kenya and then are sent to one of our fifty-four parks or reserves. But even for those who've grown up in small villages, a ranger's life can be hard and lonely. They might be stationed at a boundary post far from the park's main offices and have only one or two colleagues for company for months at a stretch. When I took over Wildlife, most didn't have a vehicle. They were expected to patrol on foot, carrying antiquated World War I–vintage rifles, which they referred to as "shoot-and-wait" weapons because they performed erratically. Our rangers did all this on a salary of about forty dollars a month, a miserable sum I wanted to increase if I ever found the money to do so. In the meantime, I could at least visit them and offer my support, encouragement, and thanks for their hard work.

Sibiloi National Park lies well off the tourist track and attracts only the hardiest of visitors. It's often called the "Cradle of Mankind" park, since, in addition to being home to a wonderful range of desert wildlife, it protects the sites where my team and I had made most of our important early human fossil discoveries in the '60s and '70s. Indeed, a member of my team found the fossil that really launched my career (the badly broken skull of a hominid about 2 million years old, which we called by its field number, "1470") on one of Sibiloi's dry, rocky hills in 1972.

Because fossils are easy to find at Sibiloi—they are scattered everywhere, although only rarely are they the bones of hominids—Meave and I used to worry that people more interested in souvenirs than scientific specimens might come "treasure hunting" when we weren't in the field. To protect Sibiloi's fossil bounty and the wildlife in the area, I proposed that the government make the region from Lake Turkana's Alia Bay to the Ethiopian border a national park, which it did in 1972.

Included in that six hundred-square-mile chunk of land is a strip of lakeshore where African short grass flourishes—the kind of browse most appealing to desert antelopes, such as the oryx and topi, and the rare Grevy's zebra. There are also found sleek, cinnamon-colored gerenuk, an antelope that stands on its hind legs to reach a shrub's uppermost leaves, as well as cheetahs and lions. Flamingoes, pelicans, egrets, herons, and crowned plovers crowd the water's edge, along with some very large crocodiles. After a hot day working in the fossil deposits at Turkana, Meave and I often enjoyed taking short walks on this narrow, green swathe between the alkaline waters of the lake and the barren hills of Sibiloi. Sometimes we saw lions. More often we saw a few oryx. After spotting us, they'd stand alertly, pointing their gray-and-black faces in our direction until one would turn and bolt, leading the others in a madcap race into the desert beyond. It always pleased me that because of our fossil discoveries these animals, whose populations were never very large, would also be protected.

The formation of this new park, however, also raised some problems. For centuries, the Turkana Desert has been home to nomadic tribes who herd their camels, sheep, cattle, and goats to the lakeshore for grazing and water during the extreme dry months. These include the Dassanatch (also known as the Merille), who come down from the northern end of the lake, near the Ethiopian border; the Gabbra, who normally live well east of the lake but also take advantage of the grasses by the lakeshore in very bad years; and the Rendille, who travel up from the south. All are tribes with long-standing warrior traditions, and when their paths cross, they engage in fierce fighting.

Large herds of livestock can quickly wreak havoc on an environment as fragile as that at Sibiloi. In the past, tribal fighting had kept over-grazing from being a major problem. Herders went to the region only warily and didn't stay for long. Once the park was established, that dynamic changed. Now rangers, backed by the Kenyan government, patrolled the lakeshore. They discouraged fights and did their best to stop such incidents once they started. Sibiloi was no longer a dangerous place for the nomads but instead a secure haven in an otherwise incon-stant world. They arrived with their livestock and didn't leave. Sibiloi's fragile desert vegetation quickly began to suffer.

I would never begrudge a nomad pasture for grazing his animals. For nearly twenty years I worked every summer among the nomadic peoples of Lake Turkana; I had come to know them and greatly admired their ability to survive in that harsh land. Allowing the Sibiloi National Park to become a permanent home to thousands of sheep, goats, cattle, and camels, however, was no answer. The area would be reduced to complete desert in no time at all and eventually neither domestic nor wild animals would survive there.

There are now such human demands on the park that the long-term survival of the wildlife we set out to protect is in doubt. The sheep and goats will graze the grasses until not a nubbin remains; the nomads will kill the lion and cheetah to protect their herds and families. Sibiloi could well be reduced to a barren dust bowl.

Sibiloi represents a microcosm of a major dilemma we face in Kenya: balancing the needs of our citizens with the needs of our wildlife. If there is going to be any balance at all in that equation, we are going to have to make many tough—and sometimes unpleasant—choices. And as Wildlife director, I knew that many of those choices were going to be up to me.

I touched down on Sibiloi's dirt landing strip a little after 8 A.M. on a cloudless May morning. A senior sergeant was waiting in the park's sole Land Rover, and he jumped out at once to welcome me and introduce me to his deputy. We shook hands, then drove to the park's head-quarters, a sad-looking, ochre-colored building with badly peeling paint and trash strewn about. A ragged line of rangers stood at attention off to one side. I took one look at them and sighed. Of the eight men, three had shoes and only two had hats. All were dressed in an odd mix of uniform and street dress.

I walked up to them, with the warden hovering anxiously at my side.

"Look at you," I began, shaking my head. "Is this the best you can do? Where are your boots?" I asked one skinny fellow.

"I have none, sir," he replied.

I asked the others similar questions. Some didn't have any shoes; others had them, but had simply forgotten to wear them, as they sheepishly informed me.

"Well, we've got to do better than this," I said, addressing them in Swahili. "You represent Kenya. When tourists come to our parks, you're often the first people they see. We want them to feel confident, certain of their safety so they will want to return. I'm counting on you—Kenya is counting on you—to see to it that they do. We're all in this together, and I'll do what I can to help."

I continued in that vein for a few minutes, urging them to treat their responsibilities seriously and assuring them that things were going to change. I would see to it that they got new uniforms and boots; they were to wear these properly. I also told them that I was always available, that they could bring any problems or concerns to me.

I noticed that most of the men were struggling to suppress broad smiles. It was the first time a director of Wildlife had ever addressed them, had ever visited them or their park for that matter. Although I was upbraiding them for being lackadaisical, they were pleased by the attention—so much so that I felt a little embarrassed. I often read biographies of leaders, particularly those who have had to command armed services. One of my favorites was about the late Lord Louis Mountbatten, for it taught me a way of understanding the relationship between a leader and his men. Successful generals care deeply about their men. They are tough with them and expect them to give their all—but they also feel deep concern for them. In return, the men give their best, as well as their trust and loyalty. Already I had caught a glimpse of that in these rangers' eyes and felt moved. It was a new feeling for me, and I wasn't quite sure what it meant. I did know that I was going to get boots for these rangers.

I had heard a lot from my senior staff in Nairobi about the dilapidated state of most of the buildings in our parks. The condition of our headquarters building in Nairobi was also nothing to brag about; it was in dreadful shape. Still, it was, to say the least, dispiriting to walk through the buildings at Sibiloi. All the equipment, from trucks to typewriters, was rundown, damaged, or broken. I could only shake my head. There wasn't much point in itemizing each thing that needed fixing—it would have almost been better to move in with a bulldozer, knock everything down, and start over. I told the warden that I understood they had no money, but to try and tidy things up. Perhaps they might find some paint in the park's stores and cover the peeling buildings. I again emphasized how important the Wildlife Department and parks were to Kenya, to its image and economic well-being. He and his deputy nodded their heads. I had inspired him, he said, over and over again; and the next time I came, he promised, I would see a new Sibiloi.

I hoped that was even a little bit true. But that night, in a room at my Koobi Fora camp, I recorded in my diary the bleakness of it all: *The park facilities are beyond description—it is dreadful and I cannot begin to see how we are going to sort things out.*

I woke once again with a knot in my stomach.

The situation wasn't any better at Tsavo National Park, to which I flew the next day after a brief trip home. Tsavo lies about 150 miles to the east of Nairobi.

Tsavo is actually made up of two large, adjoining parks, called Tsavo East and Tsavo West. Together they comprise the biggest wildlife preserve in Kenya, covering some eight thousand square miles (about half the size of Rhode Island). Tsavo West touches on the border with Tanzania; on clear days the summit of Africa's tallest mountain, Mount Kilimanjaro, at 19,340 feet, is clearly visible. Of the two parks, Tsavo West has more varied terrain, with rugged escarpments and gently undulating hills covered with open woodland, such as the Chyulus. Tsavo East is the larger of the two parks and consists mostly of flat, dry thornbush country that extends north and east into the heart of Kenya. Each park is bisected by a large river: the Galana in Tsavo East, and the Tsavo River in Tsavo West. Besides the vast amount of space they offer, the varied terrain—from woodland to scrubby thornbush to riverine—makes the two Tsavos a wildlife paradise.

Here live lions, cheetahs, leopards, buffalo, hippos, five different species of antelope, giraffes, and zebra—and, to this day, Kenya's largest population of elephants. Tsavo is on every tourist's "must-see" list. The elephants are a particular draw, since the herds are large and easy to find. But, as I've already noted, Tsavo had also become one of the poachers' favorite haunts. We'd been losing elephants here at an astonishing rate. Frankly, I was surprised we had as many as five thousand left. While that number may sound impressive, it was a far cry from the masses of elephants Iain Douglas-Hamilton had witnessed when he flew over Tsavo in 1969 to make an aerial count. Herds of thousands of elephants were common then. He once told me he'd seen almost "no end to them." Indeed, he had counted elephants nearly all the way to the Indian Ocean.

How different was my flight two decades later! Of course, I wasn't flying low enough for counting purposes, but an animal the size of an elephant stands out in the bush. It's not difficult to spot them from the air, particularly if there are many of them. I started looking for herds as soon as I crossed Tsavo's border and did spot a few small ones, one with maybe two hundred elephants. But it was readily apparent that the elephants no longer stretched like chunky stepping stones from Tsavo's wilderness to the sea.

I also spotted a few bloated gray carcasses—the bodies of elephants that the poachers had left behind. From the air, they looked like rounded boulders, the kind vultures use as perches, since trails of white droppings covered them. They could not have been killed very long before, I thought, as I banked lower to take a closer look. These were the first poached elephants I had seen. They lay scattered across the landscape, some adults, others juveniles: probably a family group trying to run away from their tormentors. Even from this height there was something so very still and silent and ineffably sad about that scene. I didn't circle again but flew on to Tsavo West National Park headquarters at Kamboyo and from there drove about ten miles to the Kilanguni tourist lodge.

I don't stay in tourist lodges as a rule. I prefer a tent or, better still, sleeping under the stars. But after my long flight and the depressing view of the dead elephants, the lodge, with its bright bougainvillea and tall palms, was a welcome sight. I had arranged to meet the parks' top wardens: Joe Kioko, who directed Tsavo East, and Bill Woodley, who oversaw Tsavo West (and who has now, sadly, passed away). The two came from very different backgrounds—Kioko was from the Kamba tribe, and had grown up in a village on the edge of the Ngong Hills, hunting zebras and antelope with his father. Woodley was a white African who'd come to Kenya as a British civil servant at the end of World War II. Both worked for the park service for most of their lives.

Bill had played a major role in shaping Kenya's National Parks system and lived and worked at several of its most famous preserves, including the Aberdare Mountains, Mount Kenya, and Mount Elgon, for almost forty years. A thin, rather nervous, chain-smoking man, he was unquestionably devoted to Kenya's wildlife, and I valued his expertise. Bill was of the old colonial school and had fought against the Nationalists during Mau Mau, the name given to a Nationalist movement that fought for independence from the British administration in the 1950s. He could be patronizing toward Africans, and sometimes this presented a problem.

Joe Kioko was about fifteen years younger than Bill and equally dedicated to the park service. Mild-mannered, good-humored, and trustworthy, he'd been one of the first students to attend Kenya's Moyaka College of Wildlife Management when it opened in 1968. He joined the service immediately on graduation two years later. Joe had worked with Bill as a junior officer in the Aberdare Mountains, so the two knew and respected each other. Both men were also pilots and had turned over much of the day-to-day management of their parks to their deputies in an effort to curtail the poaching with daily surveillance flights.

"It's tough," Joe said to me, taking a sip of cool Tusker beer. "Some days, it seems we see carcasses everywhere. I've seen ten to fifteen at a time so the five you saw today don't surprise me."

"I think we spotted them a couple of days ago," added Bill. "Looked like a small poaching party, maybe six men. The tusks were gone. I saw another three elephants killed near the Chuylu Hills yesterday."

The poaching wasn't my only worry. Just before I took office, two groups of tourists had been attacked on a dirt road linking Tsavo East with Amboseli National Park, a popular route leading from one park to the other. In both incidents, the bandits suddenly appeared among the rocks and boulders in broad daylight and fired their AK-47s at the minivans, wounding several travelers and their drivers. They'd then de-manded money, jewelry, and cameras. I didn't want anymore such trou-bles—this sort of activity, and publicity, was the last thing that Kenya needed.

I asked Joe and Bill what they needed to stop these poachers. The week before, I had sent four of the new Land Rovers I had purchased to Tsavo, along with a big shipment of fuel both for these vehicles and the park's air-craft—giving a boost to the rangers' morale, the two wardens assured me. But their men were still missing so many things: boots, radios for com-municating during antipoaching operations, decent rifles. Like the rangers at Sibiloi, rangers here were equipped with bolt-action .303 weapons, the same Enfield rifles the British had used against the Germans in the East Africa campaign during World War I. You couldn't expect a man armed with a .303 to take on someone wielding a modern assault rifle. Joe and Bill also wondered what should be done about corruption in the park ser-vice. It was well known that several employees had assisted the poachers. Some had even killed elephants using their government-issue rifles.

Others issued false tickets or overcharged tourists and pocketed the proceeds. What was I going to do about these bad eggs?

"It's going to take some time," I said, "but, yes, they've got to go." I didn't tell them that I had already brought this up with President Moi. He'd agreed in principle to ridding the service of corrupt staff, but he'd also said it would be difficult, since rangers were civil servants. As anyone who's ever worked for a government knows, firing civil servants is not a simple matter. But I wanted honest, trustworthy men I could rely on, and who could rely on each other.

That afternoon, I made a brief tour of the ranger units and gave my "we're all in this together" pep talk. I wanted to believe in what I was telling them, although I also knew that some of the men lined up before me were trying to undercut me. We had poachers in our own ranks, and we had to identify and remove them. Then we could go after the bandits.

CHAPTER 6

By the end of my first month at the Wildlife Department, I have to say that I thought all the rumors I had heard about it were true: it was one of the most—if not *the* most—corrupt organization in the government. I suspected that one cause was the rangers' and wardens' arduous life of long hours, isolation, and low pay. Rangers earned barely enough to feed and clothe their families, certainly not enough to pay their children's school fees, too. In Kenya, all students pay to attend school. Primary education is free, but parents must cover the cost of books, meals, uniforms, and activity fees. At the secondary level, tuition fees are also charged and can run several hundred dollars a year. Relative to average incomes, the actual cost of putting a child through school is very high. Many schools are ill equipped in terms of books and learning materials, with the consequence that a growing number of children do not graduate. It is no wonder that rangers, wardens, and indeed many in public service look for ways to augment their official earnings.

This isn't to say that the entire field staff had engaged in illegal practices—or that I condoned the behavior of those who had. I could understand why some had gone astray, but I was far more sympathetic to those rangers who'd remained honest despite the hardships and especially to those who had put their own necks at risk to report and document the criminal activities of their colleagues. For example, two senior officers at the two Tsavos had compiled a list of the crimes that some of their fellow rangers and wardens had committed in the mid-1980s. These transgressions ranged from the slaughter of elephants to theft of government property to murder. Yet none of these men had ever been charged with any crime, although reports of their wrongdoings had been given to previous directors and the police.

In numerous cases, the tracks of government-owned Wildlife Department Land Rovers were found next to the carcasses of elephants. Casings from .303 bullets were even recovered near the dead animals. The rangers referred to these types of killings as "roadsiders," because the elephants had obviously been killed by someone pulling up beside them in a car and shooting them point-blank. It's difficult to say how many of the thousands of poached elephants were slaughtered in this manner, but I'm afraid it was a sizable proportion. To give some idea, a report from March 1988 states that a two-day aerial reconnaissance in and around Tsavo East turned up twenty-five fresh elephant carcasses. Nearly all the animals had been shot close to roads.

As Patrick Hamilton, one of the officers, said to me, "It was motorized poaching—and it was Wildlife Department personnel who were doing it. They were using government bullets, fired from government firearms, from government vehicles, driven by government drivers, and fueled by taxpayer's fuel. And the whole thing was being supervised by government officers, some of them being top wardens in the Wildlife Department."

Some rangers worked together as poaching teams, using coded messages to alert their fellow criminals about when and where an aerial survey, for instance, was to take place. "If I took off from Voi [a town near Tsavo]," Hamilton told me, "that information would go out in coded form over the radio network. I used to think nothing of those messages. They sounded innocent, usually referring to the weather, whether the skies were cloudy or clear. But it was a code, indicating how active the aircraft was. We often found that more elephants were killed when our aircraft were grounded—and the skies were clear."

Sadly, ranger poachers were at work not only in Tsavo East and West but in Meru National Park and Marsabit National Reserve as well. They weren't always the ones pulling the trigger. Sometimes, they simply looked the other way while others did the dirty work, then took a cut of the loot. At Meru, for example, I discovered that senior park officers were almost certainly involved in the killing of the five white rhinos in their *boma* (an enclosure similar to a corral), although this was never proved. The circumstances, however, spoke for themselves. The poachers had entered the park in broad daylight and shot the animals (which were supposedly being guarded by rangers) scarcely a mile from the park's headquarters. No shots were fired at the poachers, and no arrests were ever made. I'm sure that some park officials received a handsome payoff for those rhinos' horns.

More rare than elephant ivory, rhino horn has been banned as an item of international trade for some years but fetches very high prices on the black market. A single rhino horn can attract several thousand dollars at the first point of sale, and by the time it reaches Taiwan or China, can be worth almost ten times that. The main market used to be the Middle East, where it was used for ceremonial dagger handles, but this has changed in recent years because good imitation plastics have become popular.

The new market is in China and other Eastern countries, where the alternative medical therapy trade is flourishing. Powdered horn is reputed to be good for many health problems and valued far more as an aphrodisiac. Viagra and plastics are not enough to save the rhino at present.

The secret report that had been given to George Muhoho clearly spelled out the level of the collusion between government employees and poachers. When I challenged him about revealing the parties involved, Muhoho claimed that it did not name anyone important. At the time I didn't believe Muhoho, and I don't think the press or anyone reading his statements in the newspapers did either. So it was with some anticipation that I opened Dr. Olindo's copy of the report after I was named director. He'd left it in a drawer, right on top, where it was easy to find. I pulled it out and thumbed through the pages, each one marked

SECRET. In one section, the names of corrupt wardens, assistant wardens, and rangers were listed and their crimes delineated. But the report did not, alas, connect these men to anyone higher up in government office. Yet clearly someone in the government *had* protected the malefactors, otherwise they would have been dismissed long ago, their crimes were so blatant.

Dr. Olindo had attempted to rid the department of these unsavory characters, but he'd only been partially successful. He'd written the preface to the report, and in it alluded to the difficulties he'd faced when he tried to dismiss the men. Mind you, he wasn't charging them with any crimes; he was simply trying to transfer them from his department to some other branch of service. "I reorganized the personnel," he wrote, "and I was immediately rebuffed by very strong forces from within the Wildlife Department and elsewhere in the government." He'd been "forced," he continued, "to reverse the transfers" he'd arranged for the worst offenders. Dr. Olindo didn't say who had "forced" him, but it was clear that he had not had the government's (that is, President Moi's) full backing to clean up the department.

But I did—at least so far. Since my first meeting with President Moi, he'd continued to profess his complete support and hadn't waffled over granting any of my requests, even burning the ivory. Now, after my visits to Tsavo and Sibiloi, I knew I needed to take up this matter of the corrupt personnel quickly. The same people who had thwarted Dr. Olindo's efforts would be watching to see what I would do.

Dr. Olindo had managed to rid the department of eleven officers, among them some of the very worst offenders. Another seventy, however, were equally as bad, as the report made clear. These were the men Dr. Olindo had attempted to sack. At the end of my first week in office, I had sent the names to the permanent secretary, with a note attached, saying that based on the results of an internal investigation, I wanted these men dismissed from the department immediately.

To my astonishment, they were. They were either given early retirement or transferred to some other department, where they could do no harm to mine—or to the elephants. Some have asked me why I didn't prosecute them. My answer was that I didn't have the time. I had far more important things to do than worrying over prosecutions and court cases. I simply wanted the dishonest employees gone.

The dismissal sent the signal that I had the government's authority to clean house, and that I was going to do it. Those seventy were simply the most obvious transgressors. There were others in the ranks working against me and the honest rangers and staff. I wasn't certain yet how I was going to remove them, but it had to be done were we to build a fighting force capable of taking on the well-armed poachers. If I was going to equip them with automatic weapons, I had to be certain of the rangers' trustworthiness.

After transferring the seventy rotten employees, I brought in new people and promoted deserving junior officers. All this temporarily stopped the ranger poachers—there were no new reports of "roadsiders." The lull in these attacks bought us some time. We could now concentrate our efforts on the outsiders who were still gunning down our elephants.

From the beginning of my tenure at Wildlife, I realized that everyone thought the poachers were invincible. Rangers, police, reporters, international conservationists, the man on the street—everyone regarded these gangs as highly trained, SWATlike teams. And indeed, some of the poachers were veterans of Somalia's armed forces and had fought in the 1977 invasion of Ethiopia (an attempt to claim the southern part of that country, the Ogaden), or in the civil wars that resulted after Somalia was defeated. That was how they'd come by their AK-47s, grenade launchers, and high-caliber machine guns. Kenya's citizens had grown used to seeing headlines about poachers killing rangers and policemen. Some twenty men on active duty had been killed on wildlife-related patrols in the year prior to my appointment, while merely five poachers had been killed by the government team. We couldn't change those proportions overnight, but we could do something about the public's perception of the poaching gangs.

A few weeks into my job, I gave the press a briefing on our progress, emphasizing the effect that our new Land Rovers and the donations pouring in would have on our efforts. One journalist asked if I was going to bring in personnel from abroad to help in the war against the poachers. Here was my opportunity.

"No," I replied. "There's no need." The poachers, I said, were a useless bunch who'd failed to eliminate the elephants in spite of having no opposition and indeed often having help from our own people in the parks. Now we were fighting back, and I expected that the few Somali poachers would leave the parks forever and that elephant poaching would soon be a thing of the past.

Another reporter asked if I could arrange for the press to photograph dead elephants.

"No, because there aren't going to be any more dead elephants. Soon the press will not be asking permission to film dead elephants but to film dead poachers."

This was simply bluff and bravado, but Kenyan newspapers carried headlines bearing my strong statements—and you could almost sense a new national pride. We weren't going to be defeated by these small terrorist gangs after all! (My statements were read very differently in the Western press. Many reporters and human rights activists thought I was completely serious and came to regard me as some kind of a Clint Eastwood–character running amok in the savanna. I am still attacked by human rights people over that quote.)

More was involved than elephant poaching in Kenya. It was widely believed that Somali incursions were simply the first step in a full-fledged invasion, similar to Somalia's attack on Ethiopia. When the European powers divided East Africa in the nineteenth century, they'd drawn the borders of Kenya and Ethiopia in such a way that these two countries included land that Somalia regarded as its own. To Somalia, large tracts of northern Kenya should rightfully fall within its boundaries, and the poaching came to be seen as part of an effort by Somalia's president Muhammad Siad Barre to ruin Kenya's economy and destabilize its government. I was never sure how much credence to give such rumors;

but in 1987, *New African* magazine, a London-based publication, published a letter, reputedly signed by Barre, authorizing "Comrades Omer Hassan Khayare and Hussein Barre Hassan to bring elephant tusks from Kenya to Somalia." The Somali Embassy in Nairobi vehemently denied the authenticity of the letter, but the magazine's editor insisted that it was genuine and had come from someone within Barre's office. Rumors soon surfaced that Somalia was using the elephant ivory to finance its war chest.

Several of my top wardens believed the rumor was true, and with some reason. Undercover investigators discovered that members of the South African and Angolan military forces were using poached ivory and rhino horns to fund their wars. They could see no other reason for the poachers to be toting mortars and heavy machine guns with them through the deserts. But I wasn't so sure. Somalia had collapsed into civil war. I thought these poachers were more likely deserters or rebels, people who had nothing to lose. Time and again they'd proven themselves to be ruthless. The rangers and police often talked about what fierce fighters the poachers were. Even on the rare occasions when they were outgunned, they fought to the last man.

Everyone was afraid of them. The poachers knew this, too. They used to send taunting messages to our rangers via small goat-herding boys: "Muhammad says he's going to be in those hills today, killing elephants. So unless you want to die, Muhammad says not to go there."

They tried the same tactic with me. Not long after the newspapers carried the stories with my bold statements about ending the poaching, a ranger found a written note stuck in the crotch of a thorntree at a prominent watering hole in Tsavo East. It was addressed to me. "Leakey!" it read, "We're going to kill you!"

When it was handed to me, I flipped the paper over and wrote on the back, "Perhaps, but my men will get you first!" I then had a ranger stick it back in the tree.

Again, all bluff on my part. I wanted the poachers to think that I was as ruthless as they were, and I wanted my men to believe that they could win this bush battle.

❖ ❖ ❖

In early June 1989, we got our first chance to begin turning the tide. Only this time, sadly, more than dead elephants were at stake.

On the afternoon of June 7, I was in Mombassa, on the coast, meeting with President Moi and some of the senior members of his government team. We were engaged in a heated discussion about revamping the Wildlife Department, debating whether or not it should be transformed into a "parastatal" agency—an organization financially independent of the government. The basic measure had already been approved during Dr. Olindo's tenure, but there were many details to be worked out, such as the need to override Kenya's laws pertaining to semiautomatic rifles. If we were going to arm the rangers, we first needed the legal authority to do so.

Sometime after lunch, one of the president's aides brought me a message. Something told me that that it wasn't good news.

"Well?" I asked.

The aide told me there'd been an attack in Tsavo. Tourists, maybe Americans, were the victims. People had been shot and robbed. Some might have been killed.

I had the aide summon a driver and we set off at once to the airport. Moments later I was at the controls of my plane, flying to Tsavo East.

Joe Kioko met me on the ground, looking very grim.

"They killed one this time," he said. "The driver's wounded. Shot in the leg. But he'll survive."

Joe added that the driver had shown great courage. The gang had shot out the tires of the tourist van, but he'd still somehow managed to get it to the closest National Parks gate, some thirty miles away, where the rangers had raised the alarm and sought help. Joe had immediately driven to the gate and from there had sent a radio message to my office; my secretary had then contacted the aide in Mombassa.

Joe had learned as much as he could about what had happened from the driver. Like many tour groups in Kenya, these tourists had hired a minivan for their safari. They'd been traveling together for several days through the game parks and had just finished their tour of Tsavo West. Next on their list was Amboseli, and to save time the driver had chosen to use the dirt road linking the two parks. (There'd been two earlier attacks on tourists on this track before I had taken over the department, and as I listened to Joe's story I decided right there and then to close it. I didn't want any more tourists harmed on my watch.) One particularly bad stretch cut through a black rock lava flow and was full of rocks and big potholes. That was where the gunmen had suddenly appeared, firing their assault rifles as they ran out from behind the rocks and bushes. They had killed one poor woman and wounded the driver. Ignoring the screaming of the terrified tourists, they'd stuck their rifles into the van's windows and yelled, "Money! Dollars! Cameras!" The tourists readily complied, even handing over their shoes when the bandits pointed to them.

Taking their loot, the thieves had escaped back into the black lava rock field. There were at least seven of them and possibly more who'd stayed hidden in the rocks.

"We've got to find them," I said, as Joe finished his story. "Do whatever you need to do, but bring these bandits in." The last thing we needed just then was bad press in Europe and the States, from which most of our tourists originated. To reassure the traveling public, quick action and results would be crucial and I had to move fast.

Joe nodded. "I've got our top antipoaching unit here now," he said.

The unit of ten men stood at attention at the park's headquarters, waiting for their orders. I had seen to it that new boots had been issued to everyone on these antipoaching patrols, and though the rest of their uniforms were still raggedy, their boots gleamed in the afternoon sun. The rangers were mostly tall, thin, hardy young men from Kenya's desert regions—men who knew the desert and its ways and were as tough as the outlaws they were chasing. That was part of our new strategy: if the killers walked all day in the blazing desert sun, our rangers would, too.

Shoulders back, eyes looking straight ahead, they stood on a parade ground. I told them that I was counting on them—Kenya was counting on them—to find the *shifta* (Swahili for Somali bandits) who'd robbed our tourists. I had see to it that they'd get whatever provisions they needed for the job. The one thing I couldn't give them was a decent weapon. They would be chasing men carrying AK-47s and would be outgunned if caught in an ambush. Some of them were likely to be wounded or even killed. In the past wounded rangers received only minimal medical care. I had heard of one brave ranger who'd been shot in the leg by poachers. It was a simple bullet wound, but he had had to wait three or four days before getting any medical assistance. By then, gangrene had set in and he'd lost both legs. I didn't want any more such mishaps. I told the men I knew their mission was dangerous, but that if any one of them got wounded I would have a plane dispatched immediately to evacuate him to Nairobi's finest hospital.

"We're not going to lose any ranger to any bandit," I said.

In return, I wanted them to find these murderous thieves.

"Get them or eliminate them. I don't care if you have to walk to Somalia. If you get to Mombassa and find that they've crossed the ocean to India, I'll see to it that a ship is waiting for you. Wherever they go, find them."

The unit's commanding officer, Peter Leitoro, later told me that my words had fired up his men in a way that he'd never seen before. Lacking proper training, weapons, and support, they'd been cowed into thinking that the poachers were always going to have the upper hand. I wanted to change that attitude, and to do that I needed to show them first that change had to come at the top.

There was one complication. Kenyan police were also sending in a team and the wardens had to await their arrival before setting off. So rather then marching off smartly into the savanna following my "stirring" speech, the unit was dismissed. At the time, Wildlife rangers were regarded as incompetent, and the government had ordered the police to take part in any serious missions. Commissioner of Police Philip Kilonzo argued that crimes involving theft and murder were rightfully his department's concern, not mine. Besides, the police, and their paramilitary General Services Unit, were well-trained, well-armed men, capable of pursuing and dealing with armed criminals. Still, this seemed like a ludicrous way to chase poachers. Precious time was lost while the wardens waited for the police to arrive. Then, more time was lost while wardens and police worked out a plan of action. By the time the joint team (in which the police acted as the "senior" partner) headed into the field, the gang had been given a long head start—in this case, nearly a full day.

None of this would change until our rangers were better trained and equipped. That was why in my very first meeting with President Moi, I had insisted that we find a way to deal with the firearms issue. If he wanted his "shoot-to-kill" policy against poachers enforced, our rangers had to be issued modern guns. Kenya's Firearms Act states that only the military and police forces are authorized to use semiautomatic and other sophisticated weapons. Somehow, the president had to find a way to exempt the Wildlife rangers from this restriction. All he really had to do was issue a presidential order to this effect. President Moi was reluctant to do this because it would set a precedent. Once Wildlife rangers were allowed such arms, other groups would want them as well and there might be a serious escalation in violence. All the same, I continued to press our case.

Police Commissioner Philip Kilonzo was actively campaigning for exactly the opposite and he, too, had Moi's ear. He suggested to the president that his department form a special police unit responsible for providing protection for wildlife and tourists within our national parks and that the rangers be disarmed. Not long after I took office, Kilonzo called a meeting to discuss the merits of his plan. I went to the meeting. Flanking their boss were at least eighteen police officers, their uniforms starched and pressed, their boots and buttons brightly polished. Kilonzo started laying out his plan, explaining that it was a necessary move given that the rangers were undisciplined. They had, he said, abused their weapons, using them in numerous crimes—cattle rustling, robberies, even poaching. How could such rabble be given semiautomatic weapons?

I took a deep breath and plunged in, countering that the police department also had its share of corruption, and was known for dealing incompetently with straightforward urban crimes. I didn't think policemen would perform any better inside our parks. It made far better sense to clean up the ranger units and keep the police out. Indeed, my mandate was to put an effective ranger force into place, and that was what I intended to do.

Looking Commissioner Kilonzo straight in the eye, I concluded by saying, "Your plan is unrealistic, top-heavy, and costly. It should be dropped forthwith."

The temperature in the room seemed to drop with every word I uttered; and by the time I finished, you could almost see the icicles hanging in the air. A contemptuous sneer had settled on several officers' faces. I braced myself for what was to come.

One by one the officers fired questions at me like bullets. Did I have any idea of what I was talking about? What experience did I have? What did I know about commanding men-at-arms?

Difficult questions. I had hated the cadet force that I had been made to join in secondary school, I was never a Boy Scout, and I loathe firearms.

By the end of the meeting, the icicles had melted. In their place hung a palpable air of derision. I was left in no doubt that the Kenya police would oppose my plans, especially on the matter of arming the rangers with semiautomatic rifles.

So went my first big fight with "big" people, as important officials and political figures are referred to in Kenya. I wasn't prepared to give in, and neither were they.

The Tsavo incident raised the matter again. A few days after the joint operation finally got underway, I flew back to the park with Kilonzo to discuss park security and to evaluate progress in the hunt for the killers. This was the first and only time I wore the Wildlife Department director's uniform. I knew that all the police and Wildlife personnel would be uniformed, and I felt I had to dress the part. I also had that earlier meeting in mind, remembering how imposing Commissioner Kilonzo and his eighteen officers looked in their spotless gear. A uniform lends an air of authority that a suit and tie do not. So I donned the ghastly, pea green uniform that had never been worn and instantly felt like a fool. I knew I looked like a new recruit. But I didn't have the good sense to take it off.

From the moment I boarded the plane, I felt conspicuous and self-conscious. I didn't have the uniform's beret on quite right, and instead of exuding that casual, confident air of a uniformed officer in the field, I was tight and anxious. Commissioner Kilonzo was very polite and said not a word.

At the Tsavo airfield, various people in uniform saluted us as we walked from the plane. I watched the commissioner and copied his responses. I didn't realize that I was supposed to acknowledge my officers as well as the police saluting their boss. There was a sort of flurry of salutes, which I somehow got through, and then we covered the short distance to Kilaguni Lodge, where our meeting was to take place.

Suddenly, the police field commander of the operation, Mr. Abdul Bashir, appeared at my side. "Sir," he said.

I stopped. "Yes?"

"Let me just help you, sir," Mr. Bashir said. With a twinkle in his eye, he reached up, took my beret, and pulled it smartly to one side, setting it at its proper angle.

"Sorry, sir, but you know, sir, if you're going to wear a beret, this is how you wear it, sir," he said.

It was done with such deference that I was deeply grateful, though I'm certain he was thinking I was a complete idiot. He did say that he thought perhaps I had never worn a uniform before—and I'm sure he wanted to add that I should never wear one again. I couldn't take the beret off. I knew I would never get the silly thing back on. How I longed for my suit and tie.

My bungling seemed to lighten the mood, and all of us—Wildlife officers and the police team alike—entered the lodge in good spirits. They didn't last long, however, for it soon became clear that our joint operation to get the culprits wasn't getting anywhere. Despite their smart uniforms and salutes, the police were totally disorganized; they had neither the fuel nor money to handle this kind of investigation properly. Later I met privately with Peter Leitoro, the officer in charge of our side of the operation. He told me some local Maasai tribesmen had told the police where the gang's hideout was and had actually led them to it. The police had decided it would be too dangerous to engage the bandits and had withdrawn. The gang moved on the next day. The police had started off in pursuit but had found the going too tough and quit.

I was appalled—and immediately convinced that were we to make our parks safe for tourists and wildlife, we would have to do it ourselves. Creating a crack antipoaching unit was now a top priority.

Another incident only two days later strengthened my resolve. Our combined forces had finally made contact with the gang. A gun battle ensued. One police officer and two of the bandits were killed, and many of the tourists' stolen possessions were recovered. This was our first success since I had taken office, and I thought it would be a good thing if I went straight to the scene and congratulated the men personally. Commissioner Kilonzo could not come but sent his deputy.

We flew down in a police helicopter, landed, and climbed out onto the dry savanna grass. It was hot. The sickly smell of death permeated the air. Around me were my men, lying prone, guns pointing outward in a defensive action—the standard procedure to protect me against possible assault. They looked exhausted, grim, and grimy. It looked like a scene from a war movie—except this was real. I had wisely left my uniform in the closet but knew I needed to give the impression of being in command. My men were watching me, and so was the deputy commissioner of police.

I acknowledged the platoon commander's salute. He led us over to view the dead and explained what had happened. Ten rangers and five policemen had gone up against nine armed outlaws. Our men had sneaked up on the gang at dawn. The response came instantly. The bandits opened fire, and within seconds, a young policeman was killed. His body lay in the shade of a tree, covered with a blanket. The deputy commissioner had apparently been a close friend of this young man, and he stood next to the tree, his eyes filling with tears.

I understood the deputy's sorrow, but all I could feel was infuriated. This man's death had been so unnecessary. It was a wonder that the entire team wasn't killed. I asked to see one of my men's .303 rifles and looked at the date stamped on the barrel: 1911. I passed it to the deputy commissioner of police.

"Let's see how quickly you can get a bullet into the breach and shoot that tree," I challenged him, pointing to a nearby tree.

My men gathered behind us to watch. The deputy got off one shot, then the bolt jammed. Cursing, he yanked it back, and started to reload.

I stopped him. "Don't waste the ammunition. The poachers would have killed you by now anyway."

"You're absolutely right," he replied. I knew then and there that I had won over at least one important policeman. I had also scored points with my rangers by demonstrating the seriousness of their situation.

Two weeks later, I received the first shipment of semiautomatic weapons for my men—three hundred G-3s, the assault rifles originally developed for use by NATO forces. They had been issued by order of President Moi.

CHAPTER 7

I knew that by arming our antipoaching units with a few semiautomatic weapons and by giving them eighteen new vehicles for patrols, I was doing the right thing; but I couldn't help feeling how wrong things were. Our National Parks should not have been battlegrounds for small-scale guerilla wars against poachers and thieves but places of tranquil beauty where binoculars and field guides were the only equipment rangers would carry. But I knew that would take time to happen. In the meantime, I had to turn these men into a strike force—one that would respond instantly and effectively to any violent crimes in our parks. Two things were essential to accomplish that.

First, we had to adopt what is called a "code of discipline," that is, procedures and rules for everyone in a uniform: everything from who and when to salute to what happens in the event of misconduct. Most important, its intent was to ensure that should a commanding officer give an order, the men would follow it unquestioningly. Several military people told me that it was absolutely necessary we have such a code, even though we were not a military unit. The sentiment was it would greatly reduce the risks of insubordination.

Second, we had to train our rangers in the use of their new weapons. With help from the police department's paramilitary unit, we set up a facility in Tsavo West, where the men went through four months of intensive training. They learned general weapons handling, ambush and counterattack tactics, and strategies of bush warfare.

At the same time, help was pouring into the Wildlife Department from around the world. Since taking office, I had done a number of television interviews on such shows as *Good Morning, America* and print interviews with a number of journalists. I talked about Kenya's fight to preserve its elephants and the difficulties we faced. I often emphasized how unfair it was for a poor country such as Kenya to shoulder all the costs of conservation. The preservation of our wildlife was of worldwide concern. I seemed to strike a sympathetic chord with many people, who sent in financial contributions or offered other forms of assistance, such as vehicles.

In late May 1989, I made a trip to the United States to meet with potential donors and donor agencies, and raised $250,000 for the immediate purchase of several new aircraft, fuel, and spare parts.

All this goodwill could vanish in an instant, I knew, if we didn't make our parks secure. And that was going to take more than outside donations.

All the reports I got indicated that the worst problems continued to occur in the two Tsavos and in Meru. The wardens would almost always report that people had been killed—either poachers or rangers or both—or that they had found dead elephants. (The one bright spot was that we were no longer getting reports of "roadsiders.") If anything, the bandits had escalated their operations. They were testing my resolve.

In the early days I received encrypted radio messages, telephoned through to my home where I kept the code keys from the wardens. Later I had a small radio installed so that I could be in direct communication with the field units at any time of day or night. I had a similar radio installed in the aircraft that I used. Wherever I went an assistant aide traveled with me, carrying a briefcase radio link.

It was reassuring to the men in the field that I was always available. It did, however, cause some tensions in my home life. Often I would receive a message classified as SECRET that I could not share with Meave and my family. Too often I would return to the dinner table looking vexed and acting distant, spoiling the atmosphere. It was not easy for Meave to be on the "outside."

There were reports of unbelievable, heartbreaking fiascos. One of the worst occurred in Tsavo. Before President Moi had authorized the new weapons, our rangers were still engaging in joint operations with the police. Not long after the murder of the woman tourist, they had received a tip about another poaching gang's hideout. As one of our planes was circling overhead to direct the combined forces to its location, the pilot suddenly realized that the poachers had set up an ambush. But without radio communications, he had no way of warning the rangers and police below and could only watch helplessly as the commanding police officer was gunned down.

Such incidents left me terribly shaken—and all the more determined to equip our men properly.

Despite such tragedies we did not let up on the pressure, and soon it seemed that our efforts were beginning to pay off. On July 3, 1989, I wrote in my diary: *On the poaching scene, we seem to be making good progress. I believe the number of poachers killed during June was 22 and about 7 captured or wounded. We have had some casualties, but the situation is so much better than it was.*

Only two days later, however, I wrote the following: *Two tourists shot at Meru. Damn.* A young couple, honeymooners from France, had come to Kenya on their first visit to East Africa. They had decided to organize everything themselves and tour the parks on their own, as many independent-minded visitors enjoy doing. They'd driven their rental vehicle north from Nairobi to Meru and were motoring down a dirt track through a forested area when they stumbled on a group of poachers carving up a zebra, probably for a meal. The poachers shot the two point-blank, killing them instantaneously.

Early the next morning I flew to Meru, where a joint ranger-police force was getting ready to head into the field after the culprits. We were getting better at mounting timely responses but weren't yet as swift off the starting block as I'd hoped. Despite an extensive search, our team found nothing. The killers seemed to have vanished, and the men weren't able to pick up their trail.

These murders were different from the one in Tsavo. There the gang had been after the tourists' money. This time nothing was taken from the couples' car. Very likely it was a case of mistaken identity: the poachers heard the tourists' car approaching and assumed that it was driven by Wildlife rangers coming to arrest them, so they fired away. That did not absolve the poachers of their crime. It only illustrated how strong their determination was not to be caught. I suspected that we hadn't seen the last of this gang and advised our rangers to keep on their toes.

Although there had been firefights with poachers in other parks, such as in Mount Elgon, situated on the border with Uganda, the two Tsavos and Meru remained the most dangerous. All three lie adjacent to areas inhabited by nomads—Somalis, Borans, Oromos—who regard the land as their own, not Kenya's. This is, as I've described, wide-open country, more desertlike than savanna, thick in some places with thornbush but mostly sparsely vegetated. It's sparsely inhabited, too. Dirt tracks lead to a few towns, where there's usually not much more than a mosque, little mud-and-earth tea houses, and *dukas* (shops) selling soap, cooking oil, aluminum pans, and bolts of brightly colored cloth. The nomadic people come to these towns occasionally. Most spend their lives, as they have for centuries, on the move, seeking grass and water for their animals.

The tribes here are known for their incredible endurance and fiercely warlike ways. They have close-knit family clans; family ties can stretch from Nairobi to Mogadishu, Somalia's capital. Such strong ties are critical to a family's long-term survival in the harsh desert. But they also provide an underground network that protects the poachers. The outlaws can always find food and shelter as they move about.

That made our job harder, as did the fact that many nomadic peoples had settled in our parks with their livestock. They built tree thorn *bomas* (corrals) to harbor their herds of humped cattle, camels, and goats throughout the northern and eastern areas of Tsavo East and Meru. The owners—typically a few men, although women and children are sometimes also present—stay with the animals in crude, oval huts they've made by throwing leather skins over a framework of branches. Theoretically, these *bomas* and huts are illegal, but in hard times (such as during droughts, for instance) it is often the practice to look the other way. Because we had so few rangers in these border areas, and neither the vehicles nor the fuel for patrolling them, the crude *bomas* had turned into year-round settlements. By the time I took office, some nomads had been living in the parks for almost a decade.

The wardens complained that the illegal settlements gave the poachers easy access to the elephants, since they could blend in with the herders (to whom they might be related) and enter our parks unnoticed. There was no easy way to distinguish poachers from herders; some even slipped from one role to the other. "They do double duty that way," one of my wardens once said to me, "herding cattle one day, killing elephants the next." The herders were themselves usually armed (often illegally so), because several of the tribes bear ancient grudges against each other and regularly stage raids, killing people, abducting women, and stealing livestock. In short, this part of Kenya was like the nineteenth-century American West—a lawless land of guns and short tempers where people did more or less as they pleased.

The best evidence of what our men were up against was provided by the warden pilots themselves. Here's how Sacha Cook, then working in the Meru National Park, described some of his experiences: "Herder groups always had armed men with them. Anytime you flew down over a herd of cattle, there'd be men with spears and firearms with them— AK-47s and G-3s—although with all the dust, you couldn't always tell who was armed and who was not. So you were never sure who was going to stand up and shoot at you. But they'd do that. They'd shoot at our planes."

Once, Cook flew down below the clouds along Meru's northern border and found three large herds of Somali cattle. The herds fairly bristled with armed men. Ammunition belts crisscrossing their bodies glinted in the sun.

"I didn't realize what they were at first," he recalled. "I thought they were poachers so I came around to get a better look; and as soon as I did, every single armed man—there were about seventy of them—shot off a blast at the plane. I could see the fire trails from their guns."

Cook didn't wait to see more and flew back up into the clouds. "I didn't even hesitate—and I didn't bother with them: they were cattle raiders. I guess they'd been successful."

Poachers usually traveled in smaller gangs, some with as few as three men. Not all of them had clan members deep inside Kenya and had resorted to raiding to get what they needed. Our rangers heard many complaints from isolated farmers and from people living in tiny villages who'd been terrorized.

"They'd harass the local people," explained Moses Lelesiit, a platoon commander. "They cannot travel without tea; it's what gives them strength. They'd come into someone's home, pointing their guns and shouting, 'We need *chai! chai!* [Swahili for tea].' "

The poachers would demand food, too, forcing villagers to kill and roast goats for them. Anyone who refused was shot or badly beaten. And, as in the Arab slave-trading days, they'd kidnap young men to carry the ivory tusks for them, making them walk as far as the coast (where they loaded the ivory on *dhows*) or across the Kenya-Somali frontier.

"Most of the time, after they'd killed elephants, they'd cut out the tusks and bury them," says Julius Leperes, a senior Wildlife pilot. "They could not move fast if they were carrying ivory. So they would dig a hole and hide it in a place they knew well. Then they'd come back quietly, without shooting or killing anything. But the tusks can be quite heavy, so they'd make some young men from the villages help them carry the ivory."

It was obviously going to take time to bring law and order to these areas. But the stories from the field gave me some ideas. I knew there must be villagers who were angry with the poachers. We needed to recruit them as our eyes and ears in remote areas and to alert us when they heard about gangs moving through their part of the country. Initially, such recruitment would not be easy, because in all honesty the Wildlife Department did not have the best reputation among people living close to our parks. The rangers sent out on these patrols had not been well trained. They were notorious for grabbing any men they found near the parks, accusing them of being poachers, and beating them.

As Adan Dullo, a warden I appointed head of our intelligence operations, told me, "They beat everybody, the poachers and the non-poachers. If anyone saw a Wildlife vehicle or rangers coming, he had to run and disappear in the bush because these antipoaching fellows were beating people senseless. So at that time, there was quite a bit of resentment."

I insisted on an immediate end to this kind of indiscriminate behavior. I wanted the villagers to be our allies not our enemies.

I was also aware of how desperate the poachers were; they seemed to have little more than their rifles and the clothes on their backs. Some of them had taken up poaching because they had no opportunity for an honest job. I told my rangers to spread the word that we were ready to forgive any poachers who turned themselves in to us and gave us information we could use, such as what routes they had traveled, who had given them shelter, what watering holes they had used. When rangers captured poachers (sadly, a rare event, since the poachers tended to prefer to fight to the last man), we told them the same thing. We always provided medical treatment for wounded poachers; and while all captives were interrogated, I ordered our rangers not to be cruel to these men—again I hoped we might convert them to our allies.

I also offered jobs in our Wildlife Department to "reformed" poachers. I thought they'd make excellent members of our antipoaching teams since they knew the terrain and techniques. Several of them readily signed on, glad to be earning a steady wage. Some of the worst poachers are today among our best rangers.

My ultimate goal was to build an intelligence network, with informers who would notify us about when and where bandits and poaching gangs entered the National Parks and other wildlife areas. At this stage, we were always at least one step behind them. I intended to change that. Soon enough, the poachers and not us would be on the run.

Informers and gun battles were only part of my overall strategy. An even more important element was ending the ivory trade, since that would take away the poachers' market. If no one bought ivory, the poachers would have nowhere to unload their ill-gotten gains. It would no longer be worth their while to walk the deserts, killing elephants, fighting rangers, and terrorizing villagers.

Eliminating the market seemed such a logical thing to do that I was surprised to discover that the idea was highly controversial. Indeed, until 1988, very few conservation organizations had called for a ban on the ivory trade. In February of that year, the African Wildlife Foundation (AWF), a Washington, D.C.,–based group, took the lead, launching a "Don't Buy Ivory" campaign and declaring 1988 "The Year of the Elephant." Ivory jewelry and trinkets were still being sold in the States, but AWF's campaign began to stigmatize the commodity. The AWF placed ads in several major newspapers, showing a gruesome photograph of an elephant with its face hacked away. Very few people wanted to wear a bracelet that evoked this kind of image. The organization also began lobbying the U.S. government to ban the import of ivory and to give elephants the highest form of protection internationally. This meant upgrading their status within CITES, the treaty that governs the international trade in products made from wild animals. AWF—and a growing number of other conservation organizations—wanted to see the elephants upgraded from Appendix II to Appendix I. Such a move would effectively end the ivory trade. It was just what we needed.

The idea, however, wasn't popular with all conservationists or with African governments, which depended on the sale of ivory for income. In fact, until my appointment, Kenya had been against the ban. My predecessor at Wildlife as well as other wildlife people both within and outside Africa argued that not only should African countries be free to manage their natural resources as they saw fit but that a ban would in fact increase the poaching. Since ivory was already a scarce commodity, their thinking went, a ban would only make it scarcer and therefore more valuable, giving poachers an even greater incentive to kill elephants. They based their reasoning in part on what had happened to the rhinoceros, which was listed on Appendix I. Despite the trading ban in rhino horn, the animals continued be slaughtered. The ban only drove up the price, they argued.

I listened to both sides and carefully weighed their arguments. Certainly, any increase in the value of ivory would be a disaster for Kenya—and my plans for the Wildlife Department. But I didn't feel that comparing the ivory trade to that in rhino horn was correct. The buyers were two very different types of people. As I've mentioned, rhino horn is used to make dagger handles in the Middle East or is ground into a powder for use as a treatment for various ills (such as backaches and cancers) and as an aphrodisiac in the Far East. These are old traditions—the latter steeped in superstition, the former influenced by cultural perceptions of manhood—and beyond the reach of a Western-style media campaign. It's a trade that will be very difficult to stop.

Banning the ivory trade would be a different matter. Statistics showed that in 1988, 40 percent of the ivory that left Africa ended up in North America and Europe, mostly in the form of bangles, trinkets, and cheap art. Another forty percent of the ivory was being used in Japan, and the balance was used in the Middle East, Asia, and a little within Africa itself. If a significant proportion of the trade was for things people used to adorn themselves, and it was possible to make the same people feel ashamed of their souvenirs, then, I thought, demand would drop. And if the demand dropped by, say, 45 percent, prices would fall simply because there would be more ivory on the market than there were buyers. The combination of an international trading ban and an anti-ivory movement would end the trade once and for all.

I had discussed all this with President Moi, and persuaded him during one of our first meetings that we in Kenya should take the lead in

promoting the ban. He gave me the go-ahead to submit a formal proposal for the African elephant to be moved to Appendix I of CITES.

Time was of the essence. CITES was due to have its next meeting
to vote on this matter in October 1989, and proposals of this kind have
to be given to the CITES secretariat at least five months beforehand.
That meant that we had to get our proposal in by the middle of May.
I had learned from Iain Douglas-Hamilton that the Tanzanian government was also preparing a proposal, one based on surveys he and other
wildlife biologists had made of elephant populations across Africa and
the effect the heavy poaching was having on their health and numbers.
Ironically, Iain and the others preparing the proposal had first offered it
to Dr. Olindo, hoping that Kenya would change its position and pro-
mote the ban. Dr. Olindo had turned them down, believing that Kenya's
best interests would be served by a limited and regulated trade. Clearly
the large stockpile of confiscated tusks must have influenced this position. Conservation efforts in Kenya then needed the money. I felt
strongly that Kenya should be the first in with a proposal, so that we
could link our leadership on this issue to the burning of the ivory. But
I had no one capable of writing it.

Good fortune sometimes comes from the most unexpected quarters,
and only a few days after Iain told me about the Tanzanians' proposal,
I received a call from Israel. A passionate conservationist named Bill
Clark, whom I had met when I was the director of the National Museums, called to tell me that he had a draft proposal in hand that, as he
put it, "would meet the minimum requirements" of the CITES secretariat. We'd only have to spend a few hours typing in the correct names
and addresses the document required and adding some figures on elephant demographics that Iain could supply.

Some people were surprised to learn that I planned to "steal Tanzania's thunder," as one friend put it. But that was exactly my intention,
one I still feel no need to apologize for. There's no question that the
Tanzanian proposal, which was largely written by Joyce Poole, an elephant expert, and Jorgen Thomsen, a close friend of Joyce's and a program officer at TRAFFIC, a wildlife monitoring organization backed by

the World Wildlife Fund and IUCN (or World Conservation Unit), was far better than ours. But the symbolic value of being first was far more important. Clark's proposal did the job, and we got it in just ahead of the Tanzanians. (Later, Joyce Poole told me that she'd called my counterpart in Tanzania, Costa Mlay, to tell him that Kenya was going to be the first to announce its backing of the Appendix I listing. To his credit, Costa replied, "It doesn't matter. If Kenya wants the limelight, that's okay. The important thing is to get the listing.")

However, proposing that an animal be listed on Appendix I and actually getting it listed are two different things. Our move initially brought us the international publicity I hoped for and increased support for the growing anti-ivory movement. In early June 1989, Pres. George Bush announced that ivory could no longer be imported into the United States; and a few weeks later, Britain's prime minister Margaret Thatcher followed suit. Department and jewelry stores in both countries stopped selling ivory. Sotheby's auction house issued a statement saying they would no longer auction elephant tusks or anything made of ivory.

Although public opinion was on our side in these countries, this wasn't the case in Africa. We faced a number of opponents, particularly in South Africa, Zimbabwe, and Botswana. Wildlife officials and conservationists in these countries insisted that they had no major poaching problem. Instead, they had precisely the opposite problem to ours: far too many elephants. Unless they were allowed to cull their herds and sell the ivory to fund their national parks and conservation programs, they would not be able to manage their elephants and parks effectively.

I knew their argument, but I thought they'd be open to some form of compromise—after all, we were all African countries. It made sense for us to pull together for the good of the continent. Not until I met these men face-to-face did I realize the almost visceral attachment they had to their policies. Nothing and no one was going to change them.

My first run-in with the southern African elephant contingent occurred in early July 1989, not long after the French tourists were killed, at a meeting of the CITES African Elephant Working Group. This group had been formed in 1987 to look at the effects of the ivory trade and any problems it caused. The meeting was held in Gaborone, the capital of Botswana. Delegates came from most of the major ivory-producing African countries and from the ivory-consuming countries, such as the United States, Japan, and Hong Kong. It was Kenya's turn to chair the meeting, so I assumed this role. The rules of the meeting stipulated that, as chairman, I was to remain neutral; I was not to speak out on any issue. This amused me, since the CITES secretary-general, Eugene Lapointe, had recently admitted to the press that the organization's Ivory Control Unit in Lausanne, Switzerland, which supposedly oversaw the ivory trade, had happily accepted contributions totaling two hundred thousand dollars from ivory dealers in Hong Kong and Japan. Many of us were beginning to feel that having CITES oversee and regulate the ivory trade was a bit like letting the fox watch the hen house.

The main topic on the agenda was the proposal to place the African elephant on Appendix I. By now, five African countries—Kenya, Tanzania, Somalia, Ethiopia, and Zaire—were calling for this change. Costa Mlay of Tanzania phrased it most eloquently, telling the gathering: "Every worthwhile action requires an element of sacrifice. Loss of profits alone does not constitute an argument against a ban. We are talking of the survival of a species that is important to mankind and to Africa. Every generation will be judged by its moral courage to protect species that are in danger of extinction."

Mlay stressed, too, the cost of the trade in human terms. "Ivory," he said, concluding his speech, "is not used to protect the health of humans or to produce medicines. But people in our country and in others are now losing their lives, not just their livelihoods, because of ivory. It is too big a sacrifice that our people should die so that a few people beyond our borders can make a living."

With the deaths of the tourists, rangers, and policemen uppermost in my mind, I heartily applauded Mlay's words. I expected the other delegates from Africa to be equally sympathetic to him and to the problems we, in East Africa, faced. So I was appalled when the delegation from Zimbabwe, headed by a beefy, ruddy-faced white African named

Rowan Martin, responded instead by mocking us. He was the kind of man who gave white Rhodesians a bad name. We took an instant disliking to each other. It was well known that in a few days time we were going to burn our stash of ivory in Kenya. Martin seemed to regard this event as a personal affront and took to referring to me as the "bunny-hugger." He and the other members of his delegation even composed a limerick about the ivory burning. They sang it together like a band of British schoolboys:

> We cheered when they burned the first bra,
> Lady Chatterley was going too far.
> But the whole world mocks
> When ivory stocks
> Go up in smoke in Kenya

(Zimbabweans pronounce "Kenya" with a broad accent, placing an "ar" sound on Kenya's last syllable to make it rhyme with "far.")

If Costa Mlay secured the moral high ground with his speech, the position of the Zimbabwean delegation laid claim to the other end of the spectrum. I thought they made fools of themselves in the meeting when they claimed that Zimbabwe's elephants had an astonishingly high reproductive rate, the females giving birth at nine years of age. Several elephant experts in the room broke into loud, derisive laughter at this statement, since it was well known that female African elephants do not reach puberty until their teenage years. Even I found it hard to suppress a smile and only halfheartedly called for order.

In general, however, I followed the rules, breaking them only once, when a delegate from the Congo told the gathering, "The extinction of elephants is inevitable in Africa. They will surely disappear one of these days." I couldn't abide that kind of fatalistic, doomsday nonsense and spoke up at once.

"As chairman of the meeting, I agreed to be neutral," I said, "but as an expert in evolution I have to make it clear that the extinction of the

African elephant is no more inevitable than the extinction of human beings is inevitable."

I wanted to say more but stopped myself. Here again was that passive cynicism; it was almost exactly the same attitude that the rangers and police had about the poachers. They couldn't win their battles against the poachers; Africa couldn't save its elephants. Somehow that frame of mind had to change.

The Gaborone meeting ended without reaching a consensus about whether or not to put the elephants on Appendix I.

Three days later, on the morning of July 18, I joined President Moi on a grassy glade just below the Wildlife Department's headquarters at Nairobi National Park. A huge pyramid of more than two thousand elephant tusks rose some twenty feet above us in a sort of macabre sculpture. Many of the tusks had been painted with a clear, highly flammable plastic, and placed around a stack of straw bales and firewood. A mixture of kerosene and petrol would be pumped into the straw bales under pressure. It would produce "a huge, spectacular fire," Robin Hollister, the special-effects man, had promised me. I had alerted the press well in advance, and the world's media turned out in force to broadcast the event. ABC set up a live satellite link with the *Good Morning America* television studios in New York.

I walked around the tower of tusks with President Moi. Out of earshot of the press, he whispered to me that he hoped for our sakes that the fire destroyed the ivory because if it didn't, we would look like fools. Clearly this still worried him, and I reassured him as best I could. He also asked, with a big smile, if I really thought this was a good idea. "Yes," I replied. "And anyway, it's far too late to back out now. So we'd better get it over with." Moi laughed at that and, shaking his head, walked to a podium placed in front of the ivory tower.

Secretly, I crossed my fingers that Robin was right. I was fairly sure we were going to have an enormous fire simply because of all the fuel that was going to be pumped in. But whether the pile was going to be reduced to ashes, or worse, explode and blow the president and all his men across the park—well, such concerns did cross my mind.

The president stepped to a podium. With the TV cameras rolling, Moi's voice boomed across our park and out to the world beyond.

"To stop the poacher, the trader must also be stopped. And to stop the trader, the final buyer must be convinced not to buy ivory. I appeal to people all over the world to stop buying ivory."

I then handed him a lit taper, and we walked together to the edge of the ivory pile. Without hesitation, President Moi plunged it into the kerosene-soaked straw. In a flash, flames leaped skyward, engulfing the ivory in a hot, red-orange blaze. Several young people in the audience cheered, shouting, "Burn, ivory, burn!" And much to the amazement of several cynical white conservationists, whom I noticed out of the corner of my eye and who had predicted the ivory would never burn, it did. The gleaming white tusks burst into flame like well-dried kindling. (Later, these same people spread a rumor that I had cheated everyone: the tusks were fake, they said, made of plastic by some clever technicians. I had actually made a deal with President Moi to sell the real ivory and split the profits.)

President Moi, well-pleased with the fire, stayed for over an hour before taking his leave. The fire burned hot for almost seventy-two hours. At the end, there was a pile of white and gray ash, and some flakes of blue-black enamel no bigger than a coin.

The next day pictures of the ivory fire filled the front pages of newspapers around the world. It was estimated that between the TV coverage and the pictures in magazines and newspapers, some 850 million people saw the elephant tusks burn. The whole world now knew about the African elephant crisis, and Kenya had taken the lead.

CHAPTER 8

The price of ivory did not immediately collapse after we burned the tusks, but there were signs that our message had been heard. In mid-August 1989, the European Economic Community formally banned further ivory imports, and piano manufacturers there and in Japan announced that they were switching from ivory to plastic keys. The event generated a phenomenal amount of publicity. Kenya and its elephants remained in the news for weeks afterward, and this, I was certain, bolstered the position of those of us who wanted the African elephant listed on Appendix I. I was now regularly sought out by reporters, giving me many opportunities to emphasize that we needed to give the animals the fullest possible protection. There were, of course, many who said Kenya would have been better off using the $3 million for conservation projects. I believe strongly it was well worth that amount to convey to the world the message that we desperately needed to destroy the ivory trade.

Our ivory burn had also scored points for the Wildlife Department with Kenya's citizens. The major daily newspapers, the *Daily Nation* and the *Standard*, ran editorials and letters approving of our action and of the overall changes being made in the department. My photo appeared with several articles about the burning and antipoaching efforts, and consequently I became a recognizable figure in and around Nairobi.

The Kenyan government and President Moi were also basking in the glow of worldwide approval of the ivory burning. Privately, the president told me that he'd enjoyed himself at this event, and, perhaps because of that, was more open than ever to the idea of reforming the Wildlife Department. The most important reform, I felt, would be transforming it into a parastatal agency—a state-owned corporation that could be run like a business, and, as I have mentioned, be financed and operate independently of the Civil Service and its endless regulations. That change was essential to freeing the department of its remaining corrupt employees. It was also necessary if I were going to hire the people I wanted to hire and pay them a competitive wage, one not limited by the Civil Service. So I was delighted when President Moi told me in mid-August that the government had approved the formation of a new agency, and that this would be formally announced in October 1989. Nothing would change the department more drastically than liberating it of all the "dead wood" employees, and hiring a fresh, energetic crew.

The ivory burning seemed to have stunned the poachers, too. For almost a month, we had no more reports of elephants being poached or tourists being attacked. We also started getting more cooperation from villagers close to the parks—and even from some poachers we'd captured, whose assistance helped us recover eighty-seven buried tusks. I was beginning to hope that perhaps the poachers had got the message, realized the ivory trade was going to be shut down, and packed up their weapons and moved back to Somalia.

It was wishful thinking. Just after dinner on August 20, 1989, the telephone rang at home. The line crackled and buzzed, but I heard a faint voice saying, "Can you hear me? Over." It was a radio telephone call, which meant that it must be coming from some remote corner of Kenya. I shouted back, "Yes. Go ahead. Over."

"Ahhh, Richard, is that you? I'm afraid I have bad news." It was a white Kenyan who ran a private cattle ranch in northern Kenya, close to Meru but whose name I've forgotten.

I urged him to go ahead.

"George Adamson's been shot. Killed. It happened about noon. Can you do something to get some security to the area? It is desperate."

The news left me deeply shaken. The rancher didn't know much more, but it was clear we had a crisis—one of potentially international dimensions—on our hands. I did not know him well, but George Adamson was a legendary figure, a revered conservationist and the hero of *Born Free* and *Living Free*, enormously popular accounts his wife, Joy, had written about their work returning lions to the wild. Joy had died some years before, apparently murdered by a camp cook she'd fired. For the previous twenty years, George had been living in a reserve called Kora, close to Meru National Park, where he'd continued to teach abandoned lion cubs how to live on their own in the wild. Knowing how "tame" lions can revert to their wild ways in an instant, I thought that perhaps the caller was mistaken, that George in fact had been killed by one of his animals. But the rancher was adamant: George had been shot by a gang of bandits.

Loved around the world and in Kenya, where he was called *Baba Simba*, "Father of the Lions," George was eighty-three when he was killed. I knew his murder would soon be on front pages everywhere. It would be very bad publicity for Kenya, and we had to be ready to respond. We also had to find his killers.

Some weeks before President Moi had insisted that I have a "hot line" installed in my home so that I could reach him at a moment's notice. Despite the late hour, as soon as the rancher hung up, I dialed the president.

Moi, too, was dismayed by the news. I could hear the worry in his voice. "Do whatever needs to be done, Richard," he said.

My next call was to Police Commissioner Philip Kilonzo. He also had not heard the news. Why, he wondered, were we learning about this so late in the day? I wondered the same thing. We agreed to alert our units at once and immediately arranged for a detachment of 150 men to descend on Kora at daybreak and search for the bandits. At 5:30 the next morning, I met Kilonzo and his top officers at the Kenya

Air Force Base, where a military helicopter was waiting to ferry us to Kora.

Kora lies about 150 miles northeast of Nairobi. Its northern border follows the meandering Tana River, and just touches the southern edge of Meru National Park. Ironically, only a few weeks before the government had agreed to give Kora the status of a national park. This was something George had lobbied hard over for many years, believing that park status would make it easier to keep out of Kora the domestic herds that were constantly in conflict with the lions and other wildlife. As Wildlife director, I was pleased to have the new park, but the presence of George and his "tame" lions worried me a great deal. I was sure that, in time, the lions would get into trouble with tourists.

By 6:45 A.M., we were hovering over George's camp—"Lion Camp," as he'd called it. Some of our ranger and police units had already arrived, and the dusty compound looked a little like a military encampment. Adamson had moved here in 1970, building a simple camp of thatched-roofed huts for himself and his staff and larger wooden enclosures for his lion cubs.

We landed right next to the compound and were met by a couple of police officers as well as by members of Adamson's staff. Commissioner Kilonzo was taken into one hut to see Adamson's corpse and those of two of George's assistants who had also been killed, while I was guided to another hut to meet the three survivors. One was a young German woman, Inge Ledersteil, who had been working as George's principal assistant and whom the bandits had roughed up. She wasn't seriously injured but was extremely shaken and in a state of shock, mostly because of George's death, which she had witnessed. George's camp assistant, Mohamed Maru, and his driver, Abdi Bitatscha, had also survived. Mohamed emerged from the ordeal unscathed, but Abdi had been beaten with a crowbar and shot. Both his legs were shattered, and as there were no painkillers in the camp, he was in agony. Inge and Abdi would be airlifted back to Nairobi with us.

They told us what had happened. George had been expecting a small group of visitors to arrive by plane. A little after noon, when he heard the sound of a plane circling overhead, he dispatched Inge and Abdi to his landing strip about three miles away to meet the guests. Two miles along the bush-lined dirt track, they heard a loud bang; Inge thought at first they had blown a tire. But then there was another sharp explosion, and suddenly three men burst out of the bush and stood in the center of the road. One was dressed in a khaki-colored uniform; the others wore simple, long-sleeved shirts and the plaid *kikois* (sarong-style skirts) favored by Somali men. All three carried assault rifles. They signaled for Abdi to slow down, then calmly took aim and shot out all the tires.

In an instant the bandits surrounded the car, shouting at Inge and Abdi to get out. Abdi opened his door, raised his hands in the air, and pleaded with them that they had no money, that they were simply on their way to the landing strip. They shoved him aside, and one then pulled Inge from the car.

"I pulled my pockets inside-out to show I had no money or valuables," she told me, her voice soft and trembling. "I pleaded with them, but they could not understand. He just kept shouting, 'Money! Money! Money!' " and shoved the rifle barrel into her stomach. She pulled up her shirt to show that she wasn't hiding any cash and Abdi undid his sarong to do the same, but the men only became angrier. The one with Inge beat her across the face and shoulders, knocking her to the ground; while another one beat Bitatscha with a crowbar he'd found in the Land Rover.

Back at the camp, Adamson had been typing a letter to a friend when the first shots rang out. Mohamed rushed into George's room and asked if he'd heard the gunfire. Adamson stopped typing in midsentence and told Mohamed to get his rifle, one of the old .303s, and two other men. He grabbed a revolver, too, and thus armed, he and the three others jumped in a Land Rover and sped toward the landing strip.

The bandits heard him coming. One stepped into the middle of the track. The other two turned momentarily from their two victims and then also stepped into the middle of the track.

In the Land Rover, Mohamed sat holding the .303 in the front seat, next to George. "We came around a bend, and suddenly the gangsters were there," Mohamed said. "I shouted to George to stop, they are *shifta*, but he just stepped on the accelerator." George apparently had seen that one man was harassing Inge and he pulled out his revolver, aimed it out the window, and, stepping on the gas, drove full throttle at the bandit in the middle of the road, presumably intending to knock him down. Mohamed, however, didn't wait to see more; he jumped from the vehicle, still holding the .303, and rolled into the bush. "I watched as the gangsters riddled the Land Rover. George hadn't stopped. He was still driving, but he didn't have a chance. I'm not sure if he even got off a shot."

Raked by bullets, the Land Rover swerved off the road into the thornbush. George and his two assistants were probably killed almost instantly. Bullets had hit him in his left thigh, chest, and back.

Meanwhile, Adamson's visitors had landed at the airstrip, but, hearing the gunfire, the pilot wisely took off again and circled the area. From the air, the pilot could see George's Land Rover and several bodies, and he headed to Meru to file a report. The bandits apparently thought the plane was connected to the police or Wildlife Department since they scattered as soon as it appeared. Inge and the others ran and hid; late that evening, rangers stationed on the edge of Kora rescued them.

Frustratingly, and as was so often the case in these situations, no one had really taken any immediate action. The pilot told the warden at Meru what he'd seen; the warden in turn alerted the police, but they had decided they needed some verification before responding. Now, nearly twenty-four hours had passed since the murders, and we still did not have men on the bandits' trail. We had to train our men, rangers and police, to respond more quickly to urgent messages, and I promised myself—and George—that this would become a new priority.

I stepped briefly inside George's main hut. There was a camp bed, a shelf with books, a simple wooden table with his old manual typewriter, and the half-finished letter. Adamson had been a brave man, a wildlife lover and conservationist to the core. In some ways, perhaps it was fitting that he'd died confronting men whom I'm sure were part of a poaching gang. But his death seemed tragic and unnecessary.

Outside, Commissioner Kilonzo was giving orders to his men. By now, there were a good number of police and some rangers in the camp. In my view, they should not have been there at all, waiting for orders. If I had been in charge, they would have been out in the field long ago, casting a wide net that could be drawn toward the center. But I wasn't calling the shots—at least, not yet.

George Adamson's murder did make headlines around the world, and there were, of course, many editorials questioning whether Kenya was safe for travel. The United States even briefly considered issuing a travel warning on our country, a move that would have ruined our tourist industry and national parks. That worried President Moi as much as it did me, and he pressed me again to do everything possible to give our visitors the utmost security.

"There's nothing that I'd like to do more," I replied, "but you know as well as I that until the rangers are fully trained and equipped, and we're directing operations, we're always going to fall short of our goal. We must be given full responsibility for security in our parks and the means to accomplish that."

President Moi nodded his head as I spoke. We sat next to each other in well-cushioned armchairs. The president, I had discovered, liked to sit somewhat close to the person to whom he was talking; he would bend his head down and listen gravely as I spoke, then raise his head to reply. We had already had this particular conversation several times; and while he had permitted the rangers to be armed with assault rifles, he continued to insist that the operations be directed by the police. After each meeting, however, he seemed to lean a little more strongly in my direction. Perhaps it was simply a matter of proving ourselves and earning his trust.

"We must go slowly on that, Richard," he said, repeating the answer he'd given me in every other discussion on this topic. "But surely there is more we can do to make our parks secure?"

I looked him straight in the eye. "As much as I dislike the idea, we could improve security enormously by removing the nomads who've settled in the Tsavos and Meru. It'll put us at risk of being denounced by human rights organizations and possibly by the American Congress," I warned, "but it will save lives—those of our men and our visitors."

Moi didn't hesitate. "Then you must do it."

Shortly after this meeting, the president was quoted in the press as again saying that poachers were to be shot on sight. I don't know when or where or even if he made this statement; he may have simply been reiterating the directive he had made when Dr. Olindo was Wildlife director. Whether or not he ever made such a statement, the report in the newspapers caused me further difficulties with the Western press and human rights organizations. The news stories made it sound as if we were going to shoot any poor soul with a spear found wandering inside a game reserve. I had several calls from reporters asking if that was our intention. Absolutely not, I told them. We were looking only for "armed gangsters" and would never harm "innocent *wananchi* [citizens]. All tourists and all Kenyans should feel free to see the wildlife without fear."

I used the opportunity to make another statement about the poachers, just to let them know that I was as serious as ever: "This is the last stroke for the marauders in our national parks and game reserves. If they're wise, they'll leave these areas—*now*."

I summoned the senior wardens from all the parks to Nairobi and told them we had to step up our antipoaching efforts.

"We've got to pressure these gangs, give them no rest, so that they leave the parks and keep out and stay out," I said. "I want you to make it hot for them."

Our wildlife-protection units, as we'd renamed the antipoaching teams, were far better trained now, and I issued an order to keep them out in the field on a regular basis. I wanted foot patrols on the ground, watching, listening, leaving their mark behind in the remotest parts of the parks. "Every ranger's footprint will send a message to the poachers," I said. "We're going to tell them, 'We're here and here and everywhere; we're looking for you and we will find you. And when we do, that's the end.' So the next time a poacher sees a ranger's footprint, he'll know it's time to leave."

Within days of that meeting, one of our wildlife-protection units in Tsavo tracked down a poaching gang, killing three in an early morning operation. Rangers recovered two G3 assault rifles and eighty-three rounds of ammunition. That was the kind of news I wanted to hear. Our men needed to know how pleased I was with their success; and as soon as I heard the report, I grabbed my coat and headed out my office door for Wilson Airport.

"Cancel my appointments," I told my secretary on my way out. "If anyone asks, tell them that I'm in the field."

Two hours later I landed at the Kilanguni Airstrip in Tsavo West. As usual, Joe Kioko, the senior park warden, met me and gave me a quick briefing. He knew the men's position in the field, and we took off at once, flying north to one of the most remote corners of Tsavo East. By now, I had seen to it that these teams had radios for ground-to-air communication; and as we flew overhead, they directed us to a fairly level, grassy plain nearby where we could land. It was about a ten-minute walk from there to the scene of the shoot-out, and once again I was struck by the surreal atmosphere. Here we were, truly in the middle of nowhere, in an area of peace and tranquillity, looking at the remains of a battlefield. The scent of death was heavy in the air.

Our rangers had been in the field for a week and looked it. They were sweaty, grimy, and weary, but pride shone in their eyes. They stood at attention as I appeared, but I set them at ease at once and said that I had only come to congratulate them on a job well done.

"You've done exactly what we need to do to win back our parks," I told them. "I know—and Kenya will soon know—how hard you're working. And now, you must tell me what else you need."

The men smiled shyly. One asked softly if we perhaps had some cigarettes, and Joe quickly produced several packs. Smoking and sipping tea, they told us about the shoot-out, how they'd got word from some herding boys that a gang had moved into the park and was shooting elephants. Another ranger had spotted freshly killed carcasses in the area from the air and guided the rangers to the site. They'd found an old camp and started tracking the gang, following it for days. The poachers seemed to know they were being tracked and did everything they could to leave a confusing trail: wearing sandals, then removing them and walking barefoot; at times stepping only on stones or on the balls of their feet; breaking up into smaller groups, which then headed off in three different directions, then meeting up again two days later. But these rangers all hailed from the northern deserts themselves and knew the same tricks. They studied the poachers' signs, puzzled out every misleading clue, and knew at last that they were closing in.

The poachers had made camp under a shady bush; and while some slept or brewed tea, others stood guard. Our team had spotted them the night before and drew back a short ways, leaving two men behind to watch. Just before first light, the rangers moved in, calling out to the poachers to surrender. Instead, the men in the camp immediately opened fire. The rangers scrambled to return fire. Bullets whizzed across the desert, pinging on rocks and kicking up trails in the sand. The battle lasted nearly two hours. When it was over, three poachers had been killed and two had escaped, one grabbing the rifle of a fallen companion.

"That's why, sir," one ranger told me, "we have only the two weapons from these poachers."

"Well done," I said again, thinking to myself how utterly changed these rangers were from the motley crew I had met only a few months before. Their uniforms were still tattered, but they no longer had that sheepish, insecure air about them. They were now men with a purpose.

I took a brief look at the three dead poachers. They were tall, gaunt men, and their sharp angular features and dress—long-sleeved shirts and patterned sarongs—labeled them as hailing from Somalia. Around their waists, thick leather belts, stained red, secured their sharply curved daggers. They'd each carried a heavy ammo belt, too, and these lay to one side, glinting in the sun. They'd probably walked seven hundred miles before meeting their deaths in this sandy wash—and for what? A chance to make a little money with an ivory tusk. How I wished that some of the "conservationists" from Zimbabwe, or the head of CITES, or anyone who kept insisting that the ivory trade caused no real harm, could see this. How differently they might have felt.

When we were airborne, I turned to Joe. "You know, I used to wonder if we could really stop these poachers. But now I know we can. The poaching is going to end, and much sooner than we used to think."

Joe smiled broadly. "You're right, Richard. We're finally winning this war."

Despite my initial misgivings about the joint police-ranger operation in Kora, we seemed to be making progress there, too. Only five days after Adamson's death, the police arrested three men and charged them with the crime, although the evidence against them, I'm afraid, was very scant and circumstantial. (For instance, one had a firearm that had belonged to George. The man claimed he had purchased it from a trader, which was plausible. Weapons in that region change hands very quickly.) But we'd beefed up our forces in the Meru-Kora area and the two Tsavos, and for a period were engaging almost daily in shoot-outs. We lost some fine young men; others suffered terrible injuries; we killed and captured many armed bandits; and we moved the nomads out of northern Meru, a necessary and unhappy strategy. It was a grim business and I kept turning over and over in my mind how we could bring it to a close. In the Kenyan newspapers it was described simply as a necessary action, the legal removal of illegal squatters from inside a national park. The squatters knew they were living there illegally, and as unpleasant a task as it was, it nevertheless saved lives.

Not every operation went smoothly. Not long after Adamson's death, our joint forces encountered another band of armed poachers. As usual, the police were in charge, but they hadn't been trained in guerilla warfare and inadvertently led their command into an ambush. It was the worst disaster yet. Mortars and grenades struck two trucks, killing sixteen rangers and policemen. Only two rangers escaped. They were forced to abandon another vehicle and the twenty-plus assault rifles and hundreds of rounds of ammunition inside. The entire arsenal fell into the hands of the bandits—the same gang, I was certain, that had killed the two young French tourists.

Hearing about it in a debriefing room at Meru, I could only shake my head in dismay. All the optimism I had felt at Tsavo faded away.

A few days later, I flew back to Kora to attend the funeral of George Adamson. Although he was not a personal friend, George's years as a game warden and ardent conservationist made him one of "us," and I felt he should be laid to rest with full honors. Six rangers carried his coffin to a place near some hills overlooking the Tana River, where his brother Terrence and two of George's beloved lions (which had died from natural causes some years before) were also buried. I gave a short eulogy, praising Adamson's service to Kenya and his courage, and vowing that we would bring his killers to justice. Then, with military precision, twelve rangers marched smartly to the grave site and fired a gun salute into the air. A bugler played the "Last Post," and as the notes dwindled on the wind, George Adamson's coffin was lowered into the ground.

More than a hundred people attended George's funeral. Many were visibly moved by the ceremony. Standing among them, I found myself thinking that only two weeks had passed since his murder, and, in that brief time, many more good men had also met their end; more elephants had been killed; herders and their stock had been forced to move, for reasons they failed to comprehend. And it all seemed such a waste.

I knew the fighting would continue. But there was one battle I could end: the one with the police. I called President Moi early the next morning and asked if I could have a quick meeting with him.

"By all means. Come now," he said.

I was standing in his office half an hour later.

"I believe I have the solution to our problem," I announced.

President Moi looked at me quizzically.

"We need to reassure the police that our armed ranger units are going to act as controlled, disciplined forces. I think the best way to do that is to appoint a police officer as commander of our wildlife-protection units. Give me one of their top officers, a man they trust."

Moi smiled. "Yes. I think this could work. Do you have an officer in mind?"

Indeed I did: Abdul Bashir, the fellow with the twinkle in his eye who'd helped straighten my beret in Tsavo months earlier. He was deputy commander of the General Services Unit, the police's paramilitary force. Since the beret incident, I had seen him at other meetings and had always been impressed with his demeanor, as well as the respect and loyalty his men showed him. And I liked his forthright personality. He was just the man I wanted. I wrote his name down for President Moi.

"Fine. I'll see that he's released to you straightaway."

Moi smiled again, but this time it was only fleeting. A look of concern settled on his face.

"I have something I must tell you, Richard," he said, bending his head close to mine. "You must have a bodyguard," he told me in a half-whisper. "You must—no, I insist," he added, holding up his hand to stop my protest. "There are those who want to harm you."

He would not say more, other than that he'd arrange the best security for me.

I did not tell Meave that night about the bodyguard; she was worried enough by all the gun battles and poaching. Instead, I confided Moi's words to my diary.

President Moi is worried about my safety, I wrote. *I wonder what he knows?*

CHAPTER 9

Kenya's politics are rough. It may be because our country is young, or because its numerous tribes are constantly vying for power and money, or because of the insecurity of our leaders. But anyone who gains influence with the president or is perceived as a threat to him can be in danger. My years with the Kenyan government had taught me that proximity to President Moi was seldom long-term and would certainly create powerful adversaries. I knew of several good men who'd been in high-profile jobs one day, out on the street the next. Government officials and politicians had been beaten and imprisoned; others had vanished mysteriously. The same was true under Moi's predecessor, Jomo Kenyatta, Kenya's first president. Three popular politicians were assassinated—two of them gunned down on the streets of Nairobi—during his tenure. In all three cases, the evidence suggested that high government officials were involved, and there has always been considerable speculation about who they might be. None of these crimes was ever solved.

Meave and I had both known when I took over the Wildlife Department that my life would be at risk, if for no other reason than my determination to stop the illegal ivory trade. Now that I was trying to halt the trade in its entirety—legal as well as illegal—I was even more of a target. But I wasn't sure that it was the ivory traders President Moi was warning me about when he whispered to me about my need for bodyguards. Far more likely, the threats had come from people who were unhappy about my success in overhauling the Wildlife Department—and the fact that I had the president's full backing. I had rid the department of some of its worst employees, and now was planning another round of dismissals and transfers. Perhaps someone was plotting to stop me from doing that.

I had also made several enemies. The former vice president, Josephat Karanja, was certainly no friend of mine. He had tried to have me ousted from the museum directorship after I criticized George Muhoho but had ended up losing his own job instead. Neither was Muhoho, whom President Moi had moved to another ministry after I took office. But I doubted whether anyone would have been angry enough to want me killed.

I was concerned the threat had to do with the transfers I had engineered. Since ousting the first seventy rotten employees, I had managed to get rid of another two hundred, and I hoped to free the department of even more. I had made enemies not only of those who were transferred or given early retirement (none were actually fired; that involves a cumbersome and painstakingly slow procedure in the Civil Service), but of their families and friends who had presumably helped get them their jobs in the first place. That was the way, unfortunately, that our Public Service worked. It becomes almost incumbent for someone who gets an influential position in the government to find jobs for his brothers and sisters, aunts and uncles, cousins and distant cousins. It doesn't matter whether there's actually any work for these people to do; if there isn't, a "job" is created. A person may be hired simply to bring tea to the boss in the mornings and afternoons or to buy the morning newspaper. If he has nothing to do the rest of the day except sit on his hands, that's what he does. And that is why our government offices and hallways are filled with people looking bored, and why the government is inefficient.

Now here I was, tampering with this well-established, inefficient, and corrupt system. *Of course* someone wanted me gone.

That's how I explained my need for bodyguards to Meave, which I did the next day. She was understandably alarmed. From now on, and at all times, an armed guard would be riding with me in my car, while other guards followed behind in a separate car. More guards would be posted at our house, day and night. They would come from the Wildlife Department and be rotated regularly so that it would be hard to enlist any of them in an attempt against my life. Meave listened attentively as I described the changes to our routine and home, then sighed.

"I don't like it," she said. "I don't like any of it. But if that's the way it must be . . ."

Her voice trailed off, and she forced a smile. Then, with more bravado than I'm sure she felt, she added, "Well, at least they've warned you."

As hard as it was for me to tell her about President Moi's cautionary words, it was even harder for her to hear them, given that she'd come very close to losing me once before.

In 1969, as I mentioned earlier, I had been diagnosed with a terminal kidney disease, the result of a throat infection that had spread to my kidneys. I was twenty-four at the time, and the doctors gave me between six months and ten years to live. Their diagnosis seemed unreal. I was healthy and strong. I had just been appointed administrative director at Kenya's National Museums and received my first major National Geographic grant to lead a fossil-hunting expedition of my own. And I had fallen in love with Meave. How could I possibly be terminally ill? I decided to put the matter out of my mind and carry on as if I were completely well—which was how I felt.

Meave had agreed with my decision; and after we married in 1971, we decided to have a family in spite of the doctors' grim prognosis. Our two daughters, Louise and Samira, were born in 1972 and 1974. By then we'd made numerous wonderful fossil discoveries that had landed us not just in the pages of the *National Geographic* but on the front pages of newspapers around the world. I had been named full director of Kenya's National Museums and was busy building the Nairobi Museum into a major research institution. We had built a comfortable field camp on the shores of Lake Turkana, our major field site. Life was full.

However, I had also begun to notice some of the symptoms the doctors had warned me about. My blood pressure was excessively high, and as a result I had pounding headaches every day, which were signs of my deteriorating kidneys. There was little my doctor could do for me other than to say that this was the usual course of the disease, and that I might want to refrain from eating certain foods. Her list included most of the foods I like, such as salted meats and wines, and I decided to ignore her advice. What, after all, was the point of living if you couldn't enjoy the things you liked?

My kidneys lasted a little longer than the first doctors had predicted. But in the summer of 1979, Meave and I had to face the inevitable. My kidneys were barely functioning. We traveled to England, where I was put on dialysis. Although I had never discussed my illness with anyone in my family aside from Meave, as soon as my three brothers heard about my problem they each offered me a kidney. I'm still overwhelmed by their generosity. Each sent a blood sample for testing. The kidney of my younger brother, Philip, proved to be the best match. In November 1979, Philip gave me the gift of life: a new kidney.

It wasn't as simple as that, of course. Philip suffered mightily from the operation. And three weeks later I nearly lost the kidney. I had been warned that although the operation appeared successful, my body might still reject this foreign organ. Unfortunately, that is indeed what happened, and I was readmitted to the hospital.

The doctors did what they could, giving me massive doses of drugs to suppress my immune system. That halted the rejection and luckily the kidney was not damaged by this ordeal. The high doses of immunosuppressive drugs, however, left me without an immune system and therefore highly susceptible to infection. A few days later, I developed a viral infection that quickly progressed to severe pneumonia, complicated by septicemia and pleurisy, a painful inflammation of the lining of the lungs. In the early hours of the morning of January 20, 1980, I was again rushed to the hospital, this time in an ambulance.

The doctors thought my chances of recovery were far from certain, even though I was given every possible medical care and massive antibiotic treatment. But I am quite sure that it was Meave who pulled me through. At one point in our twenty-four-hour ordeal, I nearly died. I had a classic out-of-body experience. Looking down on the hospital room scene, I saw my body lying stretched out on the bed. Nurses and doctors bustled about. Everyone looked very anxious. I, on the other hand, felt peaceful and calm. I remember wondering what all the fuss was about. I had no desire to return to my body. Then I saw Meave sitting beside me, clutching my hand. She was talking to me very insistently.

"Richard! You can't die now, Richard," she said. "You're not leaving me. Breathe, Richard, breathe."

Her words made me fight. I don't remember returning to my body. Suddenly, I was feeling all the pain again and struggling hard to take a breath, then another one.

That experience built a lasting bond between us. It also took away any fear I had of dying.

Neither of us mentioned my kidney failure or that long night of years earlier, but I could see the worry on Meave's face when I told her about the bodyguards.

"Let's not dwell on this," I said. "They aren't going to get me. Whoever 'they' are."

The possibility of my being assassinated brought us closer together than we had been for some time. As Meave had predicted, our life had drastically changed since my appointment. I was consumed with getting money for the department, solving the poaching crisis, finding good employees, staying on the government's good side. I seldom had a moment to myself, let alone any real time with Meave. For the first time in years, however, she went to Lake Turkana without me, leading a team of scientists and fossil hunters to an area on the western shores.

In 1984, Kamoya Kimeu, the head of our fossil-hunting team, had discovered the skeleton of a young boy who'd died nearly two million years ago. The boy belonged to *Homo erectus*, the human species that directly precedes our own, *Homo sapiens*. Over the next few years, we uncovered almost every bone of the boy's skeleton, making it the first nearly complete *Homo erectus* skeleton ever discovered. It was a remarkable find.

It was not long before Meave began to have considerable success in her discoveries. She began at a locality known as Lothagam, a very beautiful but very desolate location on the western side of the lake, working on sites that were older than those that I had been involved with on the eastern side. The new finds gave her well-deserved recognition and support. Although I was totally preoccupied with my own problems and with the battle for the elephants, I keenly missed the fossil work that had been so much a part of my life. I made a few visits to Meave's camp, but it was not the same; I had dropped out and I no longer felt like a part of the action.

If my enemies thought they could stop me from cleaning up the Wildlife Department with assassination threats, they were wrong. About a week after that meeting with Moi, an old friend, and one of my former bosses, stopped by my office to say hello. His name was David Mwiraria, and he'd been one of the country's most experienced civil servants. David had risen through the ranks to serve in many top positions, eventually becoming permanent secretary in a number of key ministries. In one of these positions the National Museums had been on his schedule of responsibilities, and I had reported to him. In time, he also became chairman of the Museum's board. I enjoyed working for him and over the years, we'd become good friends. A short, rotund man with a ready laugh, David has a quick, incisive mind and a ready appreciation for peoples' strengths and weaknesses. He also was a masterful technocrat and knew how to get things done within Kenya's Civil Service.

In 1987, however, David fell out of favor with the government. He had a disagreement with one of the ministers about a land issue. David did not have enough political influence to survive. One day David, along with the rest of Kenya, learned from a radio announcement that the government had replaced him with a new man. He was unceremoniously sacked.

Because I knew David to be a good man and a dedicated public servant, I found the government's move perplexing. Firing David confirmed that the system unquestionably favored people who were corrupt, readily accepted bribes, and stole government property. Very seldom were these sorts dismissed. It was always those who were doing their best for the public interest who were fired. Outsiders generally assumed that the president arrived at these decisions alone, but I am certain that he was intentionally misinformed by his inner circle of advisers and senior ministers.

I had not seen David since becoming the Wildlife director, and so I was delighted when he walked through my office door in late August 1989. To my surprise, he was using a cane. He'd been in a bad car accident, he told me, and was still recovering from his injuries.

"To tell you the truth, Richard, it's been a miserable month," he said. "I've got these pains and I'm not busy the way I'd like to be. I'm just sitting around at home."

I knew he wasn't asking me for a job, but it suddenly occurred to me that David's experience and expertise could be very helpful.

"Why don't you come and join me here?" I asked.

David grinned and chuckled. "You're joking. Anyway, the government won't let you hire me."

"I'm not joking. I need you. You wouldn't believe what a mess I'm faced with here. We're slowly turning it around. We're going to become an independent, parastatal agency, and we're going to need a solid, five-year growth plan when that happens. Will you help me put that together?"

David didn't hesitate. "When do I start?"

"Tomorrow. And don't worry about the government; I'll explain why I need you."

I wanted to get David started immediately on a review of our remaining forty-five hundred employees. He knew the inner workings of the Civil Service and would find a way to free us of the remaining corrupt and ineffectual workers.

Most important, David and I knew we could trust each other. Once, over dinner in my Lamu home when I was still at the Museum and he was permanent secretary in the vice president's office, I had spoken my mind to other "friends" in the government about the way the civil servant system had destroyed one of their colleagues, a senior government official. One of them passed my words on to the authorities. About ten days later, I received a curt summons to David's office. Customary courtesies were dispensed with. I was given a stern dressing down. David eyed me coldly and told me that the government had received a full report of the views I had expressed at my dinner, and that the government was not amused. I was to desist immediately from thinking and speaking in this manner. If I did not, I would be sacked without further ado.

I responded to David's lecture with a wink, since I knew his own views were similar to mine. In the most sincere tones I could muster, I agreed that I would not express my thoughts in the presence of senior government officials, but I was unable to offer any promises on the thoughts themselves. Indeed, I suggested that my thoughts on this issue might be much darker than those I had expressed so far. David smiled at this, came round the side of his desk, and shook my hand. He'd been only acting "under orders," he whispered, and now it was time for some tea. Then in hushed tones, we shared our thoughts on the matter and found that they matched very closely.

I knew we would work well together at Wildlife. I looked forward to having someone in my department I could trust entirely, and who could be counted on to tell me when I was wrong.

In my next meeting with President Moi, he raised David Mwiraria's name. He'd heard I was giving him a job and was not happy about it.

"I would like to keep him," I replied. "He's a man of great experience, and I need his guidance. He will help me enormously."

The president looked at me with exasperation.

"Seriously," I added, "I really do need his help."

President Moi studied me for a moment. "You're a difficult man, Richard," he said. He looked away and didn't say anything for a long minute.

I myself learned a number of lessons about the inner workings of Kenya's government during the twenty years I served as the Museum's director. I was embroiled in several intrigues, and various employees (people I had hired) plotted to oust me. They saw my position as a stepping stone to greater glories in the government and, sadly, felt no commitment to the Museum itself. I survived those crises, once with the direct help of President Moi. He listened to my appeal and then did the right thing to solve my problem. His action saved our museum system.

That experience convinced me that if he were provided with the right information, Moi would be inclined to act on it in the right way; that unlike many of his cronies, he had Kenya's best interests at heart. Yet one event brought home very clearly to me how uncertain politics in Kenya could be.

Beginning in 1983 and lasting well into 1984, a public inquiry was held into the conduct of the minister for Constitutional Affairs, Charles Njonjo. The inquiry had been launched by someone within President Moi's inner circle who had managed to convince Moi that Charles was a threat and that he was plotting to become president himself. The first attacks against Charles came in Parliament, where for almost a year members routinely stood up to accuse Charles of one thing and another. Every allegation against him was printed in the newspapers, while his defense and explanations were barely mentioned. It was apparent that some sort of political war was underway, and that Charles was losing.

Finally, the president set up a judicial committee of inquiry to investigate these charges. It was such an obvious "kangaroo court" and the charges against Charles were so blatantly false that I could barely bring myself to read anything about it. Besides, Charles was an old family friend. My grandparents had educated his parents at their mission school in the 1920s. Charles himself had gone to a mission school then to England for a law degree. He'd helped draft Kenya's Constitution and served as attorney general under both Kenyatta and Moi. He was the best of public servants, and I had often turned to him for guidance and advice in my own career.

Many of Charles's friends cut him off during this inquiry, but Meave and I kept in touch with him and continued to visit him and his family at their home. (Indeed, I never made a secret about my disapproval of this investigation. This was the matter I had raised with other government colleagues at my Lamu home, and for which David Mwiraria had reprimanded me.) The Special Branch (a secret police unit) kept a surveillance post on the road leading to Charles's home to see who came and went. On several occasions I was warned by them that I if wanted to remain director of Kenya's Museums, I should end my friendship with him. My brother Philip was then a member of Parliament, and he, too, urged me to abandon Charles. Philip was a stalwart member of the ruling KANU Party and always got behind party policy. The policy now became to attack Njonjo. Philip even suggested that it would be wise for me to denounce Charles to the press, speaking out against him as he, Philip, had done in Parliament. I wasn't proud of my brother for that, particularly since Charles had helped Philip in the early days of his political career, and told him so. Needless to say, our different perspectives on the matter cooled our relationship. But I still wasn't about to abandon Charles, particularly in the face of this ridiculous inquiry.

Nothing was ever proved in the "court," but Charles became a "nonperson" for a while. Before the inquiry, he had resigned from his position as minister and member of Parliament. The government stripped him of his passport. It was as if he had never existed, had never served his country.

Charles was still a "nonperson" in the government's eyes when I was appointed Wildlife director. Ironically, it was partly because of Charles that I had become the director. He had a deep interest in our country's flora and fauna, and it was he who had urged me many years before to join the East African Wildlife Society and then to become its chairman.

He was understandably pleased when I was put in charge of the Wildlife Department, but several times he had urged me to be careful.

Charles's words echoed in my ears every time I went to the State House. President Moi always seemed happy to see me and pleased with everything I was doing, but some of his ministers were not. The president never mentioned David Mwiraria's name again. He was pleased with my performance, and I found I could use his pleasure to get more things done. But after what had happened to Charles Njonjo, I was always wary of his inner circle of advisers.

There were a number of reasons why the government put up with me in spite of my demands and my obstinacy. I think most people in positions of authority wanted the poaching stopped, and they wanted to keep tourists coming to Kenya. My fossil discoveries had also made me an international figure and given me a certain level of clout in government and business circles outside of Kenya. Mine was one of the better-known Kenyan names. That made it possible for me to bring in the kind of funds we needed to improve the Wildlife Department. I had already raised several hundred thousand dollars. To truly turn the department around, however, I needed millions.

In early October 1989, I went to Europe and the United States on a two-week fund-raising tour. I planned to visit the World Bank, various U.S. senators and congressmen, and a number of other leaders. Since the ivory burning, Kenya had achieved a new status in the eyes of the world. We were now seen as being seriously committed to saving our wildlife, and the developed countries were ready to help us out.

My travels made it impossible for me to attend the next CITES meeting in Lausanne, Switzerland, at which the delegates would be voting on whether or not to list the African elephant on Appendix I. International support for an ivory ban was growing daily, fueled by our bonfire, the campaigns of various conservation organizations, and by all the media coverage. Eugene Lapointe, the head of CITES, maintained that the best way to save elephants was to continue the trade. Only if elephants brought in money, he argued, would African countries have a financial incentive to protect them. Rowan Martin and his Zimbabwean team, as well as representatives from other southern African countries, rallied behind Lapointe's position. So did the ivory-buying countries of Japan and Hong Kong. Given that a strong cast of East African elephant experts, including Iain Douglas-Hamilton, were going to be on hand to combat the protrade group, I didn't feel it was necessary that I be present. But I did give them an extra boost beforehand.

Since George Adamson's death, our rangers and police had had frequent run-ins with poachers in Meru and the two Tsavos. We were driving the poachers hard, and for a while few elephants were killed. I didn't want the protrade people, however, to get wind of this. I knew the poachers would strike again; and when they did, I wanted to make use of their attack.

In late September 1989, the poachers obliged me, gunning down eleven elephants in the two Tsavos. I held on to the news for a few days, then released it to the press at the beginning of October. Because there hadn't been any stories about dead elephants for a while, and because eleven was a considerable number, the papers ran our announcement as front-page, headline news—exactly as I had hoped. The story came out just as the CITES meeting was opening. "This is why it's so important for the elephants to be given full, international protection," I was quoted as saying. "We can only end this carnage by putting the elephant on CITES Appendix I."

I must confess, though, that I didn't think that the Appendix I listing would actually stop the trade. I thought that was far more likely to happen from publicity generated by the ivory burning and the ad campaigns that were making ivory taboo. On that score, I was wrong.

I later learned from my colleagues that the CITES meeting was a closely fought battle with lots of jockeying among the various African countries. In the end, our side—and the elephants—won. The elephants were elevated to Appendix I status. The legal trade in ivory was largely halted, but sadly, the illegal trafficking was to continue.

I was in New York State, giving a lecture at the University of Rochester the night the vote was taken. When I returned to my hotel, the desk clerk handed me a note. Someone had called to tell me the good news. I jotted it down in my diary, noting that those who'd lost were most certainly going to attempt to find some way around the ban: *October 17. CITES puts elephant on Appendix I. 76 for, 11 against, and 4 abstentions. We shall have to make a major campaign now to keep up public pressures.*

Some of the people who'd been tracking the ivory trade carefully may have known what was going to happen next. I did not. Almost overnight, the price of ivory collapsed. The day before the meeting, a pound of ivory sold for more than one hundred dollars; the day after, a seller would have been lucky to get five dollars.

I was astonished and delighted. I hoped this would drive the poachers out of our parks and give us a chance to rebuild them. For once there seemed to be a glimmer of hope on the horizon.

CHAPTER 10

It would be some time before we saw any positive effects from the ban. The southern African countries, Zimbabwe in particular, were telling the press that they were going to do everything possible to overturn the decision at the next conference in three years, and that they might continue to trade outside the ban with those countries not signatory to the CITES convention. They continued to argue that they needed to sell ivory in order to support their national parks, and felt that they were being unfairly punished for successfully managing their elephants.

I didn't think that they were all that successful. For instance, Zimbabwean officials asserted that, between 1987 and 1989, Zimbabwe's elephant population had increased by seventeen thousand, a phenomenal and unlikely surge. About nine thousand of these "new" elephants had been counted in Hwange Park, which lies along the border with Botswana.

Then Allan Thornton and Dave Currey from the Environmental Investigation Agency in London, who were investigating the ivory trade, got wind that the Zimbabweans had constructed a number of small dams in Hwange. It wasn't clear whether these dams were new or old, but whenever Botswana suffered from droughts, its elephants crossed the border into Zimbabwe to drink water from them. Botswana and Zimbabwe may have counted the same nine thousand elephants as their own, creating the false impression that each country was being overrun with elephants. Thornton and Currey also produced evidence suggesting that poaching was a bigger problem than officials ever acknowledged. One thousand elephant carcasses had been found in a Zimbabwe park bordering Mozambique; and since the Zimbabwean army occupied the park, there was little question as to who was responsible.

All this sleuthing, however, didn't help us much. The Zimbabweans continued to insist that they were going to keep the trade alive, and the poaching in East Africa only tapered off slightly. I'm sure the poachers were counting on the disgruntled countries to break the ban and resume selling ivory. Thus the elephant slaughter didn't end overnight. That would only happen with time once the poachers realized they couldn't—now or ever—sell their stockpiled tusks.

In the meantime, we would keep after the gangs inside our parks. As usual, we were having mixed success. But in late October 1989, our antipoaching unit in Meru engaged one of the worst poaching groups, the one suspected of murdering the French tourists and later killing policemen in a mortar attack. This time, the rangers shot a couple of members of the gang, including its leader. As I wrote in my diary that night, this was "excellent news."

More good news came a few days later. Abdul Bashir, the exemplary paramilitary police officer, was officially transferred to the Wildlife Department to head our security and wildlife poaching command. I was delighted. Bashir (as I always called him) was depressed. I well remember our conversation the morning he reported for duty.

"Now that you're here," I said, "what do you think?"

Bashir looked glum. "Well, I suppose I have to see what has to be done and I'll do it," he said, trying to sound positive. "But I don't like being here."

I smiled. I liked his honesty. I knew that he'd objected to the transfer, that, like his fellow police officers, he regarded the ranger force as contemptible rabble. Bashir had been the deputy commandant of a well-trained unit; he was nearly at the top of his profession and had had his eye, as he told me, on the top job. Although he was given the equivalent command at Wildlife, it was far from being equivalent in prestige. I knew this but told him that I was counting on him to turn things around, to make the antipoaching unit the best of our services. I wanted him to feel that he had a free hand.

"You need to find out what we have," I suggested, "what we're missing, and what we need. I'll put an airplane at your disposal. Fly to the parks, meet the men, and take stock. Then let's talk about it."

Bashir nodded. He still did not look happy but agreed that this was a good plan. We'd meet again in a week. From all the reports I had heard about Bashir, I knew he was someone who liked to get things done. Once he got started, I was sure he would begin to enjoy his job and give it his all. His experience and know-how would make the parks secure again.

As you can tell, Bashir's arrival boosted my spirits enormously. With his appointment and the arrival of David Mwiraria, Wildlife now had two good professionals on its side. A few weeks later, in mid-November, I got another boost: Kenya's Parliament passed the bill establishing Wildlife as a parastatal agency. We would shed our old name, Department of Wildlife and Conservation Management, and be reborn as the Kenya Wildlife Service (KWS). This by itself gave us a fresh start, since the old acronym (WCMD) was associated in many people's minds with everything that was rotten and wrong. Indeed, to this day, I like to gloss over the fact that I ever worked for WCMD. My appointment and tenure were always at KWS.

As I've explained, the plans for KWS had been under consideration for some time. My predecessor and others had established the legislative framework for a new organization that would manage the country's wildlife both inside and outside the parks and reserves. Early on it had been decided that KWS would have considerably more freedom and autonomy from the Civil Service than most government departments. It was to be run very much like a business, funding its own activities by generating revenue from tourism. And, like a business, KWS would be able to fire, hire, and reward employees without having to go through the Civil Service's central committees.

Two thorny questions had delayed the approval of KWS. One was, could an autonomous government organization be trusted to operate an armed force? Second, could such an organization become financially self-supporting within a reasonable amount of time?

Naturally, I became involved in answering these questions—or, to phrase it more accurately, in persuading the government that KWS could do both. This required some effort. KWS was not the first autonomous government corporation, and the track record of the previous parastatal agencies had been uneven. The Posts and Telecommunications, State Banks, Ports, and Insurance agencies all had pretty dismal histories of financial mismanagement and varying degrees of transparency. They had been disastrously unproductive and appallingly managed. In fact, the World Bank and several Western donor countries were then pressuring Kenya to privatize these agencies and others entirely. The government, and I imagine the president, too, was understandably concerned about forming a parastatal that had an armed force and yet was free from the direct supervision of the central government. But there were also positive examples to consider: the former Kenya National Parks organization was well run and had been a parastatal until 1976. The key difference was that KWS employees now had semiautomatic and other reasonably sophisticated weapons and were engaged in a serious, if small, bush war.

President Moi and I discussed the matter several times. I emphasized that the KWS force did not need to be large but rather to consist of a few well-trained mobile units. In fact, under the president's instruction, we were already making use of some three hundred semiautomatic rifles. They had made a real difference in stemming the activities of the poaching gangs. I knew that some of Moi's top advisers were arguing strongly against my position. This was why it took time to reach a final decision. In the end, fortunately, my request was granted. KWS would have sole responsibility for security within the National Parks.

We had fewer debates about how KWS would manage its finances. Here, the government seemed more ready to acquiesce. I was sure the parks' revenues would grow as tourism and wildlife-viewing facilities in Kenya improved and were better marketed, and I planned to raise the funds for these purposes. Revenue could be doubled simply by implementing measures to cut down on rampant theft and fraud at our parks' entry gates. In the previous year, the losses in revenue were estimated to be approximately 80 percent of the ticket sales. KWS could also add to its coffers by collecting back rent from the many lodges within the parks, all of which are privately operated and most of which were in arrears.

I added two other provisions to the proposed legislation establishing KWS. One was that KWS would not be responsible for compensating people for wildlife-related crop and stock losses, such as having a cornfield trampled and eaten by elephants or losing a cow to a lion. Nor should it compensate families for death or injuries due to wildlife. In the past, the WCMD had attempted to pay farmers for both crop and human damages, but the procedures for doing so were chaotic. Compensation claims had to pass through several stages of official approval before payments could be made, and at each stage public officers and WCMD officials made certain that "a little something" came their way. For instance, a farmer might have lost the equivalent of three bags of corn to elephant damage. The local wildlife officer would often only agree to forward the claim if it was for six bags. Further up the line, someone else would say the farmer must claim ten bags. So it went. By the time the claim reached WCMD, the cost had increased by four or five times. As this happened to almost every claim, WCMD soon ran out of money to pay. Only a fraction of the claims were ever met. And naturally, many farmers who'd lost their crops or stock were disgruntled and antiwildlife.

Under the new legislation, compensation claims were to be settled from funds that Parliament specifically appropriated for that purpose. People would apply to a new board that the government would oversee. KWS would no longer have to regulate these matters, freeing it of a huge and untenable financial burden.

The second provision I proposed would permit KWS the freedom to recruit its own staff. This meant that we wouldn't have to hire the entire staff of the old WCMD, many of whom were unsuitable. By having

Parliament approve this measure, I hoped to avoid some of the difficulties that would arise when more than sixteen hundred people found themselves without a job (David Mwararia's estimate of the number we needed to ax). They wouldn't be fired outright; the government would transfer some to other departments and retire others. However the government handled the matter, these people would be off my books, and KWS would be free to recruit better employees.

All of these provisions were indeed incorporated in the legislation creating KWS, which President Moi signed at the end of November 1989. I couldn't help feeling elated. During the summer, there were times when I wondered whether it would ever be possible to accomplish the task I had taken on. People, as well as their crops and stocks, had to be protected. The wild animals throughout Kenya's 270,000 square miles of parks also had to be protected. Tourists had to be made to feel safe, and Kenya's disillusioned public had to be reassured. There were no easy solutions, and no money for tackling them either. I found myself lying awake at night, mulling them over endlessly and wondering if I shouldn't throw in the towel and ask President Moi to appoint someone else.

The newly enacted KWS legislation changed my outlook. I was now completely confident that I had his full backing and the extraordinary powers that such support carries. For once, I allowed myself to think that I could achieve one of my major goals: establishing a wildlife agency in Kenya that would be financially self-sustaining. Kenya's commitment to the new agency gave me the green light to begin creating the kind of wildlife and conservation service I envisioned.

The official launch date for KWS was January 15, 1990. The approved legislation would help me show how serious Kenya was about its wildlife and lobby for the substantial funds we needed to succeed.

In the previous decade, most of the foreign support for the department came from nongovernmental organizations, or NGOs, such as the African Wildlife Foundation, the Wildlife Conservation Society, Conservation International, the Frankfurt Zoological Society, and the World Wildlife Fund. These and other conservation groups maintained offices in Nairobi, and their experts had played a very active role in setting the agenda for conservation. The Wildlife Department was financially weak, so donor money could and did have considerable influence in some areas. I felt that Kenya should make its own choices. We needed to recruit our own nationals as experts and have access to funds that were not specifically earmarked. Recognition and appreciation of help were quite different from simply leaving the decisions to the donors. Kenya had been dependent on foreign donors for so long that we had the mentality of welfare recipients: we were no longer able to determine our own priorities or manage our own affairs without an outsider standing over our shoulder. Most importantly, we needed to establish "ownership" of the new Wildlife Service. Those who worked for it needed to feel that they had helped to create and build it, and therefore had a stake in its success.

I do not think that many in the NGO wildlife community were particularly happy when I assumed the position at Wildlife. Although I had been chairman of the board of the East African Wildlife Society, most people regarded that position as little more than an honorary title. Nor had I actively participated in conservation causes. Consequently, I was an unknown quantity to those who ran the NGOs, an outsider in their tightly knit circle, and some of them made derisive comments to their colleagues and to the press, suggesting that I wasn't qualified for the office. I had indirectly heard the same complaint myself from David Western, one of Kenya's wildlife scientists.

Some weeks before my appointment, and after I had begun speaking out about the elephant poaching, I had lunch with Western, who was then working for Wildlife Conservation International, an America-based international NGO with a program in Nairobi. Western, a short, rather shy man with blond hair and gray eyes, had been born and raised in Tanzania and educated in conservation and ecology at Nairobi University. He had published several theoretical papers about managing wildlife in East Africa and was well regarded by the conservation crowd. Western and I had known each other informally for some years, as the National Museums were also active in wildlife studies; and the headquarters of the East African Wildlife Society (EAWS) were located on the Museum's campus. We occasionally ran into each other at meetings there. I had no real opinion of Western's conservation studies at the time, although I thought his ideas about the nomadic Maasai, with whom he claimed a special kinship, were overly romantic. He believed the Maasai still lived in harmony with the wild animals around them and felt that they should be allowed to come and go within the borders of the national parks as they had done in the past. The Maasai may in fact have lived harmoniously with the wildlife in the late 1800s, when there were far fewer people about and when the Maasai did not own fenced wheat farms or inoculate their cattle against disease. But times had changed, and Western's ideas struck me as unrealistic and anachronistic.

He and I met for this lunch because I had suggested that all the NGOs should decide on a common position regarding the elephant problem and present it to President Moi. Western's organization was one of the more influential conservation groups, and I wanted his support for my plan. He told me that it would be far better if I concentrated on fossils and allowed people who knew about conservation to worry about problems in the wildlife sector. He didn't believe it was my place to coordinate an effort that would advise the president. Naturally, I was offended and annoyed, although I tried to keep my irritation to myself. We did not part on the best of terms.

Neither of us suspected that a fortnight later I would become director of Wildlife. I decided it was best to put what Western had said out of my mind. It wouldn't be productive to conduct vendettas against people with views different from mine or who had once said something unpleasant. Since he was a highly regarded conservationist, I wanted to hear his thoughts about our problems and invited him to several of our early planning seminars. He joined in, but I couldn't shake the feeling that he disapproved of my appointment and that he thought the president had given the wrong man the job. Throughout my time at KWS, we never really spent much time together.

It was soon clear to me that some NGO conservationists felt much the same way Western did about my appointment, and, at times, I had to swallow the caustic remarks I would have liked to have said to them. At any rate, I was determined to change the relationship between the Wildlife Service and the NGOs. I wanted us to be telling them what needed to be done, rather than the other way around. They could then use their funds to support our projects.

This transition didn't always go smoothly. During one of my early fund-raising tours for KWS, I was invited to a breakfast meeting in Washington, D.C., with a director of a prominent wildlife organization, whom I would prefer not to name, and two of his top officials. They offered to channel the funds I was raising through their organization; they would match whatever sums I raised, provided they were given credit as the primary NGO building up KWS.

"To show our good faith," the director said, "we'd like to give you one hundred thousand dollars for KWS right now as an advance payment on the money we will raise together." He put a check for that amount on the table.

I didn't touch it. "That sum won't begin to buy exclusivity with KWS," I replied. "My budget is for over a hundred million dollars. So no thanks. I don't need you to conduit our money."

The three men looked at me as if they couldn't believe their ears. There was an awkward silence. I'm sure they felt terribly offended, but I was determined that KWS would retain its independence.

That meeting didn't improve my standing with other leading figures in the international conservation world. I'm sure I offended them further when I suspended plans to build a zoo outside Nairobi National Park. Bill Conway, head of the New York Zoological Society (the parent organization of Wildlife Conservation Society) in New York City, had laid the groundwork with Dr. Perez Olindo to turn the park's animal orphanage into an educational zoo.

Although it had been started with the best of intentions in the 1960s, the zoo was now a pathetic collection of pens housing poorly cared for and fly-ridden antelopes, monkeys, zebras, and other animals. The orphanage had evolved naturally: wardens in the park occasionally came across orphaned or wounded animals and brought them back to headquarters until they could be released. Someone decided that people would enjoy seeing the animals waiting to be returned to the wild. They paid a token fee for the privilege. Soon the orphanage became a popular weekend destination for Nairobi residents who lacked a car and could not drive into the park itself; and because of its popularity, it was expanded. Instead of serving as a rehabilitation center, however, it became a zoo. Its real purpose was to keep animals in captivity, and I think this was clear to all of its visitors. Certainly, foreign dignitaries realized this since they often gave gifts, such as tigers from Nepal, pygmy hippos from Liberia, and black bears from the Himalayas. Kenyans enjoyed seeing these exotic creatures.

I do not think that zoos are necessarily bad institutions; they can be useful for teaching the public about wildlife and conservation. But this zoo had none of the redeeming qualities or facilities of a modern zoo. The pens were tiny, the conditions appalling, and the standard of animal welfare shocking. Bill Conway, Dr. Olindo, and others recognized this and decided to provide better conditions for the animals and to make the facility more of a learning center.

These were laudable goals. However, it struck me that if the center was built as they had planned, there was a great risk to Nairobi national park. Like modern zoos in developed countries, this one would have no visible pens but rather moats separating people and animals. Such a sophisticated zoo would be costly and difficult to maintain. Worse, it would provide a big opening to politicians looking to get their hands on the park's valuable real estate. The refurbished orphanage would look so much like a park, I was sure they would call into question the need for the national park itself. I could easily imagine them saying, "Why do we need a park when we have a perfectly good zoo? We need the park's land for housing, so let's scrap the park. We'll leave enough to expand the zoo and sell the rest, and everyone will be happy."

I wasn't about to lay the groundwork for that scenario. Therefore, while I acknowledge that there was a very real need for wildlife education, the expanded orphanage-zoo did not seem the best way to achieve it. I told

❖ My father's birth place in Kabete, north of Nairobi (Courtesy of the Leakey Family Archives)

❖ At Lake Natron, Tanzania in 1964 with my younger brother Philip (middle) and Margaret Cropper. We were accompanied by a local Msongo tracker/guide. (GLYNN LL. ISAAC)

❖ Traveling by camel at Lake Turkana in 1969 (JOHN READER)

❖ With Dr. L.S.B. Leakey examining the skull of a monkey from Koobi Fora in May 1970. (GORDON GAHAN/NATIONAL GEOGRAPHIC IMAGE COLLECTION)

❖ With Meave excavating a fossil (BOB CAMPBELL)

❖ Family gathering in December 1982 (COURTESY OF THE LEAKEY FAMILY
ARCHIVES)

❖ Examining two early human skulls at Nariokotome, Turkana, in northern Kenya in 1985. The skull on the left is from the famous "Turkana Boy." The one on the right is a *Homo erectus* skull from Koobi Fora. The fossils are about 1.7 million years old. (VIRGINIA MORELL)

❖ Receiving an Honorary Doctorate from the University of Aberdeen (JOHN MCINTOSH, UNIVERSITY OF ABERDEEN)

❖ Double fence marking the boundary of Nakuru National Park (COURTESY OF THE LEAKEY FAMILY ARCHIVES)

❖ We found this dead elephant entangled in a wire snare with an infected trunk. (DR. ROTTCHER)

❖ Wildlife rangers carrying ivory recovered from a hideout in the Tsavo National Park in 1989 (Bob Campbell)

❖ Recovered elephant tusks, Tsavo National Park (Bob Campbell)

❖ The ivory pyre at Nairobi National Park, July 1989 (Bᴏʙ Cᴀᴍᴘʙᴇʟʟ)

❖ President Moi and Minister Katana Ngala viewing the elephant ivory pyre
(Sᴛᴇᴘʜᴇɴ Jᴏɴᴇs)

❖ President Moi lighting the pyre. Minister Ngala and I are standing behind the President. (BOB CAMPBELL)

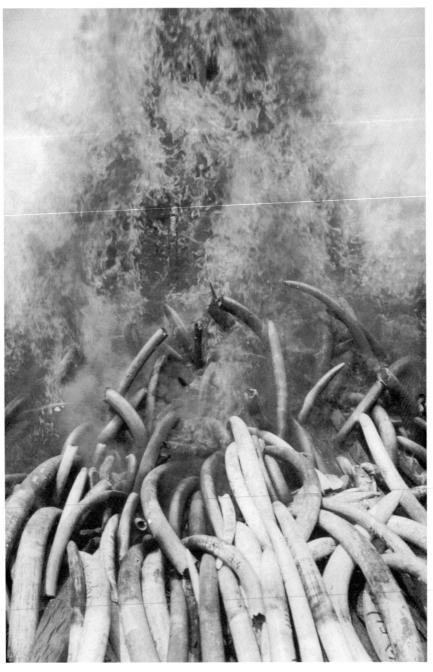

❖ Burning ivory fuelled by kerosene (COURTESY OF THE LEAKEY FAMILY ARCHIVES)

❖ My daughter Samira (left) and Dudu Douglas Hamilton (Bob Campbell)

❖ Addressing the press at the ivory burning (Stephen Jones)

❖ George Adamson with one of his lion cubs at the Kora camp shortly before his murder in August 1989 (COURTESY OF THE LEAKEY FAMILY ARCHIVES)

❖ Inspecting vehicles at Meru National Park (O. DOUGLAS HAMILTON)

❖ Loading an orphaned baby elephant into the KWS aircraft. The orphans are reared by Daphne Sheldrick for subsequent release to the wild herds. (FIONA ALEXANDER)

❖ Baby elephant, orphaned by poachers, being encouraged to board the rescue flight. (FIONA ALEXANDER)

❖ Inspecting training KWS rangers in Tsavo National Park (COURTESY OF KWS)

❖ Helicopter used by the Wildlife antipoaching units. The pilot (center) is Ted Goss of the Eden Trust. (COURTESY OF THE LEAKEY FAMILY ARCHIVES)

❖ My Cessna immediately after the crash on June 3, 1993 (Rick Mathews)

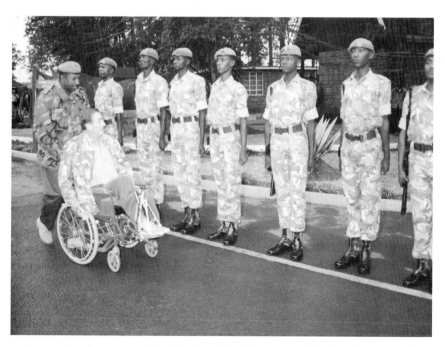

❖ Inspecting the Quarter Guard at KWS headquarters in October 1993. One leg had been amputated and the other was removed a few weeks later when I returned to the hospital in England. (Courtesy of KWS)

❖ Examining recovered ivory and animal skins after my amputations in November 1993 (Courtesy of KWS)

❖ With (l–r) President Museveni of Uganda, President Mwinyi of Tanzania, and President Moi at KWS headquarters in December 1993 (Courtesy of KWS)

Conway this. He protested that his organization had already raised $250,000 for the project and insisted that we go forward with the plans.

"I'm sorry," I replied, "I can't take that on. We have other priorities. It would be better if you gave the money to someone else." And I suspended the project. Once other priorities had been addressed, the concept could perhaps be reconsidered.

I decided that I would approach all external assistance to KWS in the same way. We would develop our own vision by coordinating a strategic business plan, policy, and approach. Then we would seek investment donors. They could participate by supplying funds or expertise. I knew this was an unorthodox approach to asking for aid. It's generally thought that the recipient should be thankful for whatever is received. Unfortunately, aid doesn't always result in clear-cut benefits; in some cases, it actually does more harm than good. This is particularly true when the recipient country hasn't been involved in the planning of a project or isn't held accountable for the end results. I had seen more than enough of these botched aid projects in our parks.

One of the worst offenders had been the World Bank. During the early 1970s, the bank had been keen to put money into Kenya's wildlife and tourism sector, which, in itself, was a very appropriate priority. However, great mistakes were made in the process, and Kenya's wildlife suffered some major setbacks. The World Bank project coerced the Kenya government to merge the Kenya National Parks and the former Game Department in the mid 1970s. As I've indicated, the merged entity, the WCMD, was to oversee all wildlife matters and to supervise the disbursement of $27 million for equipment, buildings, and infrastructure. The previously well-run National Parks suffered, corruption set in, and staff morale collapsed.

So unsupervised were the funds that enormous frauds took place. The shoddiest of materials were used in construction; buildings were badly designed; and no thought was given to their location. I was absolutely shocked at what I found when I took over and began investigating some of the bank-financed projects. One of the most egregious examples was in the Masai Mara National Reserve. The Mara, as it is commonly called, lies in the southwestern part of Kenya, right next to Tanzania, on what is actually the northern extension of the Serengeti Plains. You can cross from the Mara into Tanzania's Serengeti National Park. Together, the two parks form one of the largest wildlife preserves in East Africa. From an administrative standpoint, the Mara is unusual. Its land belongs to the Maasai people of Narok County, but legally the wildlife belong to the state. The Masai are charged with overseeing the reserve and have their own county council rangers for doing so.

For many years, the Mara was the crown jewel of Kenya's wildlife areas. Vast herds of game—elephants, rhinos, antelopes, zebras, giraffes, scores of wildebeest—crowded its green plains, and lions and cheetahs were abundant. Because lodging was limited, the number of tourists was also limited. Few parks offered the kind of wildlife experience that the Mara did. But the Narok County Council, which manages the Mara, wanted to increase tourism and asked for assistance from the World Bank's wildlife government credit.

Private investors moved in rapidly. They put up new hotels, luxury camps, and lodges, all in the expectation of better roads and infrastructure. Sadly, the bank-supported works were poorly planned. Many were left unfinished. The new tourist accommodations soon overwhelmed the roads, and visitors began driving wherever they wanted. As a result, the Mara's once-green plains are crisscrossed with tire tracks and ruts.

I visited the Mara a few months into my tenure and was shocked at how beaten-down it looked. It was far from being an "untouched" part of Kenya as it once had been, and I imagined how disappointed tourists must be. I could only guess at what they thought when they drove past the entry gates and saw the staff housing, paid for by the bank's loan. It consisted of about twenty seedy, concrete-block buildings, some with corrugated iron roofs, others covered with thatch and odd bits of metal and plastic. Weed-choked building materials—cement blocks, bags of cement, rusted pipe—were piled close to the houses. None of them had indoor toilets, and a line of filthy outhouses stood in the background. The wells for the plumbing had never been completed, either, and long lengths of plastic, PVC pipe littered the ground. It was what it looked like—a disaster. I wondered if any of the good-hearted World Bank people who had funded this project ever saw what their money had bought.

I got my chance to ask that question in the summer of 1989, when a friend took me to meet some of the bank's officers in Washington. I wanted to request funds from the bank to finish the projects it had started and left unfinished. A few of the people I met seemed vaguely aware of the problems the bank had caused; others expressed complete surprise. I was actually enjoying telling them what a mess they'd made when one officer spoke up.

"We do want to finish what we started," he said. "We're also interested in helping Kenya with a new wildlife project."

I wasn't certain how to respond. I needed—KWS needed—money desperately. Here was an offer, but from an organization that I was extremely critical of.

The bank officials went on to indicate that a fresh loan could be used to complete the Mara project, and that, following that, funding could be allocated to put KWS on its feet.

"If you were to provide new funds," I said, "the arrangements for supervision would need to be very different." I was at that moment very unsure whether I wanted to get involved with the World Bank.

Back in Kenya, without dwelling on this particular conversation in Washington, I continued to lay out with my staff my vision of what the Wildlife Service could be. From the beginning of my tenure I had spent a good deal of time thinking about this and had a very clear picture of what needed to be done. The starting point, as far as I was concerned, was addressing the issue of funding. There was simply no way of financing the conservation of Kenya's wildlife by drawing public funds from the central government; it did not have the money. All of my planning was therefore built around creating a self-sufficient, self-sustaining public enterprise able to manage the entire wildlife sector (parks, reserves, sanctuaries, and the areas outside these) not only in the immediate future but through the next decade and beyond. Few people realize just how difficult it is to conserve wildlife in national parks and elsewhere without adequate money. And if Kenya—one of the more successful of African nations in economic terms—could not manage this on government funds, I doubt if any other African country could.

I discussed this problem in detail with David Mwiraria and others on my staff. We decided that were KWS to generate its own revenue, it needed a master business plan, one that clearly laid out the organization's goals for the next five years and the means to achieve them. I put David in charge of this project. We'd already had numerous discussions about what the plan's underlying principle would be. First and foremost, we needed to protect our wildlife areas, the parks, reserves, and sanctuaries that contained KWS's key resources—the beautiful landscapes and fabulous animals. These were our capital, if you will, and securing and developing them was essential to anything else the organization did. Therefore, in KWS's first five years, we would spend money on the protected areas in order to earn money from them.

I'm not a conservation theorist, but I do believe in the value of national parks and protected areas overall. By this I mean places that are managed for the benefit of the animals and plants that live there and from which humans are largely banned or their movements constrained. I know that a significant number of others, such as David Western, have a different view, and see the human communities living adjacent to the parks as part of the natural landscape. They believe that the parks in Kenya are foreign-imposed institutions that have disrupted the natural ecosystem, and that the future of the plants and animals would be more secure were people able to wander as freely in these areas as they used to. They also fear that, in time, as the people gain more political clout, they will demand the return of this parkland; and that, at some point, inevitably, it will be given to them.

I disagree with this philosophy because Kenya is no longer in the nineteenth century. When people say that parks are a colonial relic, or unnatural, my response is to ask, "Isn't a city unnatural? A cattle dip [to protect cows against tick-borne diseases]? Immunizations and electricity? By using these things, are we imposing Western values?" I don't think any educated Kenyan intends to give up either his trousers or his telephone. Then, too, Kenya has experienced a population boom since the nineteenth century. When there are only six hundred people near a wildlife area it may be possible to live in harmony with the animals, but not when there are six hundred thousand. It has always been necessary to enforce park boundaries, whether in America, Europe, or Africa. If you don't, the people will destroy them. Lastly, we would be doing a great injustice to future generations of Kenyans, and to the wildlife inside the parks, not to do our utmost to protect our parks and reserves.

When I met again with World Bank officials in December 1989, I emphasized that KWS's primary focus in the next few years would be on the protected areas. I gave an estimate of the funding I thought KWS needed to resolve all the wildlife problems and secure its parks, reserves, and sanctuaries: $300 million, to be spent over a ten-year period.

"But if you gave us this sum and then it was badly managed, you would be permanently harming Kenya's wildlife and parks," I said. "It's not enough to just give the money, it must be wisely spent upon agreed priorities and plans, and the government side must hold firm to the agreed upon policies."

Funds should be bound by certain conditions, I continued, and there had to be a commitment by the bank to stand behind them. If KWS did not meet them, funding would be withdrawn. I said again that enormous sums of money do not have neutral effects, and that I was concerned that unsupervised donor funds can easily transform a situation from bad to worse—as the first World Bank project demonstrated.

My discussions with senior officials at the World Bank convinced me that we were using a new approach, and that environmental as well as governance issues were very much at the top of the agenda. We seemed to be speaking the same language, and they seemed genuinely eager to help. They weren't put off by the sum of money I had mentioned either and were very supportive about my plans to make KWS into a self-sufficient agency.

They agreed that Kenya should secure its parks and reserves, and build up its wildlife and tourism businesses, since they were our prime means for earning foreign currency. Once we made our parks secure and more amenable to tourists by repairing the roads, bridges, and buildings, we could have the finest wildlife parks in the world. That was my ultimate goal. We could then increase the fees we charged tourists. I estimated that KWS could earn enough money from park entry and lodging fees alone to be self-supporting in five years' time.

"Enough tourists come to Kenya's parks that we shouldn't be operating in the red," I said. "We should be earning profits. That's what I want to achieve: to make KWS a profit-earning business."

I also made it very clear that we didn't want a project officer telling us how to do this. Instead, we at KWS would write the five-year plan—indeed, we had already begun doing this—but the bank would provide consultants and experts to offer advice. It was imperative for the KWS staff to have ownership of the project: they had to feel that it was something they had created. This is the way the most successful businesses are run in the United States. If giving Americans a personal stake in their jobs—shares of stocks for example—motivated them, why wouldn't the same be true for Kenyans?

By the end of several meetings, both in Nairobi and Washington, we had reached a broad agreement. What remained was to work out the details of a loan from the World Bank for $60 million. From other donors (the United Kingdom, Japan, the United States, and Netherlands), we expected to raise another $85 million. Moreover, if KWS and Kenya met all the terms of the loan, we would negotiate a second loan for another $150 million in five years. The bank would also oversee the funds that other donor countries wanted to give. In exchange, KWS would work to become self-supporting. It would also address the human-wildlife conflicts. Methods had to be found to keep the parks' wildlife from trampling crops and people. KWS was expected to become a more streamlined operation, too, and yet also to employ the professionals it needed in order to create the professional organization we envisioned. This was particularly important given the large sums of money KWS would be receiving and spending. We would need business consultants to advise us on procurement procedures, payment schedules, and other financial matters. Further, I would expect to manage KWS and the project without outside interference from any source. This was what President Moi had promised me and what I, in turn, had pledged to the World Bank and other donors. For them, this was an especially crucial part of our agreement—so many aid projects had been ruined by nepotism and corruption within the public sector. Indeed, the bank viewed KWS as a test case for reform.

The Kenyan government was also expected to play its part by using internal government resources to rebuild and repair the road network that provided access to the main national parks. (As incredible as it may seem, this was the main reason tourism was beginning to fall off. Deep ruts and potholes large enough to swallow a small bus were not uncommon, and understandably visitors complained about the bone-jarring trips they had to endure simply to reach a park's gates.) There would be money earmarked for new headquarters buildings in some parks, such as Sibiloi, and for better staff quarters in others. Funds were also earmarked for assisting communities close to our parks and reserves to develop tourism projects so that they would benefit from the wildlife. And there would be money to raise the salaries of rangers and other staff members. I wanted to free my staff from the Civil Service pay scale, which was barely above subsistence level, and offer them wages comparable to what they would receive in the private sector. If we paid a good salary, we would naturally attract more qualified employees.

I was well aware that the money we were getting, either as a soft loan or as a grant, came out of the pockets of hard-working people in other countries. I did not want to see that money misspent or lost to bribes. The bank officers discussed this with me several times, and we finally came up with a plan. KWS would receive funds through a special account set up by the government. Disbursement from this fund would require that World Bank and KWS officials agreed jointly on the specifics of project expenditure and followed a procurement system. President Moi seemed extremely pleased to hear about these plans and the large sums I was bringing into Kenya, particularly at a time when overall donor aid to Kenya was being cut back. He praised me several times, sometimes when members of his cabinet were present. Those men smiled, too, but I also saw some dark looks.

I met with President Moi just before leaving for a two-week Christmas holiday at our house on the island of Lamu in the Indian Ocean. I had been at the helm of Wildlife for a steady nine months and needed a break. Our Lamu home is built in the simple coastal style with thick, whitewashed block walls, a thatched roof, and an airy, open floor plan. There were always odd maintenance items to be seen to, and I set about attending to these. I also had a small sailboat (something I had given myself after surviving my kidney transplant), and I spent the mornings sailing, enjoying the peace of the sea. On our boat, at least, no telephones were ringing, and Meave and I had some time to relax together.

Louise and Samira joined us, as did my mother, Mary, who was then seventy-six. She was always an opinionated woman who freely told people, including her sons, what she thought about them. At one point she had disapproved of the way I was handling a particularly knotty problem about the dating of a fossil hominid. She thought the people I viewed as unfair critics were right to attack me and my team and told me so.

Like Meave, my mother was extremely worried about the pressures my new job put on my health and also about the threats on my life. She seldom said anything to me on these subjects, knowing the futility of it, but told friends and family members. I chose to tell her little about what I was doing. I didn't want to add to her worries. When she spoke up one night after dinner, what she said was therefore all the more meaningful to me.

"You know, don't you, Richard, that this work you're doing for the elephants and the other wildlife is far more important than any of your fossil work?" She gave me the direct look that only my mother could give.

"You think so?" I asked, surprised at her assessment, since fossils and stone tools had been at the center of her life.

"Oh yes. Vastly more important. Finding a fossil simply can't compare with saving the elephants."

My mother was a person of few words, and having offered her opinion, didn't expand on it. Her approval was hard to come by—she'd never said anything this positive when I was working in paleontology—and it lifted my spirits.

By the end of our holiday, I was ready to enter the fray once more and lead KWS, our new wildlife agency, into a new era.

CHAPTER 11

My friend and mentor Charles Njonjo has often offered me sound advice. When at his suggestion I joined the East African Wildlife Society in 1974, he was then its chairman. Very few other indigenous Kenyans belonged to the society at the time. I was deeply concerned that the society was ineffective because it appeared to be a "whites-only" organization and urged Charles that we do something about this. I thought we should dismantle the board and appoint a new one. Charles was older and not as hotheaded as I was. "If you break something up," he told me, "be absolutely sure that you can put it back together—and that it works better when you're done."

We didn't dismantle the EAWS or its board because I realized that he was right—once broken apart, it would probably never have gotten back together at all. It was a small organization with only a few members and volunteers.

Now I was preparing to dismantle a far larger organization, the old Wildlife Department, and I paid close attention to my friend's advice. In effect, I was about to tackle what would be best described as a major restructuring exercise, taking a government department and changing its culture to that of the corporate world. Were we to succeed, we might change the way wildlife departments were managed in a number of

African nations. I didn't know if this would happen, but certainly KWS was going to be a far different entity from its predecessor. To make certain the new organization that emerged from the ashes of the old one would not only be better, but *far* better, I hired a small band of professionals, most from the private sector, to provide recommendations.

David Mwiraria, of course, topped the list. He had joined me in September 1989 and by January 1990 had finished reviewing the records of our 4,500 employees and presented me with a list of 1,640 people whose services we no longer required. (In his review, David had not only identified corrupt and inefficient workers but those retired workers whose relatives were still on the payroll and who had devised various schemes to continue drawing their pay.) I asked David to turn his attention to revamping KWS's overall organization. We needed to sort out the best chain of command—how internal departments would interact with one another and what their specific responsibilities would be.

We also needed to create an overall policy framework, explaining KWS's short-term and long-term goals, and the best path toward attaining them. I would head this effort but with David's assistance. If KWS was to become self-sufficient, it had to exercise better control over its sources of income (primarily the park entry fees) and find new ones. I also wanted to establish a conservation endowment fund that would assure a baseline of income for KWS in the future.

Abdul Bashir had come round to seeing the opportunities and excitement offered by his new job. He would help plan our ranger training and security programs, tasks that appealed to him, as did the job of helping to create our corporate identity. I wanted our staff to feel that they belonged to KWS and could be proud of the organization they worked for. I also wanted all traces of the old WCMD removed from our "staff memory" and asked Bashir to design a new KWS uniform and logo.

Finally, I asked Jim Else, an expatriate veterinarian who had worked for me for almost two decades at the Museum, to put together our Science and Research Division. Such a department hadn't existed under WCMD, yet numerous zoologists and botanists came every year to do research in Kenya's parks. KWS could benefit from coordinating their efforts and pointing them to studies that would help our wildlife. Within that department, we needed a special Office of Elephant Management, so I hired the elephant researcher, Joyce Poole, to run it. From one of the nongovernment organizations, we recruited Grace Lusiola. Bright, good-natured, and with an infectious laugh, Grace had worked for various nongovernmental organizations for the past fifteen years and had considerable experience in community-based projects.

I already had taken a few steps to improve relations between KWS and local villages. For instance, when it was clear that KWS would receive significant donor assistance, I told the press that we would share our good fortune with our neighbors by giving these local communities a percentage of our revenues down the line and help small businesses take advantage of Kenya's growing tourism. KWS would also fence parks, such as parts of Tsavo West, Shimba Hills, and Aberdares, where people suffered all too frequently from wildlife encounters.

As we had expected and wished, the World Bank and other organizations provided us with consultants as well to help in the makeover. Agi Kiss, a forthright, no-nonsense economist and ecologist, coordinated the bank's efforts. From the World Conservation Union (know as IUCN which stood for its previous name, the International Union for the Conservation of Nature) came ecologists Steve Cobb and Robert Bensted-Smith to assist in planning KWS's overall policy and its individual departments.

Every Tuesday, my team came to my office precisely at 7 A.M. for a half-hour discussion. I don't think meetings need last any longer than this, and I actually prefer even shorter ones. Time was of the essence, I reminded anyone who slouched in a few minutes late. For the moment we had the president's goodwill and that of the people as well, but if KWS didn't come up to speed quickly we would lose those good feelings. We had an unusual opportunity, I stressed, a chance to create a dynamic, can-do government agency, a rarity in Kenya.

"KWS is ours," I told them in an early pep talk. "We have what amounts to a blank slate before us, and we can use that to build an organization that actually works, where people accomplish things. We can inspire the whole country."

It may be difficult for someone who has never been to Kenya to appreciate the degree of demoralization that pervaded every sector of the government at that time. The lack of representational and accountable government explained some of this malaise, but most of it stemmed from the widespread corruption. For example, it was difficult, if not impossible, for someone to get something as ordinary as a driver's license, let alone a business permit, without paying a bribe. Many government employees viewed their jobs as "owed" to them and consequently did as little work as possible. And because of their low wages, they were always on the lookout for "something extra," either by stealing from the government or by forcing the public to pay bribes.

I made it clear that none of this would be tolerated, at any level, at KWS. But I wasn't there to lecture them. I wanted them to feel the excitement of being given a chance to succeed, of showing their fellow countrymen what Kenyans were capable of achieving.

Overnight, it seemed, change was on the way. My closest staff and I weren't the only ones arriving at six in the morning; almost everyone seemed to be coming in early and working late. A sense of purpose and energy filled the halls, and where once there had been only sour looks, now there was laughter and high spirits. Kenyans as a whole people realized that major changes were on the way, too. Newspaper articles highlighted our ideas and progress, and soon we had a steady stream of applicants seeking jobs.

Seeing a group of young women heading toward our personnel office one day, I asked them why they wanted to work at KWS.

"Because, sir, KWS is leading the way," one said. The others looked shyly away.

"To what?" I asked, teasing.

"To a better life," another answered.

"It is said that KWS is where the best jobs are," her friend added. "Everyone is saying this now."

I thought it was a bit premature to come to this conclusion but still felt very heartened. I wanted Kenyans to be proud of their wildlife and the beauty of their countryside—and of the agency that oversaw them. They could be something all Kenyans could rally around, forgetting their tribal divisions. Most of all, I hoped that in the near future, all Kenyans, even the poorest villager, would come to see the animals and the parks as belonging to them. These were their country's assets and provided the best means for building a future. In spite of the trouble the animals often caused villagers, I hoped that Kenyans would come to see the wildlife and the parks as their salvation. To me, KWS was genuinely that: *Kenya's* Wildlife Service.

Despite the World Bank's and others' promises of aid, KWS was not suddenly flush with money. It would take time before the funds were actually given, as each donor agency and country had to follow their own bureaucratic rules for requesting and dispensing aid. To keep KWS afloat, I went to Europe and the United States again in February 1990 on yet another fund-raising tour. My lectures were one way of attracting the income KWS desperately needed. They also kept the plight of the elephant before the world.

Some people may have felt that listing the elephant on CITES Appendix 1 would immediately stop the slaughter. In those first few months after the elephant was listed, however, I don't think anyone knew exactly what would happen. The southern African countries kept saying that they were going to find a way to break the ban. In mid-January 1990, Britain's prime minister Margaret Thatcher didn't help matters when she requested CITES to allow Hong Kong to sell off its stockpiles of ivory. Almost overnight we saw a fresh wave of poaching. Another twenty-one elephants were killed in Tsavo alone. I'm not normally given to despair, but I did hit a low point after hearing this news and wrote bitterly in my diary: *This is extremely serious and the upsurge in poaching and . . . trafficking has begun. We are desperate for arms, ammunition, and equipment. Our radios are useless and we do not have nearly enough people.*

So much to do! I feel quite daunted by the sheer size of the problem. Money, money, money—beg, beg, beg! How long can I do this?

Two weeks later I was on my way to England with my hat in hand. I had to keep begging. There was no other choice.

For much of the first part of 1990, my life was a blur of meetings about launching KWS and fund-raising lectures to keep it going. That didn't mean that the old problems simply disappeared. In late March 1990, our rangers and police had another nasty run-in with poachers near Kora National Park, where George Adamson had been killed.

By now, thanks to Bashir's guidance and advice, we had an effective antipoaching force. It was in general still a bit green but coming along. Bashir and I met weekly to discuss the continuing problem with bandits and poachers. We created a sort of "war room" at headquarters, where we kept a large map of Kenya's parks and reserves. Colored pins marked our units' locations and those of any contacts. One particular group of bandits in the Meru and Kora regions kept us extremely busy. That part of the map was thick with pins; and one day, when Bashir and I were reviewing our efforts, I asked him how we might best clear the area of poachers.

"Why do they keep getting away?" I asked.

"They are slippery," Bashir agreed. He had by then been with us for four months and, it was easy to see, was enjoying his job. I teased him occasionally about how he had vowed he would never "like" being here. "Well, Richard, you tricked me," he would tease back.

As unlikely as it seemed, given that I was a civilian administrator and Bashir a policeman to the core, we were becoming friends. We enjoyed each other's company and liked working together.

"What can we do to bring this gang in?" I asked again, pressing the issue.

"They are some of the worse *shifta,*" Bashir replied. "Very tough men. But we can try."

The next time the gang was sighted, Bashir organized a joint operation with the police department's Special Forces Unit.

Only twenty-four hours later, we got the news that the operation had not gone at all as planned; in fact it was a disaster. The gang managed to lead our men into an ambush and totally routed our force, killing six men and seriously wounding four others. No KWS rangers were hurt, but they panicked along with everyone else. We lost a truck, too.

With a heavy heart, I flew to the scene with Bashir. This time there were no dead bandits to celebrate, only six dead policemen to take back to their loved ones. Bashir gave our men a stern dressing-down. I gave one of my "we've got to do better than this" pep talks. That night I wrote once again in my diary, *I wish I had more men, officers and money.* It was beginning to feel like a chant but one without any magic.

I had hoped the new year would be completely different from the one before, but incidents such as the one at Kora made it seem as though nothing had changed. I tried not to let my disappointment and flagging spirits show, knowing that it would only demoralize my staff. Day in and day out I reminded myself that I needed to appear self-confident, determined, certain that we were going to succeed on all fronts. In the middle of the night, however, it was a different story. I often woke up, tossing and turning, worrying that we would never achieve our goals, never stop the poachers, never raise enough money. I would picture my daytime self—the self-confident, pep-talking Leakey—and feel nothing but contempt for the show I put on. At those low moments, I felt like a fraud and wondered that no one else seemed to notice. These were long nights. At daybreak, I gave myself a stern talking-to. I wrapped my self-confidence around me like a cloak—and wondered how long I could keep it on.

I had only a few long-standing friends I could talk to about my doubts. Most did not know how to respond. My confessions caught them off guard; and while they were sympathetic, they, too, believed in my public image more than in my private worries. Yes, it was a tough job, they agreed, but they didn't doubt that I could do it. Perhaps all they thought I needed was simple encouragement to keep up the good fight. And their words did usually help bolster my spirits, although in an odd way they also left me feeling even more alone. That old saying, "It's lonely at the top," began to make more sense to me. No one could fully understand the pressures I was under.

No one except Meave. I didn't have to tell her what she already knew—my restless nights gave that away—but I continued to say little to her about the specific reasons for my anxiety. She told me several times to take a break, to fly with her to the research camp at Lake Turkana and rest. A weekend of shoreline walks, of watching the gazelle and oryx grazing on the plains and the pelicans gliding low over the water, would do me a world of good, she said. But I couldn't take a break, not while our rangers were dying and the elephants were being slaughtered. I know it seems ironic. Here I was, director of some of the finest wildlife parks in the world, a position many would covet, and I had no time to stop to watch the birds and animals under my protection as much as I yearned to do so.

Indeed, there are few things I love more than waking before dawn in the Kenyan wilds, watching the sun's first rays turn the pink of the morning light to blue and then gold, while the soft cooing of African doves and the harsher cries of ibis and go-away birds fill the air. As a young man, guiding tourists on photographic safaris, I had lived for those moments. I had savored them, too, while hunting fossils in our northern deserts. On a few expeditions we traveled by camel over the northern deserts. I loved the simplicity of those days. We slept on the ground around our camels, and rose when the stars were still out and the desert air sharp with cold. A cup of strong tea sufficed for breakfast. For lunch we stopped long enough to bolt down boiled potatoes and strips of antelope jerky. Our eyes were always on the far horizon, the next promising hill or gully, where an ancestral fossil might be waiting. Lions were abundant around Lake Turkana in those days; and at night, after a proper meal, we built up the fire, secured the camels in a circle around it, then wrapped ourselves in our blankets and laid down beside them. On many nights, lions and hyenas came padding close to our small circle, making the camels snort with fear. More than once, when I rose to add a log to the fire, I found the glowing orange eyes of a lion staring hard at me.

For a while when I was first appointed Wildlife director, I fantasized about experiencing such special moments again. How wrong I was. My world was now a seething stew of meetings, phone calls, and overseas travel. When I did get to the parks, I was always surrounded by people with problems that needed my attention. We might drive through a park but only to get to the scene of a crime or to visit buildings or wells or fencing in urgent need of repair. The moments I had spent watching the dawn light turn the dewdrops on a spider's web to gold, or feeling the hairs on my neck rise from a lion's cold stare, felt far in the past.

Toward the end of March 1990, I arranged a whirlwind tour of two important wildlife protected areas: Amboseli National Park and the Masai Mara National Reserve. Both parks have long histories of unhappy relationships between the park management and local Maasai people. I wanted to end these feelings of ill will and get the Maasai on our side.

The problems I faced stemmed from the way these two parks were created. Prior to the British colonization of Kenya, the cattle-herding Masai inhabited much of the land in the southern part of our country; they arrived here about four hundred years ago, displacing an earlier pastoral people. With their herds, the Maasai wandered across the acacia-dotted savannas and grasslands that swept from the edge of the Rift Valley to the base of Mount Kilimanjaro, seeking fresh pasture and water. The Maasai shared their land with an abundance of wildlife—gazelles, eland, elephants, rhinos, lions, and leopards.

I don't know that people anywhere have ever lived in harmony with wild animals, despite our wishful belief that once this was so, but the Maasai came as close as anyone ever has. This is not to say they did not hunt the animals; they did. In general, however, they had cultural taboos against eating game meat except under the harshest of circumstances, such as times of drought and cattle disease.

Sometimes young Maasai warriors, called *moran*, demonstrated their bravery by killing lions (a ceremonial hunt I was once fortunate to witness) and other big game, such as buffaloes, elephants, and rhinos. They were also expected to protect their families from large, dangerous animals. If an elephant killed a Maasai, for instance, clan members would spear to death several elephants. Such "lessons" taught the wildlife living alongside the Maasai to fear these people who strode over the plains in their bold red robes.

In the late 1800s, when the first Europeans ventured into East Africa, the bounty of game in Maasailand made it look like an Edenic paradise. Herds of antelopes and zebras stretched to the horizon, a mass of animals we can only imagine. "To describe what we saw in the way of game, would be put down today as exaggeration," Ronald O. Preston, one of the builders of the Kenyan railway, wrote in a book titled *The Permanent Way*, published shortly after the turn of the twentieth century. "[B]ut to put it mildly, wherever one looked, it was nothing but one moving mass of Hartebeest, Wildebeest, Zebra and the smaller antelope."

It was in this region in 1899 that the colonial government created one of Kenya's first wildlife preserves, the thirteen-thousand-square-mile Southern Reserve. Hunting wasn't forbidden in this area; it was only controlled. Indeed, it was in this huge reserve that Teddy Roosevelt, the prince of Wales, and Ernest Hemingway chased their big-game trophies. The Maasai were also given land in the reserve as a way of protecting their unique way of life.

In principle, the reserve was a good idea. However, it introduced a racist element into conservation. The only legitimate hunters, in the government's eyes, were white Europeans; tribal hunters were "poachers." Understandably, this double standard led to great bitterness and resentment among Kenya's peoples.

That, plus the growing population, led the government over time to significantly reduce the area set aside for the animals. In 1948, a little over 1,200 square miles were set aside as the Amboseli Game Reserve; and in 1961 (two years prior to Kenya's independence), it was given to the local Kajiado County Council to manage. In 1974, President Kenyatta reduced this reserve even further. He issued a decree, setting aside an area of 150 square miles exclusively for wildlife and tourism, and formally creating Amboseli National Park. The Kajiado County Council continued to manage a small parcel where the tourist lodges were situated and to receive revenue from them and from the park.

Kenyatta's decision was popular in wildlife conservation circles; the Maasai were furious. They had lost access to their most important dry-season refuge—the lush, green swamps in the heart of the park. For centuries, they had relied on the swamps for water and pasture for their cattle; now they were expected to give them up. The animals in the park, however, would still be free to roam over Maasai land outside the park. In protest, the Maasai speared several rhinos and elephants, and eventually the government agreed to build a pipeline that would take water from the swamps to the Maasai and their cattle.

Unfortunately, it took years for the pipeline to be completed, and when it was, it was never properly maintained. Little wonder that the Maasai detested the park and treated its employees and rules with contempt. They refused to stay out of the park and continued to come in with their large herds as they had always done.

This might not have been a major problem were Amboseli as large a park as Tsavo. But it's not; it is one of our smallest. There are limited grasslands for the antelopes, zebras, and elephants to share—let alone thousands of cattle. The elephants presented a special problem. Before the heavy poaching of the 1970s and 1980s, they had migrated in and out of the park, following the rains and fresh grass. Although elephants inside Amboseli were seldom killed (the Masai detest poachers and are quick to report them), as soon as they left the park they were vulnerable. Elephants are highly intelligent animals, and it did not take them long to discover that they were safe inside the park's borders and at high risk outside, particularly in Tanzania, where hunting is legal. Instead of migrating and giving the vegetation inside Amboseli a chance to recover from their heavy feeding, they became virtual residents. As their numbers increased, so did their adverse effect on the land. Conservationists debated whether or not to cull the herds, fearing that if nothing was done, the elephants would utterly destroy Amboseli—they would eat themselves and all the other game out of a home.

The Amboseli elephants had a powerful protector in Cynthia Moss, an American who has studied their social behavior since 1972. Cynthia strongly objected to culling and had successfully blocked every attempt to reduce the Amboseli herds. Joyce Poole, whom I had recently asked to join KWS (previous commitments prevented her from starting before June 1990), was a member of Cynthia's research team. They had a camp in the park—something that some conservationists also objected to. Indeed, it was such a sticky subject that I had already discussed the matter with Jim Else, KWS's research director. Although not 100 percent against Moss's and Poole's research camp, Else didn't fully support it either. To be fair I thought I should hear the researchers' side before deciding what KWS's policy on research camps in our national parks would be.

The problems at the Masai Mara National Reserve were different from those at Amboseli, and I'll discuss them in detail further on.

At both Mara and Amboseli, I planned to meet with local Maasai leaders to discuss their grievances. I hoped to begin persuading the Maasai to recognize the importance of their parks to Kenya's welfare. While I was sympathetic to the wrongs and injustices the Maasai had suffered, I also felt it was time for the Mara and Amboseli to be managed in such a way as to benefit the whole country instead of only the Maasai.

As usual, I packed my schedule tightly. I would meet with my rangers, the Maasai leaders, and Cynthia and Joyce at Amboseli one day, then fly for meetings at Mara the next. Before I left, Joyce sent a message, inviting me to stay at their camp. I would have to stay overnight somewhere on this journey, and, as she asked, why not there? She also suggested that I might like to see the elephants she and Cynthia were studying. I really hadn't seen elephants—living ones—since taking this job, and the idea naturally appealed to me.

The long rains ended a few weeks before I flew down to Amboseli, and when I arrived the park was lush and green. Mount Kilimanjaro, which towers over the park, is often hidden by clouds. On such days you would never guess that a huge, glacier-topped mountain sits right there on the African equator. But on the day I arrived, Kilimanjaro was out in all its glory, its broad, blue flanks rising above Amboseli's emerald plains, where scores of antelopes, zebras, and elephants grazed. Even a harried wildlife director could see that it was breathtakingly beautiful. I decided right then that somehow I would squeeze in that visit to the elephants.

Francis Mukungi, Amboseli's senior warden, met me at the landing strip. He had not been at this park for very long, but he understood its problems and was doing his best to gain friends among the Maasai.

"It's good you've come, Richard," Francis said. "The elders are excited about meeting you. They've heard a great deal about the money you've raised, and they want to know how they can get some of it."

We laughed together. Everyone apparently knew about the funds the World Bank was providing to KWS. I was going to have to do some quick explaining in this meeting, I could see, as we weren't about to simply hand out shillings.

Francis had arranged for the elders from the Kajiado County Council and for other Maasai leaders to meet me in the park's Serena Lodge. This is a handsome safari hotel with broad verandas that face a green swathe of the swampy grasslands where elephant and buffalo feed and where the tourists gather. As much as I admired the scenery and animals, we had work to do. I headed inside to a windowless conference room.

The meeting was packed. Some Maasai had arrived in traditional dress: red *shukus* draped over them, beaded bracelets on their wrists, and ceremonial sticks in their hands. Others wore suit jackets and trousers. Several Kenyan tour operators were in the audience. I sensed immediately that this was a potentially friendly group. They were pleased that I had come—and curious about what I had to say—and I didn't want to lose that goodwill.

"I don't like meetings anymore than anyone else," I began, knowing that many of the Maasai had traveled a good distance to see me. "So I'll make my remarks short and to the point. Amboseli is a small park but a popular one. We want it to continue to be popular so that we can increase the revenues you earn from it."

I then briefly explained a few of the things I hoped we could accomplish with the World Bank money. I wanted to get the pipeline fixed and have other boreholes drilled outside the park so that the Maasai had adequate water and pasture for their cattle. A murmur of approval went through the audience at these words. However, in exchange, I expected the Masai to keep their livestock out of the park.

"I recognize the government made a promise long ago about water, and it has not been kept," I said. "At the same time, the Maasai made a promise that's not been kept either. But the government is the father and must keep the promise first."

I also talked about how I wanted to take some pressure off the park by increasing tourism outside of it. This could happen if the Maasai, who owned several large group ranches around the park, developed mini-parks or reserves of their own. I sketched the idea for them and told them that in a few months they could expect to meet with our community-projects director, Grace Lusiola. She would have more details. KWS would also see to it that the Maasai received a greater share of the revenues from the park so that they would benefit more directly from the tourists.

The more I spoke, the more interest I sparked in the faces before me. The elders realized that I was offering them a chance to develop a tourism industry of their own—a way to tap into revenue that now largely passed them by—and several wanted to get started on a community project that very afternoon.

I laughed with them at their enthusiasm. "This is what we need in Kenya," I said. "Our wildlife is our number-one resource, and we can develop it so that everyone benefits."

It was only a speech, but almost immediately it seemed to soften some of the hostility the Maasai felt toward the park.

Afterward, Francis took me on a quick tour of the rangers' quarters. These had once been utterly shabby, but the staff had given the exteriors a fresh coat of white paint and made other repairs. The rangers, too, looked much spiffier. They all had uniforms *and* boots, and stood smartly at attention as I walked by.

There were problems of course. We still were having trouble with the theft of gate receipts so that the park continued to lose money, and the rangers' salaries remained low. However, we hadn't lost anymore tourists to bandits on the road between Tsavo East and Amboseli, and the rangers were smiling and energized.

When Joyce appeared late that afternoon, I felt that I had earned my visit to the elephants. She arrived in a beige Toyota Jeep and suggested that I travel in her vehicle.

"The elephants are used to my car," she explained, "so we'll be able to get closer to them."

At that point I didn't realize what she meant by "closer." I suppose I thought we would be a few hundred yards from them, a safe distance that would allow us to flee if an elephant charged. As we drove off, Joyce briefly explained the studies that she and Cynthia were doing.

"This is the longest, continuous study of elephants anywhere," she said. "Cynthia's records really document the social history of several elephant families."

I nodded but, honestly, I didn't realize the full import of what she was telling me. The idea of an elephant "family" struck me as a trifle sentimental, which was what some researchers accused Cynthia of being. That was why she didn't want the elephants culled, these critics said. I decided not to say anything. I didn't know Joyce very well, but she was coming to work for me and I didn't want to alienate her. And I was her guest.

Joyce turned down a dirt track not far from the lodge and into an area of tall grass and short palms, which the Masai call *oltukai*. It was a breezy afternoon with dark clouds bunched up along Kilimanjaro's lower slopes. The grasses waved blue, purple, and gold in the afternoon light and the air smelled of wild mint and thyme. We drove through a herd of sleek zebras and dainty Thompson's gazelles and past an acacia tree laden with the basketlike nests of golden buffalo weaver birds. Then, around a bend in the road, a herd of elephants appeared. There were about twenty of them, of all ages and sizes, a wall of rippling, gray flesh that stretched across the road. To my surprise, Joyce didn't stop but drove slowly right into their midst.

All my past experiences told me that this was a supremely foolish thing to do. As a young man, I had had a few run-ins with elephants and had learned to give them a respectfully wide berth. In my late teens, I was asked once to stand in for the "hunter" at the Treetops safari lodge in the Aberdares Mountains. The "hunter's" role was essentially that of a safari guide. I was to meet the lodge's guests at the nearby Outspan Hotel (where they had lunch) and lead their convoy of minivans to the Treetops' parking lot. From there, I would escort them down a footpath through the forest to the staircase that led up to the lodge, which, as the name suggests, was built into the tops of the trees. The walk was meant to be exciting; a close brush with the "real" Africa. Forest animals are generally more wary and excitable—and, thus, more dangerous—than those found on the plains.

There were four cars in my convoy that day. I drove a Land Rover, and as we reached the edge of the forest, I signaled to the vehicles behind that everyone should be silent for a moment as I needed to listen for any sounds that might indicate danger ahead. I heard nothing, so after a suitable pause we pressed on and reached the parking lot. I had been given a very large gun to further impress my charges. I put this over my shoulder and told them to stay in their cars while I went ahead to see if the way was clear. To my utter consternation, only fifty yards down the trail I found a large herd of elephants blocking the path. No one had told me what to do if I actually came across potentially dangerous animals, and I couldn't think of anyway to get the elephants to move. I went back to my group looking rather pale and said, "I'm afraid we're going to have to take a bit of a break because there's danger ahead."

Everyone started laughing at me, saying, "Cut out the act, young man. We want to go inside and get our tea." I said, "No, no, I'm serious. There are a lot of elephants down there." I was beginning to feel a bit of a fool. "Well, go shoot one and clear the path," someone said.

I waited a little longer, then crept back, hoping that the elephants had moved along. They hadn't. In fact, there seemed to be more of them. I then made a serious mistake. I thought I could scare them and fired one volley into the air, bruising my shoulder considerably. And the next thing I knew, a very large elephant was bearing down on me, trumpeting madly. I ran as fast as I ever have in my life.

I'm sure the safari drivers thought it very funny as I dashed back to the parking lot, panting and ash white. One said dryly, "By the way, sir, in normal circumstances when this happens, we drive the cars right to the Treetops."

I blushed deeply at that but managed to reply, "That's a very good plan."

We then piled back into our vehicles and drove to the lodge. The tourists had heard my enormous boom and the trumpeting reply from the matriarch of the herd, so they realized I hadn't been joking—and my face, at least with them, was restored. But I was never again invited to be the "hunter" at Treetops.

That had been my closest encounter with elephants until this afternoon with Joyce. From my Treetops experience, I knew how agile and swift elephants could be—and how terrifying. I glanced over at this small woman beside me at the wheel of this small Toyota and hoped that she knew what she was doing.

One of the things I noticed immediately as we drove into that gray wall of flesh was that elephants are very large animals. We were about three feet off the ground in the Toyota, but that height put us at just about belly level with the adult elephants around us. Despite their bulk, they seemed to be constantly in motion: ears flapping, tails swishing at flies, trunks breaking off bunches of grass or exploring the ground or the back of another elephant. We were surrounded by munching, chewing noises, and the air smelled rich and earthy, like a barnyard. Glancing over at one elephant that shuffled past my window, I realized I could actually see the mud caked in her eyelashes from her midday mud bath. She didn't seem to take any notice of us, but instinctively, I brought my arms in close to my sides, as if by making myself feel small I might also make myself invisible. I sat very rigid and very still.

Joyce didn't seem to notice my discomfort. Of course, I was doing my best to hide how I felt, since I couldn't let on that I was actually frightened. She was busy telling me all about the elephants.

"That's Echo and Elijah," she said, pointing to two elephants, "and that big female is Estrella. She had twins once—a big surprise because we didn't know that elephants could have twins. And that's one of her other daughters, Elfrida."

All the elephants in the herd were related, Joyce explained. They were sisters and aunts, nieces and cousins. Joyce knew all about who was related to whom; what accidents and tragedies they'd had in their lives, their births and matings. She seemed to know, too, what the elephants were thinking.

"See Elfrida? How she's holding her ears down and back? She's deciding what she wants to do next. She wants to go closer to Estrella and, there now, she's moving toward her."

It was uncanny. Joyce could translate every ear and muscle twitch. Slowly it began to dawn on me that Cynthia and Joyce and their researchers had done an amazing thing: they knew elephants the way that primate watchers, such as Jane Goodall, knew chimpanzees. One of Jane's great accomplishments was showing us that chimpanzees are individuals with distinctive personalities of their own. She habituated chimps to people so that observers could sit with them and record their daily lives. Her investigations had changed almost everything scientists knew—or thought they knew—about chimpanzees and their social lives. Cynthia was doing the same for elephants I now realized. I was no longer seeing blocks of gray flesh but individual animals who were capable of thinking and had histories and family ties. Was I beginning to feel "sentimental"?

Suddenly, the Toyota began to shake and rock back and forth. My heart started pounding. I was certain one of the elephants was about to tip us over and gave Joyce a quick—and I hoped—urgent look. Surely she would start the motor and get us out of here. Instead, she was leaning out of the car and laughing.

"Look at that silly baby," she said. "That's little Eli and he's pushing us!"

I turned around, and, in fact, a very tiny elephant was nudging our car. He had what can only be described as a look of playful glee in his eyes. He pushed us awhile longer, than ran off, his trunk swinging giddily from side-to-side. Joyce and I laughed together. The antics of baby animals are always good fun to watch, but as Joyce said there are few babies as silly as baby elephants, perhaps because of their big ears and out-of-control trunks. My fear melted away. For the last few moments of our visit, I simply sat and absorbed the sights, sounds, and smells of elephants.

At Cynthia's research camp that night, I asked Joyce what she thought about having such camps in our national parks. I had already decided that the research being done here was so important that the camp should remain in the park. I was still thinking about the elephants. They had touched something inside me, although I wasn't sure what. For the first time, though, I realized that my job involved far more than merely ensuring that a certain number of elephants continued to exist in our parks. KWS was doing much more than that: we were protecting sentient creatures with babies and sisters and families. I fell asleep laughing at myself. In the space of one hour, I had become a "sentimental" convert.

CHAPTER 12

I woke before dawn the next day, just as a soft breeze rustled through the fronds of the green palms outside my tent. I had left one tent flap open, and the breeze brought with it the morning scents of Africa: a cool, earthy mix of herbs, dust, and smoke. It had been a good night. I had slept soundly, awakened occasionally by the whooping call of a hyena and once by the heavy cough of a lion. Now go-away birds, superb starlings, and fire finches piped their greetings to the sun's first rays. The time with the elephants and my night in the wild had done me a world of good. Our freewheeling dinner-table conversation had reenergized me, too. I had asked lots of questions about elephants and elephant management, and Joyce had readily debated the issues with me.

I was concerned about what we were going to do to control the elephant population now that the poaching was slowing down. Kenya's population was soaring; people needed land for their crops. Here at Amboseli, and around most of our parks, little farms and ranches were springing up. We had no ready means for keeping the elephants confined, and that meant that increasingly they would be trampling and eating peoples' crops—and killing people, too. How would we handle these problems? I tossed these issues to Joyce to see how she would respond. I knew how deeply she was attached to the elephants, but she was going to have to make some hard decisions. We floated various options: fencing, shooting rogue elephants, culling herds that had grown too large. Joyce wasn't eager to pursue any of these approaches, but she was willing to consider them and that impressed me. I knew we would work well together.

I was still mulling over our discussion when Joyce's camp cook appeared at my tent door and handed me a cup of tea. I wanted an early start so after sipping the tea, I grabbed my coat and headed outside. Joyce was up, too. I thanked her again for showing me the elephants and for the frank discussion.

"I enjoyed myself," I said, thinking how rarely I felt like this after a visit to one of the parks.

"Of course you're welcome to come anytime you want," she replied. "Sometimes the elephants come right through our camp."

I smiled at the thought. Only twenty-four hours before that kind of statement would have alarmed me. Now it seemed like the most natural thing for the elephants to do: stop by and visit their human friends.

"I don't know when I'll be back," I said. "It is hard for me to get away, but I'll see you for sure in June." That was when she would move to Nairobi to head KWS's elephant project. I looked forward to having her there.

My first real insight into elephants had been an amazing experience, but I also now recognized that these animals were going to pose a much bigger problem for KWS than I had previously thought. Managing animals is one thing. Managing animals that clearly have individuality and considerable intelligence is another for it introduces an ethical and moral dimension.

I drove back to the airfield and within an hour was on my way to the Masai Mara.

Like Amboseli, the Masai Mara lies along Kenya's southern border and is in effect the northern extension of Tanzania's vast Serengeti National Park. Together, the Serengeti and the Mara comprise some five thousand square miles of land, forming one of the world's largest wildlife refuges, though it is just barely large enough to accommodate the annual migration of wildebeests, zebras, Thomson's gazelles, and eland. In a journey that dates back to Pleistocene times, these animals follow the seasonal rains, moving from the Serengeti to the Mara when the rain falls in Tanzania and back to the Serengeti when the pattern reverses. It is a splendid sight to watch, and a prime reason that the Mara is one of Kenya's most popular parks. More than one hundred thousand tourists visit the Mara every year.

I enjoy the Mara, too. When I was in my late teens and running my safari company, I used to take our clients there regularly. It was still a hunting reserve then not a park. There were no lodges and no roads—merely a dirt track winding through the grassy plains and clumps of acacia trees. It was incredibly beautiful and unspoiled, as close as anything I've known to a pristine wilderness. I remember one morning, sitting with clients on a rise overlooking the Mara. Below us, the rolling plains stretched like a green canvas to the horizon. It was the height of the wildebeest migration and the antelopes were strung out along the savanna in long, loping lines. We could hear their cowlike *maaas* and the rhythmic tap of hooves against ground. All morning long, the wildebeests would move like this, traveling in herds that, from our hilltop vantage point, seemed to have no beginning or end. And every year for hundreds of thousands of years, the zebras, wildebeests, and other antelopes had migrated like this. It left me feeling humbled and proud: humbled because of the animals' endurance and proud because Kenyans had chosen to protect them.

I had not been back to the Mara since then, but the memory of that first trip was still strong. To say that the park had changed for the worse would be putting it mildly. I was shocked and depressed by all I saw. The land was crisscrossed with an ugly network of roads, most of them badly rutted, and there were far too many tented camps and lodges, all with unplanned—and polluted—settlements around them. There were far too many tourists in too many minivans, and they often harassed the animals. I myself saw twenty tour buses circled around one poor cheetah. How could it possibly go about its normal life under such conditions?

Such bad management practices had to change and the rules for watching game enforced. This would not be easy, as I've explained, because the reserve belonged to the Maasai and was administered by the local Narok County Council, which collected the park's entry fees as well as the income from the lodges and tented camps, and royalties from hot air–balloon safaris. Given the number of tourists that visited the park each year, the total income should have been a substantial sum.

Unfortunately, here as elsewhere, a hefty part of that sum vanished between the reserve and the bank. What money did end up in the council's hands was supposed to be used to maintain the reserve and to build schools and clinics for the local Maasai. The reserve, however, rarely saw any of this revenue nor did much of it go toward the community projects. The funds seemed to evaporate, ending up in the pockets of a few corrupt individuals. Everyone seemed to know this was the case, but no one seemed willing to do anything about it.

I hadn't come to accuse the wrongdoers. There was nothing I could do to stop them anyway. I simply intended to suggest that it would be in their best interests to change their ways. Donors, including the World Bank, had indicated a willingness to provide support for improving the reserve's infrastructure and management. I felt that KWS should help the county council restore some of the old luster to this wilderness jewel—and turn a bigger profit. That, in turn, would help everyone: the Maasai communities living near the reserve, the county council members, and most important, the people of Kenya.

I met a number of key officials from the Narok County Council at Keekorok Lodge, a comfortable, rambling, whitewashed hotel with a thatched roof. Over lunch I spoke casually and in general terms about our plans for improving the parks and reserves throughout Kenya. I've described the Maasai as a proud, independent-minded people, and I noted that they responded warily to my friendly overtures. Although they lived in one of the more remote corners of Kenya, the officials were very aware of current events and had kept abreast of the latest political news from Nairobi. Gracefully swinging their beaded fly whisks, several asked me about the new KWS organization. They were particularly keen to know if it was true that I was both chairman of the KWS board and also the chief executive officer—a question aimed at determining how much political clout I carried.

"Yes," I replied, pausing to let my single-syllable answer sink in. It suggested that I carried a very large stick indeed.

I have no proof that any of the Maasai leaders I met that day were involved in the revenue-pilfering schemes that were clearly going on. But if they were, they may have feared that I was going to close them down. All they knew for certain was that I intended to change the way they ran the Mara, and they weren't happy about that. I'm sure they later complained to their parliamentary representative, William Ntimama, who would later become one of my most severe critics.

I wanted to work with the Maasai, however, not fight them. To persuade them that my intentions were honest and that they would benefit from working with KWS, I explained that the World Bank was planning to spend about $5 million to complete water-supply housing and projects for the reserve's staff and to repair one of the key roads.

They nodded their approval at these expenditures, then listened more gravely as I explained that in exchange they were to do their part. I expected the council to spend funds on repairing the reserve's other roads, to enforce its rules so that tourists no longer drove anywhere they chose, and to reevaluate their plans to build additional lodges. If they did not begin making such changes, I warned, the Mara would start losing visitors, especially to the Serengeti, which was mounting an aggressive tourist campaign.

"It is like when you have a gourd full of milk," I said, using an analogy close to their lives, since the Maasai's traditional diet is curdled milk mixed with cows' blood. "A gourd of milk is a fine thing to have. It means you will eat well, that your future is secure. But if you don't keep the gourd in good repair, you'll lose that future. Your milk will spill onto the ground. And that's what's going to happen with your tourists. You'll lose them to the Serengeti."

The Maasai are clever businessmen, and I could see that my words were hitting home. Some, however, argued that it was up to me—and KWS—to patch the gourd.

"You should fix everything," one elder said.

I shook my head. "First you have to demonstrate that you're serious about managing the reserve. I want to see some signs—a formal plan—that you're going to maintain the Mara and deal responsibly with the needs of tourism and conservation. Bring that to me at KWS, and then we'll work together."

If they didn't, I added, pressing my point, not only would they not receive any additional World Bank funds, they might have to turn over control of the park to KWS. This was a not-so-veiled threat, and it caused an instant rumble of protests.

"The land is yours to protect now," I explained. "But if you fail, if you don't do your part and manage the land for the good of Kenya, you will lose it. It's not what we want to see happen. We don't need another park to manage. But you have a national asset—the Mara Reserve and wildlife—entrusted to you, and you must do your part to see that it contributes to our nation's development."

I could feel the elders' eyes on me, taking my measure again. Could I wrest the park from the county council's control, as I was hinting? I wanted them to think so, even though I wasn't absolutely certain myself. A little fear can be a big motivator, and I thought that the Maasai might tackle their problems at the Mara more aggressively if they thought I was serious about taking it over.

I tried to end the meeting on a positive note, emphasizing that the reserve—and its future—was in their hands. All they had to do was manage it better. KWS would see to it that more World Bank money was available for roads, bridges, and new vehicles. Despite my upbeat words, however, few in the audience were smiling. Getting the Maasai here on my side wasn't going to be easy. I made a mental note to bring up the Mara again with the government.

❖ ❖ ❖

The problems we faced at the Mara were similar to those we faced in every park, as well as in Kenya's government generally—too much corruption and too many people not held accountable for their actions. This was equally true for many other African nations. There were times when I used to wonder whether any African government was ready to face these problems and govern responsibly. The formation of KWS gave me hope that some leaders did, in fact, want their countries to work. Even more exciting—and initially unbelievable—were the changes afoot in South Africa.

From the time of my childhood, when I first learned of the racial laws in South Africa, I had despised the leaders of that country. Yet in the early months of 1990, Nelson Mandela was released from his prison cell on Robben Island, where he'd been held for forty years. I am seldom given to tears, but I wept when I learned about his freedom. The news simply overwhelmed me. Because of South Africa's apartheid and the racist colonial era in my own country, I had always in some ways felt ashamed of being a white African. Mandela's release lifted some of that shame. An African country had chosen to do the right thing. As I watched Mandela on television, walking proudly through his country after being set free, I had no doubt that he would soon become South Africa's new president. His dignity and bearing sent a powerful message to all the corrupt leaders across the African continent. Here was a man who had given up most of his life to bring change to his country; here was an example and challenge for us all.

Things were beginning to change in Kenya, too. The Cold War between America and the Soviet Union had ended, and America was now pushing the countries it had supported to fully embrace democracy. In late 1989, the U.S. State Department issued a directive to America's African ambassadors, encouraging their host governments to initiate political reforms. Smith Hempstone, a hard-talking, heavy-smoking former journalist, was then the American ambassador to Kenya. He and I had met on several occasions; and while I cannot say that I liked him, I did admire his strong support for Kenya's fledgling prodemocracy movement.

Not long after my return from the Mara, Ambassador Hempstone gave a speech at one of the Nairobi Rotarian Clubs in which he urged President Moi to repeal Kenya's repressive laws and to end the one-party political system. President Moi immediately denounced Smith, telling the press that the ambassador should not get involved in Kenya's internal affairs.

Changes, though, were coming to Kenya. Kenyans were increasingly restless for a better form of government, one that governed with their needs in mind. Some individuals were already forming political parties, even though it was still illegal to do so. I watched these developments, feeling restless myself. I agreed that Kenya a needed a two-party or multiparty form of democracy. The one-party state was hopelessly out of date and would only lead to greater dissension in the future. President Moi responded by saying that permitting two or more parties in Kenya would inevitably lead to tribal clashes. The two largest tribes, the Kikuyu and Luo, would instantly be at each other's throats in the ensuing melee, and everyone else would be forgotten. I understood the president's concerns but also thought there had to be some way to have a more open political system. For one thing that was the only way to end the rampant corruption. *Why does President Moi allow such crooks to continue about their work?* I wrote in my diary in early May. *How can I join the political debate?* I also wondered. I wanted to be in the thick of it, arguing about Kenya's future; but to do so I would have to resign from KWS, and I was far from ready to do that.

For the time being, I would leave Kenya's broad political changes to others and do what I could for this one government service.

And we were making progress. The formation of KWS had brought even more attention to and interest in Kenya's parks and wildlife from overseas donors and aid agencies, and I spent much of May 1990 on the road, often meeting with key people who could help me raise support for Kenya's wildlife. In Washington, I met with U.S. secretary of state James Baker, an avid wildlife lover who was eager to see Kenya's efforts to protect its parks succeed. Early in my tenure, Baker had arranged for a $1.5 million donation to be made to our parks' security forces, and he was a strong backer of my plans for KWS. In addition, KWS received a donation of five hundred automatic weapons from a European armaments manufacturer, a gift that was vital to ensuring our parks' security. I was also able to persuade a private donor in the States to provide nearly a half-million dollars for KWS to purchase night-surveillance equipment, particularly night-vision binoculars and gun sights. With the latter, our KWS forces could pursue poachers after dark, which was when the gangs usually gave our rangers the slip.

Everything seemed to be moving forward, and I was pushing hard. I arrived home from the United States on May 19 at four in the morning. Four hours later I was on my way with a team of conservation consultants from the World Bank to Amboseli, Tsavo, and Meru National Parks, to begin hammering out community conservation projects. I never thought about being tired. Racing from the airport to home and on to the next meeting only energized me. Rarely is anyone given an opportunity, as I was, to create and build a new government service, and I gave it my all.

Which is why I was completely unprepared when six days later I received an urgent telephone call. The government was unhappy about the *Code of Discipline* that KWS had recently published in the official government gazette. I was to publish a retraction immediately and await further instructions. This reflected a high-level concern that the KWS armed wing might be a threat to the government.

I was momentarily dumbstruck. The *Code* had been drafted long before my appointment. The commissioner of police had urged me to finalize it once we acquired automatic weapons, and I had done so with a lawyer and with full consultation with the government. The draft had been circulated among all the members of the National Security Committee, and only after getting their approval had I published it in the gazette, thereby making the *Code* legal.

Someone, obviously, was stirring up trouble—using this issue of our increasingly effective antipoaching units to worry the president. I could hardly believe that anyone was seriously concerned about KWS or thought that I might have any sinister plans to undermine the government.

The problem was that I had been ordered to retract the *Code*. Without it, controlling the armed units would be a more difficult matter, and there could indeed be danger. For the first time I began to realize that I was up against things that I did not fully understand because reason alone was inadequate to understanding them. Resigning from the directorship suddenly became a serious option.

CHAPTER **13**

Like most heads of state, the president of Kenya uses an advisorial system that is both complex and influences every major decision. A variety of individuals—some officials, others simply old friends or contacts—use an intricate variety of ways of bringing pressure to bear when they feel that it is necessary. To push through policy changes in a government program, you need allies among these people. The process differs from one situation to another, but having champions is a prerequisite of government.

My appointment to head Wildlife had followed a characteristically Kenyan process: I did not apply for the position but got it because someone, probably outside government, had managed to influence someone close to the president, and the appointment was made. The details of my own experience and suitability had not been "weighed," or if they had, it was done on an informal basis and based on the press reports about me.

In some respects this approach to hiring people for senior government jobs is practiced everywhere but is probably more common in those countries that have strong centralized authority and few checks and balances. While Kenya has a parliament and politicians serve in the cabinet, there exists another unofficial "cabinet" that is informal, unaccountable, and operates in the shadows and corridors. This so-called kitchen cabinet was where the real power lay, and I knew that a good number of the men in this group disliked me. I was not in their view a "team player." I refused to bend the KWS procurement procedures, and I was not even willing to discuss the idea of a commission or percentage on major contracts. I openly refused to give people jobs because they were someone's relative or friend, and I protected my staff when they refused to yield to the same pressure. On one occasion a very senior government official had asked me, "Why are you so ungrateful?" "Why should I be grateful?" I replied. "Having a highly stressed, personally dangerous existence with bodyguards around me all the time is hardly something to feel gratitude about." "No, no," said the official, "you misunderstand. You have been put in a very special position from which you can make a great deal of money for yourself and for us, your friends."

My stubbornness clearly annoyed a good number of people. Someone, or several perhaps, had decided that they would use the kitchen cabinet to damage my standing with the president. Whispered allegations, innuendo, and cynical remarks began to spread, and already these were proving to be a potent poison. My challenge was to fight back against the president's unstated suspicion and the breakdown of trust between us.

The whole argument about the *Code of Discipline* and control over the KWS's armed wing was being manipulated behind the scenes. I was powerless, and being outside the influential circle, my only course of action was to be patient. There was nobody I could really talk to. I felt like resigning and yet I knew that this would not be a solution to anything. My total preoccupation with wildlife matters had made it difficult to explain my innermost doubts even to Meave, and she was the one person I knew I could really trust. This whole period of deep frustration and self-doubt would all too often be punctuated by other depressing incidents.

One weekend, I had gone home in the hopes of finally pulling myself together and talking through my options with Meave. During lunch on Saturday, the phone rang. A senior warden from Tsavo was on the line reporting more bad news: one of our patrols in the northeast near the Tana River had been ambushed; and the sergeant in charge, a likable and very promising young man, was dead. My spirits sank with every word the warden uttered. This was the part of me no one saw in public: depressed and dispirited, unable even to think about how we were ever going to create a service that did more than simply deal with events on a crisis-by-crisis basis.

The officer completed his report. Somehow I mustered the energy to put some spark into my voice, although I felt none in my heart. Almost by rote, I said, "I'll be there at Garsen in the morning, and we'll get the gang that did this."

The sergeant's death kept me from sleeping. I tossed and turned and finally rose at 4:00 A.M., dressed, and was on the road a half hour later to Wilson Airport. I wanted to get in the air so that I could think.

I've mentioned that my early years were marked by a fear of small aircraft. My parents had little occasion to fly, and my father was convinced that small planes were quite unreliable and dangerous. In contrast, my mother, who had been one of the first women to fly a glider in England, was very encouraging when, in my late teens, I announced my intention to get a private pilot's license. I was convinced even then that a small plane would provide by far the best way to travel within East Africa. I know several Alaskans who feel the same way about traveling in their state. I can't say that I've ever enjoyed any aspect of flying and have always been aware of the dangers. I have never been a foolhardy or excessively daring pilot. But in 1968, when I was twenty-three, I crashed my plane close to my parents' camp at Olduvai Gorge in Tanzania and nearly killed several good friends.

Remembering that incident still makes me lose sleep. I was trying to land against the early morning sun. It was so bright that I could not see the small markers lining the grass landing strip. After aborting three landings, I began to feel that my pride was at stake. On the fourth attempt I willfully and foolishly put the plane down. I managed to hit the runway, but too close to the edge, causing the plane's wheels to hit rocks. The plane lost two wheels, the tailwing, and half of one wing. Fortunately I remained calm enough to switch off the engine, and there was no fire—everyone climbed out unharmed. The accident left me very shaken, and I did not fly again for two years.

I only resumed flying after I started leading fossil-hunting expeditions to Lake Turkana. We needed to travel long distances speedily and efficiently. Flying remained far and away the best method. Since I was then also managing the National Museums, I often had to stay behind in Nairobi to attend to administrative chores while my team of fossil hunters searched the hills. I flew up to join them—and to ferry in needed supplies—whenever an important discovery was made.

After my accident, however, flying became even more of a perfunctory task; indeed, I loathed being airborne. Nevertheless, it afforded me a chance to get away for a few hours from the phones and people.

I also enjoyed seeing Kenya from the air. The vast, wide-open landscape that unfolded beneath the plane and the earthenware colors of the land—burnt orange, dusky brown, and gray-green—never failed to stir something in me. I could catch my breath up here in the thin blue air and think.

On this particular trip to Garsen, a rough-and-rumble trading town on the right bank of the Tana River, I found myself reflecting about my first year in office. Actually, thirteen months had gone by since my appointment, and without question they had been some of the most tumultuous of my life. I had accomplished a great deal, but so much more remained to be done. Had I set myself goals that would be impossible to attain? I had wondered about this more than once; but now, after this quarrel with the government, I thought I would have to answer in the affirmative. And there were parts of the job I thoroughly disliked. Nothing was worse than this: having to investigate the death of a promising young man. I also did not like the exalted position in which many people now seemed to hold me. I saw an odd mixture of respect, fear, and admiration on the faces of some members of my staff and people in other government offices. The looks troubled me because it seemed that these people didn't actually see me but rather an image or caricature of what they wanted to see. I particularly did not like the almost obsequious, admiring glances some people gave me. I saw this on the faces of everyday people in Kenya and in audiences overseas, a sort of starstruck look. They wanted me to be heroic, like a superhuman, and, truthfully, I felt anything but that. It was an image I neither liked nor deserved. And if anything was proof of that, it was this young ranger's body lying in the bush.

I landed at Garsen a few hours later. The warden met me at the airport and brought me up to date. A patrol had pursued the gang and surprised them early that morning.

"We shot four of them, sir," he said.

"Wounded?" I asked.

"No, dead, sir."

I nodded. I can't say that I was sorry for their deaths, but I always hoped that we might bring in some of these poachers for questioning. Occasionally we did. More often, however, they refused to surrender. And in a case such as this, our men were eager for revenge.

I never liked any of this killing, although I was pleased that our men had stayed on this gang's trail and done what needed to be done. Each time we won—for lack of a better word—one of these battles, our stock went up in the bandits' eyes. They were now far more wary than they had ever been of running into KWS rangers and had stopped sending us taunting messages. We had become a force to be reckoned with.

A map of Kenya will reveal that Garsen is not close to any of our major national parks. A national reserve for Colobus monkeys, and another for the rare Hunter's antelope, lie some distance north of the town along the Tana River. The KWS patrol had not met up with the poaching gangs near either of these reserves but rather west of Garsen in the semiarid scrub brush that covers most of southeastern Kenya. This is some of the most remote terrain in the country. There are no paved roads and only an occasional two-wheel dirt track. The country is low—just a few hundred feet above sea level—flat and arid. Viewed from the air, there seems to be only mile after mile of empty bushland, dotted with whistling acacia trees and cut by dry, eroded gullies. Much of the land outside the park's boundaries is divided into huge cattle ranches that belong to groups of Wa-Pokomo and Oromo people. The poaching gangs often used the ranch lands as staging areas for their forays into the park. Not every gang traveled south from Somalia—some came out of the local villages near the park—but, in general, the poachers followed routes that led them from the northern edge of Kenya, near the Somali border, across the Tana River and into the empty area between it and Tsavo East, and then into the park itself.

The warden drove us close to the scene of the last battle and parked. We walked for twenty minutes through the bush to a hot, sandy gully with only a few small acacia trees for shade. Peter Leitoro, a slim, handsome young officer in the patrol, saluted smartly as I climbed out of the Land Rover. He was from the Rendille tribe, a nomadic people who live with their camels and goats in country very similar to where we were now. Leitoro had risen quickly through the ranks and now patrolled with one of our crack units, working out of a remote outpost on Tsavo's northeastern border. None of this bothered him, he told me later.

"You could say I trained for this as a youth when growing up," he told me. "I was used to staying in the bush without food and walking long distances without water. That's what we did as children. We went out with our animals to look for pasture in the morning, and we brought them back in the evening. Sometimes you have a drink in the morning, but you don't have another one until you return home at night."

Leitoro explained that a few days earlier his unit had been patrolling the northern border of Tsavo East when they spotted a thin trail of smoke from a campfire. The rangers knew this part of the park as well as their homeland pastures. One glance told them that the campfire was within the park's boundaries, and they set off immediately to investigate. They also called in air support, which the warden provided, flying overhead to spot the gang on the ground.

By now the poachers knew our methods. Small planes meant that rangers were on the way. They abandoned their camp and took off for the bush beyond the park. At their encampment, the rangers found the remains of a giraffe the bandits had poached and partially roasted.

"We think they'd come to recover some tusks," Leitoro told me. "We had also found three elephant carcasses a few weeks before, and we think this was all done by the same gang."

Leitoro thought that they had never gotten to those tusks, that the rangers dispersed them before they had had a chance to dig them up. Our patrol followed them for two days then lost their trail one evening. That was when the ambush occurred, and the patrol officer was killed.

"That made us only more determined," Leitoro said. "We were angry, very hot to get these bandits."

Early in the morning they surprised the gang, a team of eight, hunkered down in this gully.

"We crawled in on our bellies. I saw one sentry and shouted a warning. He turned and fired but missed. Then one of our rangers shot him."

There was a brief firefight. None of our men were wounded, but when the shooting stopped, four bandits lay dead. Their bodies were pulled off to one side of the gully and placed in the shade of some acacia trees—far enough away that the sickening smell of death didn't hang so heavily in the air.

"Well done," I said to Leitoro. "What are the chances of getting the others?"

Leitoro thought they might find them, but they would have to cross the Tana River.

"Then do so," I said. "We must never let them rest, never let them think that we feel we've done enough. Soon they'll know better than to come into our parks—or into Kenya."

In fact, the poachers were already learning this lesson. This gang, for instance, was working only in the most remote part of Tsavo East. Previously, such bandits treated this park and Tsavo West almost as their private elephant-hunting grounds.

Over the past several months we had used increasingly aggressive methods against the poaching gangs, particularly against the one that had killed sixteen policemen in that ambush between Meru and Tsavo East. That gang was heavily armed with grenade launchers and 16-mm-machine guns. We hit back hard, shooting a couple of their members and one of their leaders, but that didn't stop them. A few weeks later, they were back in the park, killing elephants.

At that point I asked the Kenyan army for some assistance. The next time one of our patrols made contact with the gang, the army flew in a helicopter—with a machine gunner stationed at the open door. Before sunset the pilot dropped down over the poachers' hideout, rotors whipping the air, while the machine gunner strafed the ground with rapid fire and heavy-gauge tracers. The poachers had scattered into the heavy bush at the first sound of the helicopter. I doubt if we killed anyone, but the tracers made an impressive amount of noise and blasted apart a number of rocks. Observers told me that the tracers lit up the landscape, making it appear as if the entire countryside was on fire. I don't know how much of our show the poachers stayed around to watch, but certainly they heard it, which was all that I wanted.

After that, the army stationed one of its helicopter-training units at Voi, a town just outside of Tsavo East. For the next four months, the trainee pilots flew their helicopters back and forth across the park almost daily. They weren't armed, but it was another big display of power.

That was really the end of poaching—and of attacks on tourists—in the central part of the two Tsavos. The bandits were particularly wary of us after the first helicopter attack. Some of our sources later told us that word had quickly spread among the poaching gangs that it wasn't safe to venture very far into the parks; that if they were found inside the boundaries, KWS would call up its helicopters and blast them out.

I took this latest encounter as a sign that the memory of the helicopters was still very strong in the poachers' minds and that we were close to securing Tsavo's borders.

I shared a cup of tea with our men, gave them a pep talk, and then drove back to Garsen with the warden. It was a hot, dusty trip, bouncing through thick bush and scrubby acacias, but I enjoyed it. Seeing KWS's rangers out here doing their jobs and fighting this battle always gave me a lift. It would be very hard, if not impossible, to resign, after seeing the pride and determination on their faces. Somehow I would find a way to settle my differences over the *Code of Discipline* with the government. And I would see to it that our dead patrol officer's family was amply rewarded for his service to Kenya.

More than a month passed before the issue of the *Code of Discipline* was finally settled. I never discussed it with President Moi. I made several appointments with him, but these were either broken for various reasons or I was kept waiting then told to come back another day. This only added to my worries that someone or some group was coming between the president's office and me. But I also knew that the president had larger matters to attend to. The American ambassador, Hempstone Smith, had not backed down from his demands that Kenya become more democratic. He wanted to see the government repeal the old law that had turned Kenya into a one-party state. Although the daily newspapers carried editorials criticizing Smith's requests, his position was gaining in influence among local groups that also wanted to see the government reformed. In June 1990, the Episcopalian Church leaders, the most powerful religious leaders in the country, announced that they, too, wanted Kenya to become a multiparty state. Some were even calling for demonstrations. President Moi clearly had his hands full. My worries at KWS must have seemed insignificant in comparison.

I continued to lead KWS as I thought best, and no one from the government interfered. Then, in mid-June, the attorney general telephoned to say that the cabinet had directed that the *Code* be revoked. It was to be degazetted. The attorney general wanted me to sign the papers immediately, and an hour later he was in my office.

"Richard, the *Code of Discipline* must be degazetted," he said. "We believe the proper steps weren't followed to establish the *Code* and consequently it does not comply with Kenya's law."

The attorney general spoke softly but gravely. President Moi wanted me to remain as director, he assured me, but the *Code* needed to be rethought.

I argued again that without a *Code*, KWS had no legal means for disciplining and controlling its armed rangers.

The attorney general nodded. "Yes, KWS needs a *Code of Discipline*. But not this one. After this one has been degazetted, then we can discuss it again. Now you must sign this paper."

He opened his briefcase and pulled out the document. I read it quickly. It was a notice of the revocation; by signing it, I would acknowledge that KWS's *Code* was repealed.

The attorney general watched me closely. I sat silently for a few minutes then picked up my pen. Part of me was thinking, *You're a fool, Leakey. You give in on this, they'll be back asking you to give in on other things.* But another part was more optimistic. The attorney general—and presumably the government overall—knew that KWS's rangers could not function without a *Code*. If they didn't already realize this, someone in the military would surely explain how dangerous it was. Maybe this was just a small stumbling block, not a large one; and if I signed the papers, we could work on a *Code* that was acceptable.

I seldom hesitate when making a decision. I've always thought it best to make decisions quickly, then get on with whatever needs to be done. I signed.

The attorney general sat back as I did so and gave me a smile. "Thank you, Richard."

I passed the papers to him, we shook hands, and he left.

Then I called in Bashir.

"We have no *Code* now," I told him.

Bashir's eyes widened. "But, sir, this can be extremely dangerous."

"I know," I replied. "But I think it's only temporary. We'll see. Let's not make an issue of it with the men. I simply wanted you to know."

The rangers admired Bashir and were devoted to him. They were also terrified of him and of his disapproving scowl. For the time being, *he* would be the *Code of Discipline*.

Had I lost an important battle? Or had I simply been maneuvered into thinking it important? I decided not to worry about it. The attorney general had acknowledged the need for a *Code*, and presumably, the government agreed with this. In the end that was all that counted, and in time I expected we would have a *Code* again.

But an inner voice also told me to be careful.

CHAPTER 14

I knew from the moment I accepted President Moi's appointment that I would have to move swiftly to succeed. From day one I'd pushed hard and worked as fast as I could. At some point, I expected to lose the privileges accorded me by having been specially appointed by the president. I just had not anticipated losing them only eighteen months into my tenure. I worried about what this meant for KWS.

There were now fifteen hundred armed men in our service, and the repeal of the legal standing of the *Code of Discipline* was a matter of deep concern to me. The KWS armed units acted on my authority. According to the legislation that established KWS, the director had the ultimate responsibility for the conduct of KWS officers and men. I had signed the repeal of the *Code* but was not convinced that everyone fully understood the implications of this action. Consequently, I continued to make every effort to see President Moi. Eventually I was granted an appointment. I could see that he wasn't particularly happy to see me and came right to the point.

"Look, KWS cannot operate this way," I said. "You may think it's dangerous for the country if I have a *Code of Discipline* for KWS, but I can assure you it's far more dangerous for the country if we don't. Can't this be reviewed?"

President Moi looked at me glumly. "Perhaps that would help," he replied. "I'll have the attorney general look at it again."

I thanked him for that, shook his hand, and left. Before all this happened, we might have shared a laugh or two. Now I could almost smell his wariness.

Without the *Code*, I knew it would only be a short while before the police once again began to insist that they be given full responsibility for handling serious crimes in the national parks. That would spell the end of KWS's wildlife-protection units and I had no doubt would launch another round of poaching and banditry. I couldn't allow that to happen. I had to find a way to turn this situation around—and I had an idea for doing just that.

One of Bashir's key duties at KWS was to build up an intelligence network. I had arranged for some specialist training for a few carefully selected officers; and by early 1990, the system was working quite effectively. We had special-intelligence officers stationed in the hottest areas— Meru, Tsavo, and Mount Elgon on the Uganda border. They were given money to pay informants and to merge into the local communities. Some opened little tea shops or newspaper kiosks where they could eavesdrop on conversations. Others disguised themselves as poachers and actually shot the odd old buffalo or gazelle to make it look like they, too, were in the poaching business. In this way we gathered a good deal of information about the people in the gangs as well as their contacts in the villages and in Nairobi.

I was still hoping to land a "big fish"—some wealthy individual who might be implicated while trying to buy illegal ivory. While angling for that kind of trophy, we caught a few smaller fry. We heard of smugglers who were trucking ivory from Kenya across the Ethiopian and Ugandan borders (that was the key reason for putting one intelligence unit at Mount Elgon) and of others who were moving it into Tanzania. Other informants led our men to sacks stuffed with ivory chopped into the little blocks that the Japanese used for making their signature *hankos*, while larger chunks were found abandoned in a pile along a road in the Rift Valley. A phone call tipped us off to the existence of a trading ring of five Koreans and one Ethiopian who had a factory for carving up tusks in the town of Kiambu, north of Nairobi.

From our informants and the people we arrested, we got more names. Soon we were able to build a database of poachers, middlemen, truckers, and ivory traders. A secret map in our "Operations Center" showed every contact, every ivory bust, every move that our men encountered in the underground world of the illegal ivory trade. We had spies watching the people named on our list, and it wasn't long before some of them could no longer take the heat.

In May 1990, one of our best agents, a Somali who went by the code name "Mamba," and who looked as sleek and dangerous as that snake, told us he had two informants who wanted to turn themselves in. They were in Somalia, but he felt confident that they would come back and in exchange for amnesty lead us to a large cache of ivory stashed near Tsavo East. I immediately agreed, but asked Mamba to wait awhile before they led us to the ivory. I wanted to make sure that our men—and not the police—got full credit for this bust. This seemed an excellent way to restore our credibility with President Moi and the government.

Toward the end of June, Mamba contacted the poachers and brought them to Tsavo. Then, early in the morning of June 27, according to plan, Stephen Gichangi, the warden of Tsavo East, telephoned to report that one of the wildlife-protection units had just uncovered a big stash of ivory. The day before, knowing that his call would come in, I had scheduled a meeting at Amboseli, at which, supposedly, Joyce Poole and I were going to show the elephants to a *National Geographic* film crew. We were thus all at Wilson Airport when Stephen's call came. I immediately changed our plans, and told everyone we were heading toward Tsavo East instead. The film crew wasn't the least bit disappointed. They would be shooting scenes of our rangers unearthing tusks—excellent footage for the film they were planning on the plight of the elephant. With everyone on board the KWS twin-engine plane, and the film crew's gear safely stowed, our chief pilot, Phil Matthews, took off for a landing strip just beyond the northern border of the park.

Theoretically, the police should have been called in. They were supposed to be involved whenever we found poached ivory, particularly when it wasn't on park property. Of course, whenever we followed the rules, the police got all the credit and KWS got none. This time was going to be different.

This cache was located some miles east of Tsavo's boundary on a large private ranch called Wanainchi. Mamba was waiting for us at the ranch's landing strip, and he escorted us to two Land Rovers while our rangers stood rigidly at attention. The photographers were busy filming every scene, and I smiled inwardly at how fine our men looked.

For about half an hour, we bumped along a dirt track through the thick bush. Mamba parked in the shade of a small tree and led us down a faint trail for another fifteen minutes to a large cluster of acacias. Several other rangers and the two poachers were waiting there, squatting on their haunches. Like most poachers we encountered, these fellows were tall and thin, dressed in traditional cotton skirts and leather sandals. I was surprised, though, at their youth. Their faces were smooth, not a whisker in sight; they couldn't have been more than teenagers. One of our rangers nudged them to a standing position, then ordered them to point to the spot where the tusks were buried. Then our men began to dig in the rust-colored sandy earth.

It didn't take them long to hit the first of the tusks. The poachers had buried them as close to the surface as possible, since they wanted to get the ivory out quickly when they returned. Still, digging up long, heavy tusks—some weighing thirty pounds—was not an easy task, and as the sun climbed higher in the sky, our rangers began to sweat heavily.

It was a grim sight: four men shoveling at the red earth, shouting when they hit a tusk, then others joining in to help pull it from its burial pit. The ivory was dirty, stained the same rusty shade as the earth, and I thought immediately of that saying, "bloody ivory." At least this time, no rangers had died while bringing in these poachers. I glanced briefly at them. They had returned to their squatting position and were idly cleaning their teeth with twigs, while two armed rangers stood on either side of them. I wondered how long it had taken them and their partners to kill these elephants, to transport the tusks to this forsaken spot, and then to bury them. It must have been a tough job—and one that had no payoff.

There were actually several ivory caches in the area. The two poachers patiently led our men to one spot after another: near this tree, close to that bush, by that stone over there. Altogether we recovered 150 tusks—the remnants of seventy-five elephants. It seemed they'd killed most of a herd, since there were tusks from adolescents, small females, and hefty matriarchs. Stacked in a pile, we estimated we had about a ton of ivory. The red-earth stains on the ivory indicated it had been buried for some time.

Joyce turned to one of the poachers and asked him in Swahili when they had killed the elephants. "In 1988," he answered, his eyes downcast. "We can't sell the ivory now," he added. "No one wants it anymore. No one will pay us for it."

I looked at the pile of tusks and shook my head. Because of my visit with Joyce to the Amboseli elephants, I could barely stand the sight. The tusks looked as inert as a pile of cordwood, yet represented what had once been a fine herd of elephants, a tightly knit society of mothers and offspring, of sisters and aunts. It was all too easy to picture the terror and horror on their faces and imagine their frightened cries as these boys and their gang blasted at them with their machine guns, then hacked open their faces with machetes to get their ivory.

The film crew, on the other hand, was delighted with this "surprise" discovery. One photographer also shot some still pictures and promised that these would be given to the Kenyan press. Our rangers began to carry the ivory back to the Land Rovers, and I lifted a tusk over my shoulder, too. It would take us several trips to transport it just this short distance; eventually the ivory would be securely stored in Nairobi.

"It's a grim business," I told the film crew. "But our rangers have done their job and done it well. That's how it's going to be from now on: no more dead elephants, only poachers turning themselves into KWS. They have no other choice."

The next day, our ivory bust was big news. RANGERS FIND HUGE IVORY CACHE; STOLEN IVORY RECOVERED FROM POACHERS trumpeted the papers' page-one headlines. The reporters wrote glowing accounts about the work KWS rangers were doing. We had the poaching nearly under control, they said, and had brought an end to the ivory trade.

That was a trifle optimistic. What counted though was the way the KWS rangers looked: proud and competent. This time there was no mention of the police. It was KWS's time to shine, and I could only hope that the government was watching.

Nothing more was said to me about the *Code of Discipline.* President Moi did ask the attorney general to review the issue, as he had promised. By early September 1990, the attorney general had yet to issue his opinion.

I didn't see the president, who continued to be under very intense pressure from a number of Western countries, led by the United States and their ambassador, Smith Hempstone, over the issue of changing Kenya to a multiparty state. Several dissidents in the country had picked up Hempstone's challenge, and throughout the summer there were demonstrations and near-riots in Nairobi. I didn't see how the government could forever stonewall what looked more and more like a grassroots uprising, but I stayed out of the debates. Only at home did Meave and I mull over what Kenya's future might hold—particularly for our daughters. And increasingly I hoped that the calls for a multiparty state would succeed. It was the best way to assure a responsible government and a healthy, growing economy, which Kenya sorely needed.

The riots, of course, didn't do Kenya's economy any good since they frightened off tourists. I was still traveling abroad regularly to raise funds for KWS and had found that I also needed to be something of an "ambassador-at-large" for Kenya as a whole. It wasn't at all dangerous for tourists to visit Kenya, I reassured my audiences. The attacks weren't aimed at our visitors; these were internal problems and, at any rate, Nairobi was still a safer city in terms of violent crime than either New York or Miami. Perhaps my words stopped some people from changing their safari plans; they may have even persuaded others to visit Kenya.

I hope so, since tourists were vital not only to Kenya's economy but to my plans for KWS. Were KWS to become the self-sufficient, revenue-generating organization that I envisioned, and that my staff was working so hard to achieve, we needed a steady stream of visitors. So whenever possible I talked up Kenya as a wildlife and holiday destination.

All this glad-handing was beginning to wear me down. Neither President Moi nor anyone else in the government seemed to notice my extra efforts—not that I expected to be patted on the head every time I did something for my country. However, given the government's suspicion over the *Code of Discipline,* I was, by early September, feeling more prickly than usual about all I had done for Kenya. The National Museums was also organizing a big sixtieth anniversary celebration, and to my puzzlement and disappointment those in charge appeared to have ignored my family and me altogether. I know this may sound like whining, but it struck me as very odd that the Leakeys weren't mentioned at all on the Museum's schedule of events for this grand fête. A Leakey had been at the Museum's helm for more than half of its sixty years. My father had been the second director of the Coryndon Museum, from 1945 to 1961, and had gone against convention and laws to open it to black Kenyans. My mother had also worked at the Museum, adding to its archaeological treasures. I had served as its director for twenty-one years, raised money for many of its buildings and laboratories, and established smaller museums across the country. And Meave continued to work there, directing the Department of Palaeontology. As a family, we'd added immeasurably to the Museum's collections and trained its technical staff. None of this was now to be mentioned at the big public ceremony at the end of September, and I decided against attending.

President Moi, however, did attend, as host of the festivities; and to my pleasure and surprise he didn't overlook my family. In fact, he praised the Leakeys so strongly that when others recalled his speech to me I was half-embarrassed—and somewhat glad, for that reason alone, that I had not been present. He recounted my career at the Museum, as well as my year directing KWS, and even mentioned my rangers' recent success in recovering the buried ivory. Then Moi looked out over the audience and intoned, "What Kenya needs most is three Richard Leakeys."

I blushed when I heard that story. But I would be dishonest if I didn't admit that I liked hearing the president's praise. It meant that he continued to support me, and that my plans for KWS could still go forward—or so I hoped.

By now I knew that I would never have a smooth ride at the helm of KWS. There were too many political interests at stake. Someone would always be jockeying to push me—and other well-intentioned civil servants—out of the way. Still, President Moi's supportive words did work in my favor. A few weeks later, the attorney general announced that he had completed his review and that the "new" *Code of Discipline* could be placed back in the government's statue books. I put "new" in quotes because the only difference I could find between the old *Code*, which had caused the president and me so much grief, and this version was that in one section the word "mutiny" had been replaced with "rebel." Apparently, the legal specialists had decided that since KWS rangers weren't part of the military, they could not legally mutiny. They might, however, rebel. I didn't think that either action was likely and had a good chuckle about the whole thing.

It was a great relief that the committee agreed with our main concern: that KWS had to have a *Code* to guide our armed units. Bashir and I breathed a sigh of relief when the *Code* was reinstated.

But even as this latest crisis abated, another one arose. I began to feel like the greek hero Hercules sent out to do battle against the hydra. This time I fell out with a powerful cabinet minister.

The government had plans to build an oil pipeline from the coast at Mombassa to Nairobi, and one day the manager of this project came to my office with several maps tucked under his arm. An affable fellow, he chatted pleasantly about how this pipeline would reduce the price of gasoline for the average Kenyan, then unrolled his map.

"You see, sir," he explained, "the best route for the pipeline crosses here"—he pointed to a spot on the map—"just inside Nairobi National Park. We've already done a survey, and this is the most efficient, cost-effective place to put it. But we do need a waiver from you. Your deputy director wouldn't give it to me so now, I'm afraid, I must trouble you. All we need is your stamp on it."

I looked at the map and the line of dashes indicating the pipeline. The map showed the pipeline entering the park on its easternmost boundary, then turning gradually north in a gentle curve. It basically paralleled the road that followed the park's boundary, only of course it was about a quarter of a mile inside the park's perimeter. The civil servant traced the pipeline's course with his finger, explaining how it would not affect the animals and how everything would be done to assure that there would be no oil spills. I let him finish his spiel, but I already knew my answer.

"I'm sorry," I said, looking him directly in the eye, "but my deputy director was correct. The pipeline can't cross Nairobi National Park. It's against our policy. I can't give you the waiver."

He looked at me blankly for a moment. "But, sir . . . ," he began again.

"No, no. There's no need to discuss this further. It can't be done. You'd be better off putting the pipeline here." I traced a route that followed that of the already-existing road.

"But the survey has been done, sir," he tried once more.

"I can't help what's been done. All I can tell you is what will *not* be done. And there will be no oil pipeline in our park."

I sat back. "Now please take your maps. I'm sorry I can't help you."

A dark look passed over the man's face. "All right," he said, then quickly and noisily rolled up his maps, stuffed them under his arm, and walked huffily out the door.

I knew I had not heard the last of this pipeline—but I also already knew that there was far more to this story than the simple routing of a pipeline. It was a silly idea, of course, given the money we were trying to attract from foreign conservationists, even to consider putting a pipe-line through a national park. But that was not the real issue. The pipeline seemed to me a ruse to grab a chunk of Nairobi National Park's extremely valuable real estate. Situated as it is on the outskirts of our capital city, the park's land is worth millions. I'm sure that many wealthy real-estate developers drive past our park every day and hungrily eye its open space. Someone had apparently cooked up a scheme to try to lay their hands on some five hundred acres of land by routing the pipeline inside the park's boundaries.

It was a clever idea, based on secret plans (about which I had also learned) to expand the road that paralleled the park into a major six-lane highway sometime in the next decade. Of course, you can't have wild animals wandering across a highway of that size, so it would naturally have to become the park's new northern boundary. Theoretically, the highway expansion would require annexing only a narrow strip of parkland. However, this oil pipeline was to be constructed first. It would be built some distance inside the park's boundaries and curve north, slicing off a nice, wide crescent of parkland. It didn't take a genius to see that the highway would then be designed to follow the curve of the pipeline, and that a nice crescent of what had been Nairobi National Park would be instantly open to real-estate speculators. Someone was planning to make more than a tidy profit.

About a week later, I met with the aforementioned cabinet minister about the pipeline. He was all warmth and smiles.

"Richard, it's good to see you," he beamed, clasping my hand.

I smiled back and asked my secretary to bring us some tea.

We exchanged a few pleasantries, and then the minister said he would get right to the point. "Why are you being so difficult about our pipeline? We'll bury it. It won't be seen by the tourists. It won't affect your animals. It'll be out of sight. Surely you can agree to this?"

I smiled back. "It does sound sensible," I replied, "and I hate being difficult. But, you see, we have to think about international opinion here. Oil pipelines don't have the best reputation. It's hard to ensure they won't leak; and I'm sure the donors who, as you know, are investing large sums in Kenya's parks now, won't approve this."

Neither of us mentioned the highway expansion. I'm certain he knew about these plans, and I was equally certain that he did not know that I knew. It was political poker, and I kept the straightest of faces.

"Well, Richard, I don't understand," the minister said, beginning to look annoyed. "You're being awfully unreasonable, don't you think? Look at it from the taxpayers' point of view. This pipeline has been surveyed at their expense. It will cost money to survey a new route, to change these plans. I think you're making a mistake."

"I'm afraid I must disagree," I said. "I'm also thinking about our taxpayers and about what is best for Kenya. An oil pipeline in one of our most popular parks will benefit neither. It can curve in the other direction, so that it follows the road," I suggested.

"So you won't grant approval?"

"No."

The minister's warm smile turned icy. He stared at me, angrily and impatiently, and tapped his fingers on my desk. "Everyone told me you were impossible to work with," he said. "You know, it's really none of your business where this pipeline goes. It is a national project, and it has priority."

"Well, I'm not budging on it," I said, staring back at him. "You can get another director of Wildlife to approve this but not me."

At that, the minister stood abruptly, turned on his heel, and left.

The next day, President Moi telephoned me, and he did not mince words.

"What's this I hear about you stopping our pipeline?" he demanded. "Who do you think you are?"

"The director of KWS, sir," I replied. "It's my job . . ."

"It's your job to take care of wildlife, Richard. You're overstepping your boundaries here. This is a national pipeline, and with all this delay Kenya is losing money. Why are you always so unreasonable?"

I took a deep breath. "Well, Mr. President, I'm not being unreasonable. The pipeline would be better if it followed the road, as I recommended to the minister."

"No one is asking you for your recommendation. We're telling you where the pipeline is going."

"Not while I'm director," I said. "It simply can't happen." I pointed out, as I had to the minister, that we were in the middle of negotiating a project with the World Bank for $150 million to rebuild our parks. The foreign conservationists who would be asked to approve our plans would not be at all happy to hear about an oil pipeline crossing this tiny park. "I guarantee you that it will be very controversial and bring us a lot of bad press, which might jeopardize our funding from the World Bank and the whole foreign wildlife sector."

Moi disagreed. The minister had assured him that the international community wouldn't object to this.

"I don't mean to cast any aspersions on the minister," I said, "but I don't think he knows these foreign donors as well as I do; and they *will* object. You can be sure of it."

Moi calmed down as I continued to talk, explaining how sensitive conservationists overseas were about these kinds of pipelines, that there'd been various catastrophes, spills that injured wildlife, giving pipelines decidedly bad reputations.

"Surely, we don't want to get involved in something like this that may turn the international donor community against us?"

"No, no." He sighed audibly. "Richard, you can be very stubborn, you know. But I see your point. I'll tell the minister. He'll have the pipeline resurveyed. It won't cross your park."

"Kenya's park, sir," I said with a soft chuckle.

"Yes, Kenya's park."

We hung up and I took a deep breath, then glanced at my calendar: November 30, 1990. The new year was little more than a month away. I wondered if I would last in this office that long.

CHAPTER 15

I've always prided myself on my ability to make decisions, to see what needs to be done and do it. It's a skill a leader needs and, for me, at least, a talent that has made up for deficits in other areas, such as my lack of a formal education. I knew what path needed to be taken to make KWS a success, and I was doing my best to follow it. I generally knew what I needed to do in my personal life as well and had made tough decisions when I felt them to be necessary. But as the end of 1990 loomed, I felt increasingly doubtful that I had achieved anything of importance and confused about my relationships and home life. I was in the grip of a general feeling of malaise—and with no ideas about how to shake it.

On December 19, I turned forty-six and in the wee hours of the morning, it suddenly dawned on me that I was facing what I had once scorned: a midlife crisis.

At forty-six years of age, I wrote in my diary, *I am not really all that I would like to be . . . I am not really sure that I am a very good family person and I have doubts about my ability to relate to the children and probably MGL [Meave] as well . . . Quite honestly, I do feel very depressed when I think about things but I am not sure how I can change anything. I never expected to be alive at forty-six and I guess this is part of the problem.*

In my twenties, I had heard about that period of self-doubt and uncertainty in one's middle years. It had all seemed silly and highly self-indulgent to me; then I had already survived a terminal disease, and the idea of wallowing in self-pity in one's middle years (which is how I viewed the "midlife crisis") struck me as ridiculous. At the time, as I'd mentioned in my diary, I didn't believe that I would live to see the age of forty. I thought then that if by some twist of fate I did live into my middle years, I would not be so foolish or self-absorbed as to suffer such a "crisis."

Fate, however, had been kinder than I would have ever imagined: I had lived long enough to experience this humbling event myself. And I was as miserable as anyone else who's found themselves adrift in their middle years.

My family had gathered for my birthday and the Christmas holidays at our home on Lamu Island, and although I did my best to disguise my low spirits I'm afraid I was fairly glum and out-of-sorts. It didn't help my mood when KWS headquarters sent news that poachers had shot and killed a ranger and wounded three others at Meru. That kind of report always left me heartsick. Meave, my three daughters, and others in the Leakey clan probably decided that it was this news and all the ups and downs of my job in recent months that was making me so unhappy. They didn't press me about what was wrong, and I tried my best to get into the holiday spirit. We joined in sailing races, ate well, laughed, and talked, but still I couldn't escape the dark cloud of self-doubt hovering over me.

On New Year's Day I wrote in my diary: *I think that 1991 is going to be a very taxing year for me and the "middle-age hump" may be the worst part of it! I must get a grip on things and move forward.*

Hard work has always helped me see things more clearly, and once back at KWS I threw myself into my job. I found myself welcoming every problem, every crisis—anything that tuned out the unhappy, self-chastising voice in my head. I had heard nothing more from President Moi since our last discussion about the oil pipeline, and I took his silence as a sign of his approval to carry on as I thought best.

As always, there was much to do. Most of January 1991 was spent putting the final polish on KWS's five-year plan and policy, our "Zebra Book," as we called it, which I presented to our board of directors at the end of the month. They gave it their full backing. A few days later the World Bank notified me that they strongly endorsed our plans and confirmed that KWS would be receiving $60 million from the bank and the remaining $90 million from other donors over the next five years.

The stage was now fully set for us to begin building the self-sustaining, revenue-generating organization that I had envisioned.

There was, however, one major fly in the ointment, one we in Kenya were helpless to do anything about: the Gulf War. The war started in mid-January 1991, two weeks before we received all our good news. I knew from the moment the war began that it would play havoc with Kenya's economy and with my plans for KWS. I didn't disagree with the American and European assessment that Iraq had wrongly invaded Kuwait and needed to be punished. And I wasn't at all surprised to see the Western powers join together to drive the Iraqis out. For our fledgling wildlife organization, however, it was the worst possible news. Almost overnight, tourist bookings to Kenya dropped by 80 percent. Tourists are generally reluctant to travel when war breaks out, and East Africa is geographically close to the Middle East, so I wasn't surprised that many people canceled their safaris. But the drastic decline in numbers—only the year before, nearly 1 million visitors had come to Kenya, and 1991 began with only a trickle—was sobering, and I was glad we had five years to build up our revenue base. We would need it.

In the meantime I forged ahead with our plans. With the World Bank's funds, we could begin hiring additional staff and short-term consultants to help us get KWS underway. We had no time to spare; the Gulf War was already setting us back. When it ended and tourism picked up again, I wanted our parks to be safe, all roads and buildings to be in order, and the landscape teeming with animals.

Some were not pleased that I employed consultants—a few of them were white expatriates—to whom we paid the wages such people expect.

I knew that before long someone would raise the issue of race, charging that I had hired these people because of my own European ancestry. I had run into the same problem at the National Museums. Every so often, an employee bent on ousting me would concoct a story about "rampant racism" at the Museum because of my Anglo roots. It was always easy to deflect such charges because they were not true.

Racial prejudice is not the burning social issue in Kenya that it is in countries such as the United States and South Africa. During Kenya's colonial period, the indigenous population did suffer gross injustices at the hands of the white settlers. Had they had their way, the settlers would have established an apartheid system like the South African whites did, but the British government did not allow this. Still, it required a rebellion, the Mau Mau uprising, for Kenya to win its independence. In the newly free country, Kenya's white population lost its dominant role and instead became its smallest minority. Only about 1 percent of Kenyans are of European ancestry. Most white Kenyans are farmers or businessmen; very few have ventured into government or politics.

None of this is to say that racism—that is, a feeling of white superiority—doesn't exist in Kenya. There are many white Kenyans who've been unable to shake the colonial legacy and whose sole contribution to our country consists of complaining about how bad things are. At the beginning of my tenure at Wildlife, a couple of white wardens who worked for the department had much this same attitude, and in time I let them go. They were older men and, unfortunately, unable to change. I don't know if these men ever voted in elections. The majority of Kenya's white citizens do not, and I often wonder why they stay in Kenya. These people are merely irritants. They have no political power, and because they are afraid that the majority population will turn against them, they generally keep a very low profile.

Of far greater concern to the average Kenyan are our country's tribal divisions. Within Kenya's boundaries are about forty different tribes; of these, the Kikuyu, Luo, and Kalenjin are the largest and have the most political clout. From the moment Kenya received its independence in 1963, tribalism has been our main worry. Smaller tribes have always feared that a tribe as big as the Kikuyu would dominate the country, particularly if all decisions were made on a simple majority basis. Kenya's first president, Jomo Kenyatta, was Kikuyu. But he was sensible enough to know that if the Kikuyu totally dominated the country, it would soon be racked by civil war. A charismatic man, Kenyatta astutely formed alliances with other tribal leaders and used his position as a national leader to preach about the need to transcend tribal roots and to pull together as Kenyans for Kenya. President Moi has for the most part followed this same path. Indeed, the original idea behind Kenya's single-partystate, which Moi helped create, was to limit the influence of tribalism in politics.

Although Kenya's Constitution and laws specifically seek to prohibit discriminatory practice, the effort to keep a balance has in some cases resulted in problems. Tribal loyalties run deep; leaders are expected to find jobs for their clansmen. Affirmative action intended to increase numbers among certain groups has on occasion lowered standards, and village ties have lead to nepotism and corruption at senior levels. Once, when I was director of the National Museums, some disciplinary actions that I took were construed as representing prejudices against a particular tribe.

At KWS, we employed people from nearly every tribe. I had even employed several members of Kenya's smallest minority, the "white tribe," because I thought it important that more white Kenyans get involved in their country's public affairs. It seemed a shame that most young white Kenyans never considered serving their country by joining the public service. Many believed that they could not work for the government, or serve in its military or police forces, or lobby for political reforms. Most grew up with little contact with their fellow citizens, aside from house servants and a few elite school friends. Yet I believed that the KWS would be the perfect career for some of them. Many white Kenyans love life in the bush and are ardent conservationists. From the beginning of my tenure, I encouraged young whites with these interests to join us. I made it clear that they were not going to get special treatment; and when I hired a few on as rangers, I sent them to boot camp along with their fellow countrymen and compatriots. They were shouted at by the same training sergeants, slept in the same uncomfortable beds, went on the same forced marches at three o'clock in the morning, and learned to work as a team. Here's how Bongo Woodley, who became a KWS pilot and assistant warden, describes that time:

> I had been born and raised in Kenya, but like most white kids I mingled more with white people than with black. So there I was in the barracks—all black Kenyans and two whites, me and my brother, Danny. Initially, it was tough; who was I going to talk to besides Danny? But I found out that all of us shared basic issues: worries about our homes and families, those who were sick or who had died. And we shared common goals: protecting the parks, building up KWS, surviving the training. So it gave me a very different feel for what Kenya is about.

No one in the government ever challenged me about hiring these young men. Hiring foreign consultants, on the other hand, was more controversial, because it implied that local Kenyans—white or black—weren't ready to take on high-level managerial jobs. Nothing could be further from the truth, but the Kenyans I wanted—bright, talented men and women in the private sector—would have had to work for low government wages, as they would be Civil Service employees, and most weren't willing to do that. Nor did I want them to give up their high-paying jobs to work for a pittance at KWS. It was far more reasonable to employ the consultants on a short-term basis, get KWS up and running, and then replace the consultants with skilled Kenyan workers once we had the money to pay them what they deserved—something I expected to happen within three or four years.

Until then I knew that sooner or later that someone hoping to score political points would run the "racism" charge up the flagpole again. And I would haul it right down, just as I had in the past.

❖   ❖   ❖

When I wasn't wallowing in my midlife blues, I could see that KWS was beginning to make real progress. My staff's morale and spirits were high; our plans to improve and upgrade the parks were coming along; I had forged alliances with other conservationists that would help to keep the elephants listed on CITES Appendix I; we were developing plans to assist the people living along our parks' boundaries; and the leader of the worst band of Orma bandits had turned himself in—to KWS. This latter event was a real coup. The fellow simply walked into the KWS warden's office on Lamu Island at the end of April 1991, gave the warden his name, and said that he wanted to surrender.

"I came to you instead of the police," the warden quoted him as saying, "because I've heard good things about KWS. You won't beat me and you may grant me amnesty."

It was my policy that KWS should act mercifully and generously to any captured bandits or poachers and especially so to those who surrendered. Bashir used to shake his head when I insisted that such men be well treated; our men, he would say, wanted revenge. I understood that feeling, but dispensing justice was not our job—it was the job of the courts—and we were not to torture or mistreat anyone. I didn't want any charges of human rights abuses leveled against KWS. Word of KWS's policy had circulated in the bush and was now paying off. We benefited not only from this bandit leader's surrender but from the details he provided about ivory stashes, poachers planning raids into Tsavo, and robbers who had recently held up several buses along the Tana River. Unfortunately, when we investigated his past we discovered that we could not guarantee him amnesty for all the crimes he had committed. He had so many murders to his name that we ultimately had to turn him over to the police.

Among other disclosures, the bandit leader said that he and many of his friends thought that KWS was gaining the upper hand in the wildlife wars and that, because of this, other poachers were also thinking of calling it quits. I hoped that he was right. I wasn't sure that we were as close to winning the war as he thought, but to hear that some of the poachers believed this to be the case was good news indeed.

We added the information about poachers and illegal dealers the bandit supplied to the database we were building on the underground ivory trade. Since the beginning of the year, we'd had numerous reports about secret stashes of ivory that poachers and traders hoped to move. Zimbabwe had recently announced that it was going to continue trading ivory, and that announcement immediately revived the illegal market. The Zimbabweans always insisted that they sold only ivory culled from elephants in their own parks, but I never believed them—and, obviously, neither did people in the trade. Some poachers were gambling that they could mix their old ivory with that from Zimbabwe, and I didn't think they would make such a bet if they weren't fairly confident of the outcome.

However, our intelligence unit was now regularly tipped off when someone recovered buried ivory or tried to smuggle tusks. We tracked several loads of tusks that were shipped from Tanzania into Kenya in the false bottoms of trucks. Since the shipments were large, we thought we might score a major bust with this ivory and land a major government figure. But, as before, only a small-time Nairobi businessman proved to be the purchaser. I was surprised there was any market for ivory at all, since, despite Zimbabwe's selfish declaration, tusks were being sold for under five dollars a pound.

It was unlikely that this trader was working alone, or that Nairobi was the ivory's final destination. It was probably headed for Egypt or the Middle East. There were frequent rumors about former South African army officers buying ivory and rhino horns from Angola helping to support Jonas Savimbi's rebellion. The details of these transactions were always murky—but it didn't surprise me that arms and ivory merchants would be working together to make money off a bush war in Angola. Were this the case—*and* we could prove it—we would hold a powerful tool for ending the ivory trade once and for all.

To track the ivory, I had members of KWS's undercover ivory unit pose as corrupt rangers and collect some of the tusks crossing the border in official KWS vehicles. I then saw to it that they weren't stopped at any of the government roadblocks, which sometimes pull over vehicles to check for smuggled goods or contraband. But as before, the trail quickly petered out. The ivory buyer turned out to be a small-time trader, and there was no evidence that he was sending the tusks to South Africa.

In the northern deserts, we had a better idea of where the ivory was going: Somalia. Every tusk poached in Meru, along the Tana River, and in northern Tsavo was either carried into Somalia through the desert or shipped to Somalia by sea. Once there, it quickly fell into the hands of avaricious associates of Siad Barre, who was then the president of Somalia. The country had few resources and selling poached ivory provided a lucrative source of revenue for the ruling couple. And, as in South Africa, many of the tusks were also being used to buy weapons—that were later used in Somalia's civil war.

A Somali trader in the Kenyan town of Isiolo was alleged to control the Kenyan end of this trade, and we kept a close watch on him. He bought any ivory for sale around Isiolo and the northern desert towns of Marsabit and Maralal, then shipped it south to Mombassa in false-bottom trucks—sometimes with the aid of a police escort. At Mombassa, the ivory was loaded onto a transport ship, the *Idris*. The trader was a big livestock merchant, too, and he generally had about two thousand cattle onboard to sell to the Middle East. The decks were stacked with bales of hay, and it was alleged that the ivory was hidden in these. I had that ship searched several times. Though we were certain there was ivory on board, we never found it.

The trader had a brother in a high position in the Kenyan military, and I suspected that was why the trader was able to use police escorts to transport his ivory. Here, at last, was a big fish. I doubted that the police officer was benefiting financially from the trade, however. More likely, he was following his tribal customs and protecting a close family member, as he was expected to do.

In early April 1991, we got a big break: news came that the Somali trader planned to move a large stash of ivory he had buried in his courtyard garden in Isiolo. A few rangers posing as mechanics stationed themselves on a nearby road next to a broken-down truck. They watched and waited . . . and waited. Several days went by, and then a new report was passed along. The ivory wasn't going to be moved after all. Apparently, the officer had learned of our plans and had warned his brother. Shortly after this near showdown, I met the officer in a government meeting about some other issue. We smiled and nodded at each other. He knew what I knew, and we let it go at that. I couldn't arrest him without evidence, and given his high position, I didn't really want to. I had no idea of what the repercussions might have been, but I'm sure the army—and perhaps the entire government—would have been shaken to its core.

Other ivory trails led to some members of Parliament and even to a permanent secretary, but again we lacked the concrete evidence necessary to arrest them. Instead, we entered their names in our database and waited. Sooner or later someone would get greedy or make a mistake. Thanks to both the Appendix I listing and our rangers' efforts, the ivory trade had slowed to a trickle, but it was still there—the poachers, traders, and buyers were still in place, waiting to make their move. All that was required was some other African country deciding to break the ban.

I believed that there were two key steps to making KWS a success: keeping the elephants listed on Appendix I so that the poaching did not start up again, and ridding the organization of corrupt employees. Despite Zimbabwe's threats and protests, we were managing the first task fairly well. And in late May 1991, after several discussions, President Moi gave me the go-ahead to work at the second task.

"If this is the only means to straighten out KWS, Richard," he told me during a phone conversation, "then you must do so. You'll have the government's support."

Previously, he had always been hesitant to agree to my request, though I had emphasized that KWS could not be restructured without first being given a clean slate. Moreover, the World Bank was counting on Kenya's government allowing KWS to be managed with a free hand, and this meant letting me hire and fire people as needed. Traditionally, as I've said before, Wildlife employees were guided by cumbersome Civil Service procedure. The work-output assessment and rapid promotion for good efforts that is so typical in the business world were not part of the public-service culture.

In the previous year I had asked the government to redeploy some 220 wildlife personnel to other parts of government. Now the situation was more difficult; I wanted to rid KWS of 1,640 employees, each of whom had been assessed as a nonperformer. My hope was that by having government reassign these employees, we would avoid having to fire them. The problem was that people knew that KWS employees were about to get better pay and benefits, and nobody wanted to go voluntarily. I braced myself for the hue and cry that would soon follow. It wouldn't be easy for the government to find all these people new jobs; some might be forced to resign from the Civil Service. And in a country where unemployment ran at close to 40 percent, losing a job was going to be very rough on them. As much as I disliked and distrusted many of these employees, I was sympathetic to the hardships they and their families would be facing.

I didn't dodge the bullet. I made the announcement myself. I also convened a special meeting of KWS's senior officers, about 150 in all, and gave them the news that close to half of them would be leaving. Many looked utterly shaken. Some followed me back to my office, asking for further explanations. There was little more I could tell them—their shortcomings were well-known among the other employees, and had they been allowed to stay, their presence would have been demoralizing. Nevertheless, telling them they were being transferred out was difficult. Indeed, this was one of the hardest days I had yet faced.

This has to happen, I kept telling myself. I didn't feel any elation at showing them the door. Still, there was a bright side. With these staff changes behind me, I could envision a revitalized team of rangers and wardens, among whom corruption would be the exception rather than the rule and whose conservation efforts would be coordinated and efficient. I believed we were finally poised to form this team.

CHAPTER 16

I was never certain how President Moi reached his decisions. At times, he seemed ready to agree to any request I put to him; at other times he was reluctant to agree to the simplest request and regarded me warily. I didn't know how to interpret his hot-and-cold behavior and decided that it had more to do with his cabinet officers and their advice than with him or me.

As I've suggested, President Moi was in a particularly tough position. After the end of the Cold War in 1987, Western nations were taking a closer look at the countries they had supported. They had become less eager to support regimes they defined as authoritarian, even those with which they long had had friendly relations, such as Kenya. The Western press and several Western leaders continued to clamor for more democracy and for investigations into human rights abuses. When Kenya didn't measure up on all counts, funding was reduced or frozen. While well-intentioned, this carrot-and-stick approach to moving Kenya and other African nations forward didn't improve life for the average Kenyan. It also made it harder for President Moi to know whom to listen to for advice. People lobbied him from all sides and sometimes even persuaded him to change his mind about decisions he had just made. I was sure that he would be under great pressure to rescind his support for my request to transfer the corrupt employees, since so many people from so many different tribes were affected. I could only hope the government had the fortitude to stay the course. Kenya's own course was far from clear. The Gulf War, mercifully, had ended in an astonishingly short amount of time. This offered some hope to our beleaguered tourism industry, although I doubted that visitor numbers would pick up as quickly as they had dropped. Poaching and bandit attacks inside Kenya's parks were virtually unheard of now. And the United States State Department lifted its warning to tourists about the dangers of visiting Kenya, an alert it had posted after the prodemocracy riots in Nairobi during the summer of 1990. But other problems soon arose.

Most distressingly, a severe drought struck northeastern Kenya and southern Somalia, killing people and livestock. Somalia was embroiled in civil war. Its autocratic ruler, Siad Barre, was driven out, leaving the country without a government, and warlords from the different clans were locked in a brutal, bloody battle for power. People were starving. They streamed across Kenya's northern frontier where our own nomadic tribes were faring little better. Some refugees were also fleeing the fighting in Somalia's capital, Mogadishu, and many brought their Kalashnikovas with them. In no time at all, these and other weapons flooded the black market in Nairobi. It was said you could pick up a used AK-47 for as little as a hundred dollars. With prices that low, I worried that ex-poachers might be tempted to return to their old trade. Fortunately, although the police had their hands full, due to a growing number of bandit attacks in Kenya's northeastern region, the ivory trade ban remained in place; and we didn't notice any marked increase in poaching.

I had other concerns. My biggest problem, now that we'd transferred the corrupt employees and curtailed the poaching, was how to control the elephants in our national parks and reserves. During all of 1990, we lost only fifty-eight elephants to poachers, compared to several hundred in 1989, and several thousand the year before that. Our success, however, carried a price. Elephants are smart animals, and it did not take them long to figure out that people were no longer shooting at them. They quickly lost their fear of humans and began boldly wandering outside our parks' boundaries. When they returned to the areas they had inhabited in the 1980s, before poaching became a serious problem, they encountered farmers and villagers—people who had moved in where the elephants had moved out. Inevitably, there were human-elephant encounters and, all too often, the humans lost.

A charging elephant is a terrifying sight. Elephants can move far faster than their size suggests, and in a split second they can be racing at you at full steam. They flare out their ears, raise their trunks to send out an ear-splitting trumpet, and generally look as wild and formidable as a moving mountain of muscle and flesh can look. A thin, two-legged biped can do little more than run. And a determined elephant will chase down a person, knock him—or her—over, then kneel on him to crush him or run him through with a tusk.

At KWS, we did not want to control elephants by shooting them except as a last resort. The rangers helping Joyce Poole keep track of crop-raiding animals disliked the idea, partly because corrupt rangers had once engaged in poaching and partly because I had emphasized from the start that KWS's mission was to protect the animals in our care. Killing problem animals did not seem a solution—although at times we had no other choice. All too often, the wrong elephant ended up being shot or, worse, wounded.

Elephants weren't the only wildlife problem. Buffaloes, lions, crocodiles, baboons, and wild pigs all caused trouble for villagers. According to the law, whether the animals lived inside or outside of a park or reserve, they were the responsibility of KWS. People, as well as their crops and stock, needed protection; the wild animals also needed protection. There are never simple solutions to such complex problems, but I hoped that by fencing off park lands where wildlife caused the most trouble we might reduce some of the animal-human conflicts.

The fencing idea was actually President Moi's. Six months before he put me in charge of Wildlife, he had suggested it in one of his speeches as a way to keep people and animals apart. I thought it was a good idea and early in my tenure proposed fencing some of the parks, only to be met with an avalanche of criticism from many conservationists. (I had also contemplated allowing hunting again on a very limited basis. Only the wealthiest people could have afforded the fees I imagined charging, and they could have hunted only certain species of antelopes and buffaloes. I later scrapped the idea when it became clear that it would be an extremely difficult program to manage and would undoubtedly provide a means by which more guns would be brought into Kenya.)

Critics of the fencing strategy complained that I wanted to turn Kenya into a zoo. Fences would disrupt the animals' migrations, involve a huge expense, and be impossible to maintain, they argued. There was a good deal of venom in their attacks, along with comments that implied that I knew nothing about the behavior of wild animals. I sometimes wondered about these critics. They could see as well as I that unless conflict between animals and humans was reduced, all of Kenya's wildlife would eventually disappear. Villagers would tolerate the animals only for so long before taking matters into their own hands. Yet very few of my critics offered any concrete proposals about how to address the problem.

In fact, Kenya already had a couple of partially fenced parks. Nairobi National Park is largely fenced, and Lake Nakuru National Park is entirely fenced. The latter lies on the outskirts of Nakuru, an agricultural town, and is home to buffalo, giraffes, lions, leopards, baboons, and many antelope species, although not to elephants. Yet these other animals—particularly baboons—caused farmers so much trouble that the only solution lay in erecting electrical fences, which was done in the 1970s. It is not a perfect solution. Animals still get out. Farmers' crops are still raided. But it helps.

I thought it more likely that Kenya would be able to keep its abundant herds of game far into the future by separating wildlife and people in other areas where the conflicts were frequent and severe. Consequently, we made the construction of wildlife barriers one of our key policies at KWS. The World Bank and other donors agreed and provided the initial funding to begin experimenting with fences and fence designs.

I never intended to fence every park or to entirely encircle any park with an electrical fence. In certain areas, such as the Masai Mara, fences would be disastrous. The large herds of wildebeest, zebra, and antelope have to migrate each year if they are to survive. Buffalo, giraffe, and many other herbivores don't need to migrate, however. In the areas where there were regular encounters between people and these animals—such as the Shimba Hills National Reserve on the coast or on the Laikipia Game Sanctuary near Mount Kenya National Park—fences could help.

We weren't going to build the fences overnight. They needed to be designed and tested before being put in place. (Early on we discovered that there was very little information available anywhere to guide us, as the concept of fencing large tracts of parkland was new.) And prior to the design stage, we needed to identify those areas where barriers would do the most good. Joyce's team was already busy collecting these data, recording every reported encounter between animals and people. To make the fences work, we also had to ensure that the local people regarded the barriers as "theirs" by involving them in the planning through community meetings and workshops. Doing so added an extra step and costs, but it was the best way to reduce the chances of vandalism and theft of fencing materials.

Telling villagers of our plans did little to soften the blow they felt when they lost food or a loved one to an elephant or other animal. Until the fences were in place, we could do little more than direct those who suffered such a loss to the government's Treasury Department, whose responsibility it was to reimburse them, according to the legislation that had created KWS.

We wanted good relations with those villagers who lived closest to our parks. At the time, conservationists worldwide were grappling with the same issues that we were, as many of the regions containing the most abundant and diverse plants and animals are also found in some of the world's poorest countries. These conservationists realized that the people who lived in the forests, deserts, and savannas—whether it was the Amazon or the Serengeti—would use the natural resources surrounding them. If a timber company was willing to pay a high price for teak, for instance, villagers would understandably cut down as many hardwood trees as possible. If there were buyers of antelope or monkey meat, people without any other means of making a living could easily be enticed into hunting these animals. Many conservationists came to the conclusion that parks only exacerbated the problem of finding a way for humans and wildlife to coexist. In some places, such as Kenya, parks had been developed by a colonial government. Local people had been forced off their land and then denied access to the natural materials in the parks. It was understandable that they would resent the parks and those who administered them. And as human populations continued to grow, the pressure to develop these parks would also grow.

This was a very bleak scenario. To counter it, some conservationists proposed that local communities be given funds raised from the parks through tourism, an idea called "community-based conservation" or CBC. Several members of my staff, such as Robert Bensted-Smith, were great CBC advocates. Initially, I was, too. I've never liked any form of human suffering and have seen far too much of it in Kenya. Whenever possible, I've tried to improve peoples' lives, even if only on a small scale. For instance, on our fossil-hunting expeditions around Lake Turkana, we always made it our practice to hire local people as camp helpers and assisted them with medicines and food if they were in desperate straits. Meave and I also supported numerous children from the Turkana, sending them to elementary school and, if they did well, on to high school. The CBC concept struck me as something along these lines. It seemed fair and, if it gave the local people a better understanding about why it was important to preserve the parks, it was well worth pursuing. (I have since decided that, in fact, it does little to save a park's plants and animal and runs the very real risk of turning villagers into welfare recipients—but more on this later.)

Grace Lusiola headed up our Community Wildlife Service, KWS's community-based Conservation Department. By June of 1991, she had already identified some key communities around Amboseli where she hoped to put in place projects that would both help the local people and raise their awareness about the importance of the park. We also hoped to extend community projects to areas where we could never build fences and where it would therefore be impossible to keep wildlife off of private land. Our initial plan was to set aside 25 percent of the parks' entry fees for financing small-scale development projects in such places. But even as we began drafting the plan, it became clear that it was going to be highly political. All sorts of people, from local leaders to members of Parliament, wanted part of the action—that is, a share of the promised revenue. And it became equally clear that we were going to have trouble convincing the villagers that this money had been generated by the wildlife in the parks—a fundamental and important connection if any community project was to work—and not by some political figure trawling for votes.

I've always been surprised at the shortness of peoples' memories. By the summer of 1991, I had been in this office for about two years. The first year was almost entirely devoted to stopping the poaching; the second to raising funds and lobbying for the new agency. Now we were ready to build it. But people expected KWS to be up and running overnight. With the poaching largely under control, elephants were no longer seen as endangered. Villagers were showing less and less tolerance for the elephants or for any animals that caused them problems and becoming increasingly impatient with what many perceived to be a wealthy government agency. We could lose all the goodwill that Kenyans had directed our way in a matter of moments if we didn't address their concerns. It was like watching a gathering storm, and we were still building the foundation of our shelter.

I had expected a political backlash from the transfer of the corrupt KWS employees. We were showing the door to more than sixteen hundred people—and all of them Civil Service employees who believed that no matter how badly they had behaved, they should have jobs for life. Inevitably, I knew, some politicians would try to use such resentment to their advantage. Still, as I noted in my diary at the end of May 1991, *with support from the top . . . we can achieve the cleanup needed.*

For most of the summer of 1991, it felt as if the future had already arrived. The employees we no longer wanted were transferred to the

Ministry of Tourism, where they were either assigned to new jobs or given retirement. Once they were gone, staff morale surged again, and we began a new round of hiring. The air at KWS was electric with anticipation and excitement. Many on my staff commented about how energized they felt. We were an example to the entire country.

I thought we would have at least a year to get things underway, that the politicians would stand back and give us a little breathing room as what we were trying to achieve was in the national interest. I was wrong.

In early August, barely six weeks after transferring the employees, I heard from the head of the Civil Service that a crisis was brewing. Someone had charged that I had fired the corrupt KWS employees because I wanted to replace them with members of the Kikuyu tribe. It was said that I had no evidence of real corruption among these employees, and that my reasons for requesting the transfers were mere ruses to mask what I was really up to: creating a Kikuyu empire at KWS. The government was considering an investigation.

I was utterly dumbfounded by the charge and telephoned President Moi immediately. He answered very coolly and said that of course people were always worried about one tribe being favored over another but that he didn't have time for a meeting with me. Instead, I arranged a meeting with the head of the Civil Service, thinking that even if he wasn't on my side, I might at least get some clues about the person—or people—behind this rumor.

We met in his office in Central Nairobi. I didn't intend to beat about the bush and addressed the matter head-on.

"These are serious allegations—and they are outrageous. You know that as well as I do," I began.

He pursed his lips in a sympathetic manner. "Yes, these are very unfortunate assertions," he agreed.

"And they are utterly false," I said.

In response, he tilted his head to one side but said nothing. I continued. "It's clear that someone is trying to get me to resign—or force the government to withdraw my appointment—and it would help enormously if I had some better idea about why these lies are being spread."

"No, no, Richard. The government backs you 100 percent," he insisted. "No one wants you to resign. But it may be necessary for you to go a little more slowly on the transfers."

"We can't go more slowly. The transfers have been done. Those people are gone, and we're hiring new people. If KWS is to succeed, we can't have corrupt employees working for us. Now, anyone from any tribe can apply for these new jobs, and we'll hire the best ones."

"Well, Richard, it might help if you added more openings for some tribes," he suggested. "Maybe you should think about hiring more Masai and Kalenjin. I hear they are underrepresented at KWS, particularly compared with the numbers of Kikuyu there." He smiled affably.

That was the clue I was looking for—someone tied to those two tribes was complaining to the government. Most likely it was the "tea room set," as I called the president's kitchen cabinet, who were again making it impossible for me to do my job. William Ntimama, the Masai member of Parliament from the Narok District, probably had stirred things up as well, perhaps by complaining to friends among Moi's advisers. He and I had already clashed over the way the Masai Mara National Reserve was now being managed, and he was upset that I had not put the Mara on the list of reserves to receive the first round of World Bank projects.

"I'm not operating KWS as a welfare agency," I countered. "And I don't think you build a good, well-run organization by catering to the whims of various MPs or by discriminating against good people in order to hire a certain number of Maasai or Samburu or whatever. KWS must be free to choose the right people for the right job regardless of their tribal affiliation. We're hiring *Kenyans*. That's what should matter."

"Yes, of course, Richard," the head of the Civil Service said. "But the public is very sensitive about tribal issues. You can't ignore that."

"I disagree. The public is only made to feel that tribal issues matter because politicians say that it does. They use tribalism as a ploy to get what they want. But I think our citizens are better than that. I think they want those of us in the public service to put Kenya first—which is what I am trying to do."

"I know that, Richard," he replied. "The government knows that. Still, think a little about hiring some more Maasai."

"It can't be done like that," I said, shaking my head. "It's not KWS's policy, and I won't bend the rules."

"Ah, Richard, you are very tough," he laughed. "Well, we need a tough man overseeing our wild animals and parks. I'm sure you're not hiring Kikuyu when you could be hiring Maasai. This will blow over. I think it does not need to be a major issue."

We shook hands and I left. I had learned what I needed to know, but there seemed little that I could do about it. I wasn't going to change KWS's policy on hiring, and I certainly wasn't going to favor one tribe over another. The meeting cleared things up a little for me but left me slightly depressed, too. Perhaps public service—at least in a position of this sort—was not my calling. That night, I wrote in my diary: *I have to give careful thought to getting out of public service. I am not willing to bend and my rigidity brings much stress.*

My meeting with the head of the Civil Service seemed to have had some effect because almost at once the rumors ceased. My energy and enthusiasm for the job were revived. *If the politicians would just leave KWS alone,* I kept saying to myself, *we could achieve everything we envisioned.* In the short eight months that KWS had been operating, there were already enormous improvements everywhere. At Amboseli, for instance, where I made a quick visit, new roads were under construction and off-road driving was becoming a thing of the past. Freshly painted buildings and signposts made the park look smart.

We needed to share our success with the public. I contacted the editor of the *Daily Nation* newspaper to suggest that once a week they devote a full page to describing one of Kenya's national parks. He liked the idea immediately and added to this a weekly profile of someone on KWS's staff, such as a ranger or field biologist. I don't think that any newspaper had ever written about these men and women before, and that column was a great hit.

Although the rumors about KWS's hiring practices seemed to have died down, the fact that they had been spread—and believed—in the first place continued to worry me. At night I found myself mulling over these allegations, wondering when and how they would surface again. Once, just as an exercise to reassure myself—and for proof if I needed it—I listed in my diary all the different tribes and the approximate number of people KWS employed from each. KWS had retained 2,867 employees from the old staff, and they came from twenty-six different tribes. It was true that the largest number of employees was Kikuyu (503), but we also had 225 Kalenjin, 260 Luhya, and 336 Luo. There were 60 Maasai on board. Of the 333 new staff members KWS had hired, the largest number came from the Samburu tribe (48). Twenty-five were Kikuyu, while 41 were Maasai, and 11 Kalenjin. *My own views are that nobody can really complain about this list,* I wrote in my diary. *The point of irritation, however, is that one has to answer such tribal sentiments.*

It was almost comical that I could be seen as having any tribal bias at all. I wasn't accused of favoring whites but of favoring a black tribe. People imagined this because my grandparents had been missionaries among the Kikuyu, and my father had been made a full member and elder in the tribe. However, I had not been raised among the Kikuyu, I didn't speak their language, and had not been inducted into the tribe. I do have many Kikuyu friends, including my mentor, Charles Njonjo. But I also have friends and advisers from other tribes, such as David Mwiraria, who is Meru. That my friendship with certain Kikuyu leaders would be used against me revealed just how afraid the government's inner circle seemed to be of this tribe.

Our country's first president, Jomo Kenyatta, was Kikuyu; and during his time in office, the Kikuyu held many of the top positions in the government. Being sensitive to this, President Kenyatta had appointed Mr. Moi as his vice president. Under Kenya's constitution, the vice president assumes the presidency in the event that the incumbent can no longer serve, and this is how President Moi initially took over. Since he was from the Kalenjin tribe, he was not seen as a threat, as another

Kikuyu leader might have been. Some political commentators have argued that those Kikuyu power brokers regarded Moi as a puppet of sorts and imagined that he could be controlled. He turned out to be far more politically savvy than they expected. Over the years, some Kalenjins appear to have benefited from Moi's presidency, just as some Kikuyu did under Kenyatta. However, observers often say that the Kikuyu are angry about losing their political influence and power, and are determined to regain control. In the summer of 1991, these sorts of rumors intensified. One rumor was that the Kikuyu were about to make a grab for power.

That KWS and I were being linked, however indirectly, to this rumor worried me enormously. Even worse, in late August 1991, another rumor surfaced, this one among the white, expatriate community. It troubled me so much that I wrote it down in my diary:

People are saying that my ambition is to become President. This is utterly nonsensical but it is very dangerous. If the current government felt it was a matter to be taken seriously, I would expect an "accident" to happen—car or plane. I cannot be complacent about this and it upsets me greatly. I have *no* interest in the top position. My honest wish is to help Kenya. Anyhow, it is very dangerous gossip and it worries me.

I had to make myself somehow less visible to the government. I did not want to be perceived either as a Kikuyu or as someone with great political ambitions. Again I found myself thinking of resigning. Life would be so much less complicated. I had started a small vineyard on the slope below my home. Tending my vines; developing a wine industry in Kenya; spending time with Meave and our daughters and doing things that we could enjoy together: these were worthy goals, too. On the weekends, while sitting on our veranda and gazing across the Rift Valley, I sometimes found myself mentally composing my resignation letter. I never wrote one, however. For now, KWS needed my guiding hand. In a year or two I would turn it over to someone else.

CHAPTER 17

Now and then one of KWS's rangers or wildlife biologists would stop by my office to tell me about the new baby elephants they'd seen in one of our parks. I was always delighted to hear such news. Perhaps because the herds weren't as anxious and harassed, a small population boom was underway. To get a better sense of the elephants' overall population, KWS, with assistance from several conservation organizations, launched a countrywide elephant count during the first week of September 1991.

After my visit to the Amboseli elephants with Joyce, I took every possible opportunity to see the animals. I didn't want to miss this survey and one weekend flew to Tsavo to join the elephant counters. Meave came along, too, as she'd always enjoyed watching elephants. The trip would give us the chance to be together again in the field, sharing in our work as we used to do.

It was the kind of day that spoils those of us who live in Kenya: the sky a clear, cerulean blue, the sun hot and baking, and the earth smelling of smoke and dust. Iain and Oria Douglas-Hamilton were helping with the count, as were several of KWS's ranger pilots and Joyce. The surveyors divided the park into one-square-kilometer blocks. Planes with two people aboard then flew low over these blocks of land. The count could be tricky, as elephants are known to travel great distances and it was possible to count the same herds two or more times. And on overcast days cloud shadows can sometimes be mistaken for an elephant's bulk. But Iain and several of the others had counted elephants across the African continent and knew exactly what to look for.

"You might think you're looking at only a big, gray boulder," Iain explained, "but then the 'boulder' waggles its ears or makes a move of some sort, or you just sense an animated quality to it. And, of course, it's really an elephant."

We met Iain and his colleagues for lunch at the Voi River, where a herd of about a hundred elephants had gathered to bathe and drink.

"Look at all the babies," Meave said. There were several babies in the herd and like any babies, they soon had everyone's attention.

"They're having a remarkable comeback," I said. "There must be at least six here."

"If they can just be left alone for a few years," added Meave.

She was right. All it would take was some protection and time. It seemed very little to ask.

We watched from a distance as the baby elephants cavorted in the cool of the river's brown waters. They sucked up the liquid, then squirted it out, like children playing with straws, or ran giddily along the muddy banks, their backs glistening from their baths, playfully trunk-wrestling with each other. A couple of adolescent males started a pushing game, locking trunks and tusks and shoving to test who was the strongest. They clashed, separated, and clashed again, the pleasing sound of ivory against ivory drifting across the plains to us.

Joyce joined us at the picnic and guided us into the minds of the elephants, pointing out the social etiquette and hierarchy that prevails among a herd, even when elephants are drinking and bathing.

"We think there are about sixty-five hundred elephants now in Tsavo East," Joyce told us. "They're doing extremely well."

I was as surprised as anyone by that. When I started as director, there were barely five thousand elephants in this park—down from forty thousand in the 1970s. I doubted that the elephants in Tsavo would ever reach those proportions again, particularly given the number of farms and ranches that had sprouted up in the Taita Hills between the two Tsavos. But a population of ten thousand was certainly feasible and sustainable, given the park's resources. Were this latest crop of babies to survive, it wouldn't be long before the Tsavo elephants reached that number.

This was the kind of news I wanted to share with Kenya's citizens. They needed to know that the battle with the poachers was largely over and that Kenya had won. I wasn't at all sure that the average Kenyan realized this, and on our flight home I mulled over the best way to get the news out. I thought I might call a press conference once the elephant survey was complete. The public had seen plenty of photos of poachers being arrested and tusks being uncovered; they rarely saw scenes of elephants bathing and playing in the brown waters of a park's river, pictures of elephants just being elephants. Such photos would lack the drama of a shoot-out or an ivory bonfire, but they would represent what I hoped KWS would ultimately achieve: a return to calm and normalcy.

I jotted this idea down, planning to bring it up first thing when I was back at the office on Monday morning. Meave liked the idea, too. We'd had a terrific day together, our first in what felt like years. We'd laughed together and watched the elephants together, and returned home feeling quite content.

That contentment lasted barely one day. On Monday, September 9, 1991, KWS began to unravel. My diary tells it best: *Crisis! Have received a presidential directive to* reinstate *1,640 people to KWS—madness and I am* not *willing to do this for a variety of reasons. I am very discouraged and confused* . . .

My enemies had once again succeeded in persuading President Moi to change his mind. For the first time, I felt utterly and completely defeated. In my heart, I knew then that it would be virtually impossible to achieve our goals at KWS. There were simply too many political stumbling blocks in our way. Yet so many dreams and hopes—not just mine, but those of the people I had hired and of many Kenyan citizens—rested on KWS's success. I would have to try to undo this damage.

The news, of course, was all over the newspapers, which was humiliating for me. Reporters had been covering the story since KWS first announced that 1,640 employees had been sent away from KWS for the government to redeploy. We had tried to arrange everything within the guidelines of the Civil Service. It was never my intention to embarrass or dishonor any of our former employees, despite the fact that many had engaged in various criminal activities. However, the Civil Service Department had not treated them well after informing them that they had been "retired" from KWS. Consequently, ex-Wildlife employees had staged several protests against both the Civil Service and KWS. In my effort not to discredit these people, I did not tell the reporters the true reasons for their removal. Now, given that the general public knew about the World Bank and other foreign-aid loans, KWS simply looked cheap and mean-spirited.

The president's directive was a blow to KWS's overall morale as well. It would be dispiriting to have to take these people back, particularly those who had been in positions of authority. It would be dangerous, too, as they would return without a loss in rank, and some would be issued firearms. They would know which employees had given information about them, which posed a potential threat for those employees and jeopardized our entire security system.

I couldn't let any of this happen. From the minute I opened the directive, I decided there was only one course of action: to fight back.

I tried to get through to the president on the telephone immediately after learning of the directive, but it took several days. When we did finally talk, his voice was as cold as steel. He agreed, however, to a meeting. From my discussions with the minister of Tourism, Mr. Ngala, and others, I learned that the president and his advisers believed the old gossip: that I was staffing KWS with more Kikuyu than with people from other tribes. It was said that I was recruiting primarily Kikuyu rangers to set up a private army that would then overthrow the government.

That the president would believe any of this nonsense pained me more than I can say. Somehow I had to persuade him that the rumors were not true—and to subtly remind him that when I accepted this job, he had assured me that if I chose to get rid of four thousand employees, he would "back me to the hilt." I grabbed the list I had written, breaking down KWS employees by tribe, and headed off to the State House. I gave the list one quick glance and thought to myself, *Surely we are the most diverse of all government agencies.*

I hadn't been to the president's office in several months. The less visible I was, I had thought, the easier it would be for me and KWS to simply get on with our work. That tactic had not worked. Others had used my absence to poison our relationship.

Regardless of the circumstances, President Moi is always unfailingly polite. Although he wasn't particularly happy to see me on this occasion, he nevertheless greeted me at his office door and escorted me inside.

As I feared, he had been misled about my hiring practices at KWS. I attempted to persuade him that his information was incorrect, and, taking a deep breath, I showed him my list.

"As you can see, sir, there aren't more Kikuyu than people from other tribes," I said, pointing to the number and varieties of people. "Indeed, almost every tribe in the country is represented at KWS. I doubt the same can be said for any other government office."

President Moi scanned my list then laid it to one side.

"It looks impressive, Richard. But anyone can produce lists and figures like this."

His words momentarily deflated me but I pressed on, arguing that if we reinstated the corrupt employees, KWS would be ruined. And he knew these men were corrupt: I had shown him the reports documenting their illegal actions and activities. There might appear to be some disparities in our hiring, I acknowledged, but that had to do solely with our policy of finding the best person for the job. For instance, our crack antipoaching rangers came primarily from Kenya's northern desert tribes, as they were the best men for fighting the poachers. I also pointed out that the World Bank was watching how the government handled the staffing at KWS; our agency was deemed a "test case" to see whether Kenya could actually clean up its dishonest and inefficient Civil Service.

President Moi listened patiently to all I had to say. I concluded by urging him to keep the list.

"Look at it after I've left," I said, "and if you need, please send one of your representatives to KWS to make your own survey of our staff. I think you'll find the list is accurate."

"I'll look it over," he agreed.

"And if it's necessary, KWS will continue to pay the salaries of these former employees. I will not, however, have them back on KWS's premises," I said, explaining the problems I foresaw were they to return.

President Moi sighed but said nothing. We shook hands, and I turned and walked out the door. Several months would pass before I saw him again. During that time I remained absolutely firm on my last point: the 1,640 would not return to KWS.

President Moi's distrust had cut me to the quick. I was now operating under a cloud of suspicion and knew my every action and move would be scrutinized. Nothing I could do would prove my integrity and commitment. I would continue to act and make decisions as I always had, with the good of KWS and Kenya foremost in my mind.

And the elephants, too. It was sometimes easy to forget that they were the reason I had taken this job in the first place. They still needed protection. The CITES group was convening again in March 1992, and Zimbabwe was working hard to convince the delegates to remove the elephants from Appendix I so that the ivory trade could resume. The Zimbabweans and their supporters (primarily the former trading countries) argued that the ivory ban had not worked and that the only way to control the trade was by opening it up to full management. As always, they were wrong. Our survey demonstrated that the elephants were on the rebound in Kenya. But our security data showed that the ivory traders were simply waiting in the wings for the illegal trade to restart. If the Zimbabweans had their way, Kenya would once again have a poaching war on its hands.

Several southern African countries, including South Africa, were allied with Zimbabwe. I hoped to lure South Africa to our side before the CITES meeting and began actively lobbying the head of their National Parks Board, Robbie Robinson. I had met Robinson in the course of my duties and liked him immediately. Tall and energetic, he has a serious but friendly manner. And he loves wildlife.

We visited each other's parks. Robinson came to see Amboseli and its elephants, and I made sure Joyce was on hand to give him what I considered "the full treatment"—her tour of the elephant mind and behavior. I often did this for visiting dignitaries and found that they returned changed in mind and spirit. For instance, Joyce and I joined Baroness Lynda Chalker, then Britain's minister for Overseas Development, on one such tour. Britain had yet to agree to participate in the World Bank project, and I thought our elephants might help nudge Lynda to our side. That day, the elephants Joyce guided us to were in a state of heightened excitement, apparently because a young female was coming into her first heat. Several large males had moved into the vicinity and stood just beyond the edge of the herd, watching this female and each other. Suddenly, elephants were trumpeting and rumbling and pushing against each other all around our car. I could see that Lynda was absolutely petrified—and elated. I will never know if the show that the elephants put on was of help in our funding, but I knew that one senior British minister would probably never forget Kenya's elephants anyway.

Robbie was similarly moved and fascinated by Joyce's ability to get into the minds of the elephants. Afterward, he invited me to the crown jewel of South Africa's national parks, Kruger. This was my first trip to South Africa since the end of apartheid, and I was curious about what kind of progress the country had made.

I'm not sure what I expected to see in Johannesburg, where I traveled first. The hotels and restaurants were still dominated by white customers, while black South Africans waited on them. Johannesburg was utterly different from any other African city I had been to. The city was built by and for Europeans—only the vast sprawling slums, and so-called townships, were African. *The "white" or European element in everything is overwhelming.* I wrote in my diary. *The sky is African but the town, roads, and feel is so unlike anything I have seen before.* The same held true at the small airport built at the entrance to the Kruger National Park, which struck me as being rather like a Hollywood movie set. Several groups of tourists had arrived and were met by young, bronzed-faced men in khaki shorts and shirts unbuttoned to show their chest hair. They loaded luggage and clients into their topless Land Rovers, adjusted their sunglasses over their blue eyes, and roared off into the bush.

Robbie and his wife, Joh, had flown from Johannesburg with me on a South African Airways flight and we were met by the chief warden and some of the park's staff.

Kruger is a large park, close to Tsavo in size. Unlike Tsavo, however, it is actively managed, meaning that certain animals, primarily buffaloes and elephants, are culled if their populations reach certain levels. Robbie thought I was overly sentimental about elephants and told me so several times. Like many wildlife authorities in South Africa, he was proud of his country's managed parks and modern wildlife-management strategies—including the culling operations. The park had a state-of-the-art abattoir for killing, butchering, and canning the different animals, and he took me to see it.

Housed in a large, concrete warehouse, the interior of the abattoir was glistening white. It was fully equipped with cranes and carving hooks for lifting the carcasses, hydraulic hoses for washing out the rooms after the butchery, and meat-processing facilities. A team of white men in shorts and white gum boots, blood stains up to their armpits, were busy preparing the meat and hides of forty-five recently culled buffalo. They worked efficiently, despite the blood and gore. The hides and tinned meat would be sold, Robbie explained, and the proceeds used for the park.

I watched for a while impressed by the size and scale of the operation but appalled that this was what wildlife "management" in the late-twentieth century had come to. Conservationists who once used to talk about the value simply of protecting nature in and of itself were now saying that wildlife and lands had to "pay" their way to survive; that unless they made money, like a factory or business enterprise, they could not expect to endure. To me this has always been a wrongheaded argument. If wildlife and wilderness were regarded solely as items that generate money, their days were surely numbered. Inevitably, someone would find a way to use them to make more money from them than protecting them does. I fear that conservationists who use bottom-line reasoning as the key argument for saving the animals they love are actually dooming them to extinction.

I tried not to show it, but the abattoir made my heart sink. The heads, hides, blood, and bodies of the buffalo were scattered about; the place was a house of horrors. Robbie and the staff talked with tremendous pride about their use of the game—but showed absolutely no sign that they knew the remains were once living creatures. Dead elephant carcasses were brought into this cold, concrete room, only to end up canned, like tuna, their tusks removed and stored (if not for the ivory ban, these would have been sold). It was a sad, shameful end for such magnificent, intelligent creatures. I found being in the abattoir nearly as hard as being in the ivory warehouse in Nairobi, and I was glad when our tour ended and we walked back out into the South African sunshine.

Robbie insisted that the culling did not affect the surviving elephants negatively in any way. Knowing how intelligent they are, and what prodigiously long memories they have, I found this difficult to believe and decided to watch the Kruger elephants closely. I was curious about how they reacted to people—and to helicopters. The rangers culled the elephants by herding them with helicopters and shooting drug-laced darts into them. The drug only paralyzes the elephants, so that their meat doesn't spoil. Later, the rangers arrive in Land Rovers, finish off the prostrate animals with gunshots, and haul their carcasses to the abattoir.

Since Robbie and his wife proposed to show me Kruger via helicopter, I would have ample opportunity to see just how the elephants responded to the sound of the rotor blades. Over the next few days, we flew over golden savannas and green plains from one end of Kruger to the other. There were several large herds of elephants, and Robbie always had the pilot fly down low so that we could get a close look. It was immediately clear to me that the noise of our helicopter terrified the elephants. They could hear us from about two miles away, and as soon as they did they ran off in a panic.

The South African rangers always killed every elephant in the herds they culled (except for the youngest babies, which they sold to zoos or game reserves, after chaining them to the dead adults to keep them from running away while trucks were brought in to move them), so that theoretically there would be no traumatized survivors. However, I had learned from Joyce that it is impossible to kill every elephant in a herd because some members are invariably off visiting relatives in other herds. Elephants also communicate by long-distance rumbles. During a cull they surely spread the news of their terror and distress far and wide. I'm certain other elephants in the park know that the cull is happening, that they are "told" about it as it is underway. And elephants are aware of death. There are frequent reports of elephants picking up and fondling the bones of dead family members, touching their remains gently with their trunks, or covering dead elephants with branches. As we flew over these panicked Kruger Park herds, I was sure the elephants associated the noise of the rotor blades with fear and death. That was why they always ran.

At first, I said nothing to Robbie and his wife about what I had observed. But after observing this same behavior several times, I said, "Look at that herd. Have you noticed that every elephant we come across in this park runs away even if it's miles from us? Just at the sound of the thrashing blades?"

Robbie raised an eyebrow but said nothing.

At dinner that evening, he sighed when I raised the issue again.

"Yes. I did notice that after you pointed it out," he said. "And yes, it troubles me."

I said little more, but not long thereafter Robbie stopped the culling operations in Kruger, and they have not since been resumed.

Robbie and I discussed the ivory ban as well. I wanted South Africa's support to keep the ban in place; and while I felt that Robbie was leaning in my direction, I could not get a firm commitment from him.

"Well, Richard, these types of decisions are hot potatoes. You know that."

"Yes, but now would be an excellent time for South Africa to break away from the pack, to stand apart from Zimbabwe. Your country has a new leader, Nelson Mandela. It strikes me as a great opportunity to forge a new wildlife policy as well," I said.

Robbie laughed. "You can be persuasive. I might do it on my own, but it's not a unilateral decision."

I understood and took Robbie's words as a hint that I would have to develop a different strategy to keep the elephants on Appendix I. We could not count on the South Africans to jump ship and join us.

I'm a firm believer in the expression "nothing ventured, nothing gained." Given that the South Africans would not switch sides, I decided to try to win over the Zimbabweans. It would have been a real coup. And it might have persuaded the South Africans to change their stance.

My relationship with Zimbabwe and its conservation leaders had always been strained at best. However, I believed that we should be able to sit down and talk about our differences. I also continued to hope that they would see the ivory ban as a solution to an African problem, and one that they as Africans should be concerned about as well.

On my way home from South Africa, I stopped in Zimbabwe and met with several conservation organizations and government officials. They were invariably polite toward me and also invariably cool toward my proposal. They continued to see ivory as money. They had sold ivory (and elephant meat from culling operations, like those used by the South Africans) to support their parks in the past, and they had no intention of changing their practice. One official bragged to me that they had several tons of ivory stored in a warehouse. And one day, he added, they would sell it.

Over and over again I was told that this was the only way to make conservation work in Africa. The parks and animals had to pay their own way—even if the "pay" meant with their lives.

I was all in favor of parks earning their keep. Indeed, that was what I intended to achieve in Kenya: establish a park system that supported itself and made a profit. I did not think, though, that it was necessary to sacrifice the animals to reach this goal. It could be attained via tourism and tourist dollars, which was a far wiser and more humane conservation method. If tourists knew that most of the money they spent in the parks was used to preserve the land and animals they loved, they would most likely not begrudge paying higher fees. It would also give visitors a sense of participating in saving the animals. And it spread the burden of preservation costs to others beyond Kenya's borders.

This latter point is particularly important and bears repeating. Kenya has set aside land that amounts to nearly one-quarter of its total area, yet it is expected to shoulder alone the expense of preserving its wildlife and wilderness. No developed country has taken such vast tracts of land away from its citizens. For Kenya to keep these parks intact, conservationists, wildlife enthusiasts, and anyone who wants to see elephants and lions continue to roam free must share in the costs. And tourism is one of the best ways to do this.

That was what I told the Zimbabweans. They listened politely but declined my invitation to join us in support of Appendix I. They saw themselves as separate from the rest of Africa and at war against the world; several jutted out their chins and said they would defy the ivory ban.

Fortunately, Kenyans continued to support the ban. On what was now known as "Elephant Day"—the day we had burned the ivory— Kenya's newspapers printed strong editorials defending that decision. "Kenya can today reflect back with pride and have the last laugh at those who assumed that the decision to burn ivory was just a wild theatre staged for publicity," wrote a writer for the *Standard*. "Today, we can no longer be worried as we were three years ago that our elephants would cease to exist. We are now confident that elephants have a future."

With Kenyans standing firm on the ban—as well as the Tanzanians and Ugandans—I, too, felt confident. We would find a way to stop the Zimbabweans and keep the ivory ban in place.

❖ ❖ ❖

I've never lived my life to be popular or made decisions that were designed to curry favor. Nevertheless, the strong editorial support for KWS's protection of the elephants pleased me. It kept the issue in the spotlight and reminded Kenyans of the value of their wildlife and National Parks. This was especially crucial given that more letters to the editor and news articles were appearing about the damage wild animals—particularly elephants—were wreaking on villagers. And, of course, there were also fewer reports about elephants being killed by poachers, since KWS rangers had nearly put an end to this activity.

The newspaper headlines often used a slang expression for the elephant, "Jumbo." Beginning in the latter half of 1991 and well into 1992, it became unfortunately all too common to read such headlines as JUMBOS GO ON THE RAMPAGE, or JUMBOS WREAK HAVOC. The news story would then quote bereaved people, telling of the horror of having one or more elephants trample their crops or, worse, kill their wife, husband, or child. Just as I had feared they would be, such incidents were on the rise. And while KWS's elephant team was doing its best testing and building fences and helping to design and test a contraceptive for elephants, we were far from ready to deal with this problem countrywide.

Yet that was exactly what KWS was expected to do. All wildlife matters throughout Kenya's 270,000 square miles were our concern. It was difficult enough to look after the animals inside the parks, let alone those outside park boundaries. I felt that it was initially more important to secure the parks and to stop the elephants from killing people within them. Once we had solved these two problems, we could turn our attention to the animals beyond the parks' borders.

Our fencing program was making steady, if slow, progress. We had installed fences of various designs along large cattle ranches on the Laikipia Plateau near Mount Kenya. Some ranches were owned by white Kenyans, others by indigenous Kenyan businessmen. They were wealthy individuals with the means and personnel at hand to make sure the fences were monitored and maintained when the KWS team wasn't present.

Electric fences, powered with solar batteries, proved to be the most cost-effective, and we built several lengthy fences of varying designs. A good jolt kept most elephants at bay. Given how intelligent elephants are, however, it wasn't a surprise that certain individual elephants quickly learned how to beat the system. Some used their tusks (which are poor conductors of electricity) to break the wires; others pushed over the fence posts with their back feet; and some especially smart elephants placed branches on the wires, causing a short circuit. One of the most effective fences I saw stood only eighteen inches off the ground. It consisted of a series of waving wires that touched the elephant below the knees, giving the animal a shock. The lowness of the fence allowed other animals to pass through unscathed, making it a good design for areas where we had migratory game.

By late 1991, my team had completed its fencing survey and reported that we needed to install almost one thousand miles of barriers, at a cost of $15 million dollars. The length of fencing and cost were staggering, but it was clear from newspaper and ranger reports that unless these fences were constructed, conflicts between humans and wildlife would only escalate. Ultimately, the animals would lose.

Several times I told reporters about our fencing tests and plans. We were moving as fast as we could, I explained, and said that in January 1992 we would begin building barriers in the Taita Hills—the area between the two Tsavos—where there seemed to be elephant-people conflicts nearly every week. Naturally, people who had just lost their crops or a loved one to an elephant didn't want to hear about what we were *going* to do. They wanted something done now. And people who lived elsewhere and who were also endangered by elephants wanted a fence built there and not in the Taita Hills.

I asked people for patience, although I knew that were I in their shoes, I would have none. Nevertheless, to succeed, this kind of fencing project had to proceed according to a plan. We now had that plan and were ready to implement it. And once the fences began going up, I was sure that Kenyans would stay on our—and the elephants'—side.

CHAPTER 18

Increasingly, my greatest hopes for KWS were pinned on the World Bank loan and on donor aid. The first $60.5 million payment was scheduled to arrive in April 1992, which was now only a few months away. These funds would enable us to make essential improvements in the National Parks and other conservation areas. I hoped that the infusion of money for roads, new buildings, and vehicles would vindicate KWS, and that the subterfuge of disgruntled politicians would end once and for all.

I stayed as far away from the State House as possible throughout the latter part of 1991, and therefore I was not privy to many of the changes underway in the government. I was thus as surprised as any person on the street when the newspapers suddenly announced that Kenya was going to switch from being a single-party state, run solely by the Kenya Africa National Union (KANU), to one with numerous political parties. A special conference of delegates from KANU had met in early December, and had voted to open up the country's political system. Lobbying by the American and German ambassadors in particular, along with the street demonstrations by Kenyans demanding change, had paid off. Kenya was on its way to becoming more of a democracy. It was a startling and enormous change, and everywhere one went people were busy discussing the new political parties that were quickly being formed and their candidates.

Equally surprising, some officials were taken into custody for further questioning about their possible links to the 1990 assassination of Kenya's foreign minister, Dr. Robert John Ouko. Dr. Ouko had been a well-liked and effective leader; and the circumstances of his assassination in February 1990 have, even to this day, yet to be explained. His burned and mutilated body was found only two miles from his family farm near Kisumu in western Kenya. The grisliness of his death and the rather casual, almost indifferent, official reaction to this terrible crime suggested that someone in the higher reaches of the government had had a hand in it. I had met Dr. Ouko a few times and always admired his spirit and energy. He was full of ideas for bettering Kenya and was working hard to improve Kenya's relations with the West.

Among his own tribe, the Luo, Dr. Ouko's assassination opened an old wound. In 1960, another talented leader, Tom Mboya, was gunned down on the streets of Nairobi. His assassins were never found; however, they were thought to be connected to the then Kikuyu-run government. After Ouko's murder, Luo and many prodemocracy activists throughout Kenya took to the streets in protest.

Britain and the United States had also taken a dim view of Dr. Ouko's death. Their representatives suggested that economic aid might be suspended unless Kenya undertook a full investigation. President Moi said he would "leave no stone unturned" in searching for the killers, and asked detectives from New Scotland Yard to assist. The government also appointed a presidential commission, headed by a respected jurist, to collect testimony from people who might shed light on the assassination. Neither the Scotland Yard detectives nor the Ouko Commission were given as free a hand as they would have liked, however. The commission was disbanded before it could render an opinion. And the Scotland Yard officers reported that they had been unable to interview a cabinet minister, Nicholas Biwott, which of course created media speculation. Mr. Hezekiah Oyugi, then the permanent secretary for Provincial Administration and Internal Security, also was caught up in the investigation. Both men were arrested and temporarily removed from office but subsequently were released for lack of evidence—a puzzling series of actions. No one was ever indicted for the crime.

Although the murder was never solved, I believe that the protests and media attention emboldened the prodemocracy movement. In some important respects, they were also helpful to organizations like KWS. We needed a press that exposed attempts by politically powerful men seeking to influence our program. Efforts to influence KWS procurement and contract awards would certainly be made, and I would have to fight hard to combat them. My hope was that the World Bank, through its Nairobi office, would be a key supporter; after all, Kenya had agreed to build a wildlife organization following the rules and guidelines developed jointly by the government and the bank. The bank had to see to it that Kenya played by those rules. If government officials tried to misuse the donor funds, the World Bank, as the lead donor, would, I hoped, suspend its disbursements—just as the United States and others had withheld assistance until Kenya agreed to become more democratic. Indeed, the bank had already demonstrated that it could stand firm if it needed to.

A minister in the government had announced that a portion of the Tsavo National Park was to be given over for the settlement of landless peasants. I understood the needs of these people and the desire of the government to alleviate their problems. The amount of land to be appropriated was not excessive, and because Tsavo was so large it could have easily survived. However, the announcement could not have come at a worse time: just when the bank was giving final approval of the loan for KWS. I also feared that unless we complained, this first appropriation of land would only be the first of many. In the end I had to do little. The representatives of the bank were persuaded that this proposal contravened the agreement between the donors and the government on protecting National Parks and took a firm stand. Much to my relief the land excision proposal was withdrawn.

The bank's action encouraged me greatly. I hoped that the bank and other donors would maintain their principled position, though I also expected that they would soon be challenged for interfering in Kenya's domestic affairs.

The early 1990s were a lively and turbulent time in Kenya. People felt emboldened to express themselves, and there were demonstrations and riots almost weekly, which did little to help Kenya's tourism but were fully understandable given the long years of political repression. I began to wonder if KANU—President Moi's party—would win the next round of elections, which were scheduled for the fall of 1992, a little less than a year away. Several of my friends were joining the new political parties that had sprung up, and I watched them with some envy. They were in high spirits, full of ideas and enthusiasm for the challenge of the moment. Directing KWS over the last year, had often given me the same feeling. I reveled in the hard-charging climate; and despite the setbacks, I was determined to keep KWS moving forward at a similar tempo. I knew this would be possible only if we could minimize or completely avoid political meddling and interference.

Christmas came and went. My family and I gathered at our Lamu Island home as usual, but like the year before, I was not in a holiday mood. The government's concern about the former 1,640 KWS employees had waned of late, but only because the multiparty issue was of far greater concern. Kenyans sensed an opportunity to put new leaders in power; and, for once, KANU seemed to be facing quite serious competition for leadership. I hadn't been summoned to the State House for some time, other than to meet Britain's Prince Philip, at his request. His invitation and private audience with me had clearly annoyed some members of our government, but I viewed it as an opportunity to beat the drums once again on the elephants' behalf. Prince Philip is a well-known and ardent conservationist and agreed that the elephants should remain on Appendix I. His backing would help, as the CITES delegates were to meet in Japan in March—and the hot topic, once again, was what to do about the African elephant.

Over the next two months I lobbied actively for the elephants. I knew we had to build a strong coalition of supporters because it appeared increasingly unlikely that South Africa and Zimbabwe would change their stance. They had offered a kind of compromise or at least they were trying to give the appearance of offering one. Instead of asking that the ban be lifted in its entirety, they suggested it be lifted only for those countries that could demonstrate they were managing their elephant populations effectively. Supposedly, Zimbabwe, South Africa, Botswana, and Namibia fit this description, although it was not clear who would define what "effective management" was. These four countries suggested that only trade in meat and hides be allowed. They relied on the money such trades brought, they said, to finance their parks and were being unfairly punished for a problem—rampant poaching—they did not have. Zimbabwe, however, wanted the elephant down listed altogether, so that it could once again trade ivory.

I was strongly opposed to any compromise. It would place the elephants in every other African country in jeopardy, and it was certain to set off a new round of poaching and on a massive scale. Even were only elephant hides and meat allowed to be sold, poachers would soon try to get in on the action, hiding the ivory for a speculative profit down the line. And if Zimbabwe had its way and was allowed to trade in ivory, poachers in East Africa were certain to find a way to sell their illegal ivory there, just as they had when CITES had attempted to regulate the trade through quotas. Indeed, there were already signs that poachers were betting that the trade would begin again. On the black market, the price for ivory had doubled from $5 to $10 a pound. And in Japan, just before the CITES meeting opened, officials confiscated twenty-seven ivory tusks from a ship docked at Kobe Harbor.

All this convinced me there was only one way to assure that there would be no poaching and no questionable ivory: having no trade at all—ever. I hoped I could persuade the other African countries, including those that wanted some form of trade, that a united African stand behind keeping the elephants on Appendix I was best for all.

I went to Kyoto at the beginning of March 1991, accompanied by a small KWS delegation that included Joyce, Richard Bagine—an expert on insects—and Christine Kabuye, a leading botanical taxonomist. Several South African conservationists attended the meeting, as did Rowan Martin, my nemesis from Zimbabwe. Shortly after spotting me and giving me a cool hello, Martin was sneering to everyone within hearing range about what a "sentimentalist" I had become.

"Leakey has gone completely soft," I heard him say. "He's even more of a bunny hugger now."

Martin's attitude had always irritated me. He spoke only of Zimbabwe's needs, not those of Africa as a whole. So long as people like Martin represented their countries, we would never be able to develop a pan-African position on the needs and problems of the elephants—or on any other issues for that matter.

My first day in Kyoto was an eye-opener. This was my first CITES meeting; I decided right there and then that it would be my last. It seemed to have less to do with conservation than with people building careers or trying to make a name for themselves. There was lots of back-slapping, posturing, and politicking. I am not a gregarious person. I don't go out to parties in Nairobi or belong to any clubs. Meave and I prefer having small dinners at our home with close friends. Here in this sea of chattering, chain-smoking conservationists, I felt ill at ease; these were not people I would have invited home.

When the meeting got underway the next day, I decided to take an aggressive stance. From the outset it was apparent that we would have to defend our position on elephants. Japan, which was hosting the CITES meeting, seemed persuaded that the resumption of the elephant-ivory trade would be a good thing. I used every possible opportunity to challenge the Zimbabwean and Southern African efforts to renew trade.

"The elephant has had only two and a half years of protection, and we're going to drop that protection now? It's because of that protection that our elephants are recovering in Kenya. For the first time in many years, we're beginning to see a small increase in our population. We're even seeing elephants in places they have avoided for years. The ivory ban has been a success for the elephant. And there's worldwide public support for it. Let's not tamper with it.

"I know my good friends from Zimbabwe and South Africa believe that they can control a limited trade. But experience shows that there is no such thing as a limited trade. And if the trade resumes and poaching begins again—which it will—elephants in many parts of Africa will disappear permanently. Make no mistake: Dollars for Zimbabwe ivory mean bullets and death for the rest of Africa's elephants."

Rowan Martin charged back hard, arguing that if East African countries couldn't manage their elephants, then at least they should have the decency to stand out of the way of those countries that could."

The exchanges were often unpleasant. I belittled and derided the arguments put forward by the southern African countries, describing them as selfish and provincial. Every argument they put forward, I was quick to rebut—sometimes with what I hoped was withering sarcasm. I may have succeeded a little too well. Out of the corner of my eye, I noticed my three Kenyan companions sinking lower and lower in their seats. And once, when I was lambasting Zimbabwe, Joyce slipped out of the hall, apparently appalled by my remarks about some of her professional friends and colleagues.

Everyone feels I was too rough on the southern Africans, I noted with some surprise in my diary that night. *I don't think so. My hope for a pan-African position is clearly not possible and I have to decide whether to go for a compromise or stick to Appendix I. There is a rather unfortunate lack of good advice or sounding boards. My closest friends seem to favor a gentle approach. My sense is to be very clear and direct.*

For the next two days I stuck to my guns, gambling that my hardline approach, as unpleasant as it was, would win. And it did. The proposal to partially down list the elephant was defeated by a vote of sixty-six to eleven, sending a strong message to the Zimbabweans and other southern African countries about the folly of their ideas.

We had won, but it wasn't a joyful victory. No one wanted to celebrate. After the vote I retreated to my hotel room alone, feeling very down. Joyce had told me that some of my remarks had embarrassed people and that I been a "little too rough," as one put it. Astonishingly, some even said that they felt sorry for the southern African countries, particularly Zimbabwe.

"They're trying hard to manage their elephants in a sustainable way and for that, they're punished," one fellow told me. "They have to carry the burden of the rest of Africa. You saw to that."

I could only shake my head. Less than three years earlier, everyone had agreed that the African elephant was in dire straits and that an ivory ban was absolutely necessary. Now some of these same people thought that the elephant—after such a short pause in the killing—was "saved." Zimbabwe was the new underdog, and I had given it a public whipping. I may have helped save the elephants, but I had not made any friends. In my diary, I wrote:

I was the big "hope" to save the elephants, I am now the "big bully" or bad guy for having done so. Even JHP [Joyce] seems to be uneasy and embarrassed.

I might be director of the Kenyan Wildlife Service, but I still did not belong with the professional wildlife-conservation community. I was now pretty sure that I would never want to.

A few weeks before leaving for the CITES meeting, I received bad news from the Masai Mara: a gang of bandits had attacked, beaten, and robbed a group of American tourists. Fortunately the thieves had not killed or severely injured anyone; but the tourists, who had been left stranded in the bush, far from their lodge, were understandably terrified. We suspected that the bandits had come from neighboring Tanzania and had retreated back across the border. The same armed gangsters had attacked four German visitors at a luxury tented camp inside the reserve in November, stealing all their possessions. And only a week before I departed for CITES, the gang struck again twice, ambushing, beating, and robbing two groups of British and Austrian tourists. In the latter attack, the thugs (who were dressed in police uniforms) killed the group's guide.

The American, German, and British embassies soon announced travel advisories, recommending that tourists exercise extra caution when visiting the Masai Mara or that they postpone their trips to the reserve. Given the Mara's popularity—it was always at the top of every visitor's list of places to visit in Kenya—the travel advisories were devastating to the tourism industry, yet there was little that I could do about it. Responsibility for the Mara's security resided with the Narok County Council; it hired and trained the reserve's guards and rangers.

Of course, had KWS been on the job, the second and third attacks would never have happened. Our men would have caught the bandits. This argued for raising yet again an issue I had raised several times with the government: turning the Mara over to KWS.

Despite my prodding, the Narok County Council had done nothing to improve the management of the reserve. Tourist vans were still being allowed to drive wherever they wanted, and council members continued to approve the construction of new lodges. Nor had they taken any steps to ensure the security of the tourists. All I got from the county council were blunt demands for "their share" of the World Bank money. They knew that for the first five years, we were giving priority to parks such as Tsavo, Nakuru, Amboseli, and Nairobi—places over which we could exercise tight financial control. I had wanted to include the Mara on that list but had told the council, on several occasions, that I would not do so until either they agreed to let KWS, or an outside firm, manage the reserve. I had repeatedly urged the government to send a high-ranking representative to explain to the council that KWS wasn't prejudiced against the Maasai and the Mara but had developed a government-approved policy to enhance tourism. The official could stress how important the Mara was to the nation as a whole and emphasize that by joining in KWS's plans, the council and the Maasai people would ultimately benefit from them.

Unfortunately, the council, in part through their local member of Parliament, William Ntimama, had considerable influence over government policy, and nobody wanted to deal head-on with these issues. A corrupt system was being sustained. As a result, the problems in the Mara were reflecting badly on Kenya's image.

The new round of gangster attacks and the resulting travel advisories gave me fresh ammunition. Just before leaving for the CITES conference, I arranged a hasty meeting with the minister of Tourism, Noah Katana Ngala.

"You know how bad the situation is in the Mara. And look what it is doing to our tourism industry. Something has to change—you know that and the rest of the ministers know that. Let's not waste time. Get KWS the authorization to make the Mara secure."

Ngala hesitated. "Well, it is really up to the county council . . ."

"And look at the job they're doing. It's ridiculous. There can't be more than one or two gangs involved. Every one of their actions suggests that they are amateurs. A decent security force would have hauled them in months ago. What are we waiting for? While we wait for the council to do something, the bandits will strike again. And how long will it then take for Kenya's tourism industry to recover?"

"Well, you're right about that, Richard. It's just a very hot political issue, as you know. The council can be very tough."

"But the government should be even tougher. This is not just a political issue; it is a *national* issue. And it's time someone in the government brought that to the Masai's attention."

"That's true, but the council will surely see this as a first step to take over the Mara," he warned. "And they will fight you to the death over that, Richard."

"Perhaps. But we need to start making decisions that benefit all of Kenya. The Maasai view the Mara as their own private kingdom, but it's not—it's part of Kenya. And all of us—including the Maasai and the county council—need to start thinking of Kenya first. It's the only way our country will progress."

Ngala agreed; he would bring up the matter with the president and his ministerial colleagues. A few weeks later, at the end of March, over protests from the Narok County Council (which continued to insist that its own personnel would find the bandits), the government ordered a joint team of KWS security forces and police into the Mara.

"The problem is not solved, but it can be solved and it *will* be solved," I said at a meeting of Kenya's organization of tour operators when news of the deployment was released. "We've put 104 security personnel into the reserve, and that includes 44 of our best KWS men." Bashir had ordered some of the men be posted at twenty-four observation stations throughout the Mara; others would patrol in vehicles and on foot, with air support.

"You can be sure we will find these bandits and bring them to justice."

The actual operation was somewhat more complicated because our undercover agents learned that the gangs (there were two involved in the attacks) came, as we had suspected, from Tanzania. The bandits had also terrorized tourists and a team of research scientists there. In one instance, they had even attacked the tourists with poison arrows and killed a young man. It didn't take much effort to persuade our Tanzanian neighbors to allow a special joint cross-border operation. The gang members were little more than village thugs and were easily found and apprehended.

We played up their arrest in the Kenyan newspapers, as I wanted to be sure that the Americans, British, and Germans knew of our efforts to make the Mara safe. By late April 1992, the latter two countries lifted their travel advisories. The Americans were more cautious, saying that there was too much overall unrest in the country to remove the warning.

Violence against tourists anywhere always gets ample media coverage. The risks of an attack in Kenya were very low; but after reading stories in the *New York Times* and other papers, many chose to go on safari somewhere else.

There was, however, some substance to their worries. Nairobi continued to experience political demonstrations, and some of them had exploded into riots close to the large tourist hotels. Even more alarming, a rash of "ethnic clashes" had broken out around the country. Although, as I've explained, Kenya has its share of tribalism, it rarely degenerates to the point where one tribe attacks and kills members of another, as happens so tragically elsewhere in Africa. Yet now, almost monthly, there were reports from the rural areas of tribes viciously attacking each other.

Most of these incidents occurred in the Rift Valley and northwestern Kenya and involved Kalenjin or Maasai attacking Kikuyu or vice versa. During the late phase of British rule in Kenya and during the early post-independence years when Kenyatta was in power, many Kikuyu farmers had bought their land from their neighbors and these neighbors were now attacking them. Many Kenyan professionals—doctors, teachers, lawyers, and businessmen—were Kikuyu. Some had Maasai or Kalenjin spouses, but none of this helped them. According to news accounts, they were being ordered to move back to "Kikuyuland." And if they didn't, the other tribes ganged up on them, attacking with spears and bows and arrows, and burning Kikuyu homes, farms, and businesses. Many were killed and badly injured in these brutal attacks, and of course, they lost all their worldly possessions. By April 1992, the death toll had risen to more than sixty people.

Because the attackers were wielding essentially nineteenth-century weapons, the raids appeared to be grassroots, spur-of-the-moment affairs. It looked as if tribes were settling old scores. Something about the attacks, however, made me doubt that this was the case, for they began to occur shortly after KANU announced that the next elections would be open to all political parties. President Moi and the government had often warned that if Kenya became more democratic, allowing multiple parties to compete, the country would dissolve into tribal warfare. The clashes suggested that the government had been right. Further, by chasing the Kikuyu out of their provinces, the Kalenjin and Maasai were ensuring that they would dominate the elections on their home turf. Most of the people in these two tribes continued to ally themselves with KANU, the president's party. Their attacks were one way of solidifying KANU's power. Rather than being a grassroots uprising, in other words, I suspected that the tribal clashes were part of some strategy, particularly since the government was curiously silent on the subject. Not once did a high government official speak out against the aggressors. It almost seemed as if the government wanted the country to slide into tribal warfare. Officials could then point their fingers at the American Embassy and say, "We told you this would happen."

Others agreed with my assessment, but took it a step further. Oginga Odinga, a respected leader of one of the new parties, actually accused the government (including KWS) of harboring terrorist groups that trained people to take part in the clashes. He claimed that the training took place in the Mara. Odinga made his charges to a newspaper reporter, and I replied by telling reporters that his accusation was rubbish.

"However," I added, "it may be that there are terrorist groups in Kenya doing this kind of training."

I found the entire business exceedingly unsavory. The clashes, plus a slew of recent human-rights violations, made me wonder yet again whether I shouldn't quit my post and join one of the new parties. Critical as it was to save the elephants and preserve Kenya's parks, I was increasingly torn up about what was happening to Kenya's citizens. More people needed to speak out on their behalf. The only ones who truly did so were members of the clergy, and several of them had received severe beatings at the hands of the police.

I wasn't the only one thinking of changing careers. In May, David Mwiraria gave notice that he would be leaving KWS in June to join the Democratic Party. David had been one of my chief sounding boards over the previous three years and had guided me through many sticky moments with the Civil Service. I would miss him. And I envied him. He was following his conscience, and his move gave mine an even bigger twinge.

Nevertheless, I continued to feel that staying at KWS's helm was the right thing to do for the time being. I had also found an indirect way to participate in the political changes. Through friends, I was able to solicit financial contributions to the Democratic Party. My daughter, Samira, was an active volunteer with the party, helping with the campaign literature. I am sure that the intelligence services were watching me closely, and I knew that if I went too far I would be sacked from KWS.

In August 1992, I thought that moment had arrived. Philip Mbithi, the head of the Civil Service and a staunch KANU loyalist, summoned me to his office. I was instantly struck by the lack of warmth in his greeting. Mbithi gazed at me stonily and announced that I was going to be fired that afternoon. I didn't think that KANU had actually found any hard evidence about my activities on behalf of the new Democratic Party, so I wondered what on earth it was that they knew. Mbithi accused me of having personally flown a KWS plane to Koobi Fora with leaders from another political party where we supposedly discussed plans to overthrow the government. He added that many government leaders were afraid of KWS because of its strengths in intelligence, communications, and mobility, not to mention its national and international reputation, access to enormous funds, and the loyalty of its men to me.

All of this was so unexpected that I laughed, then quickly apologized. "It's not that I don't take your charges seriously," I said to Mbithi, "but all of this is absurd."

I had never even met the key political figure I was supposed to have taken to Koobi Fora, and the aircraft I was accused of flying had been grounded for the last six weeks. Nor had I been to Koobi Fora in the previous two months. As to the rest of his charges, I could only tell him what I had told the government before. "How can the government be afraid of a service with less than five hundred armed men?

Mbithi listened carefully to my reply. "Well, Richard, these new political parties and this democracy have everyone upset. There's a lot of paranoia in the higher offices now. No one knows who to trust. I believe what you're telling me. You won't be sacked."

"It won't trouble me in the least if I am," I replied. "I might even join another political party. I've been asked already but have turned them down."

"I'm sure everyone wants you to stay at KWS," he said, trying to smooth things over.

The accusation, Mbithi then told me, had come from a member of Parliament. I was not surprised. This member had not been in the least happy that KWS's security forces had been ordered into the Mara. He viewed it as part of KWS's efforts to take over the Mara entirely. And he was right. I thought that if KWS could successfully prove itself in this area, I might be in a better position to argue for even more control over the reserve.

That night I did something I had not done in a long while. I telephoned President Moi. The member of Parliament had made his accusation directly to the president, Mbithi informed me, and I wanted to clear the air.

President Moi sounded pleasantly surprised to hear my voice. I was sure that Mbithi had already told him that the story was incorrect.

"I've heard that I've been accused of joining your opponents at Turkana," I said.

President Moi chuckled. "Well, there have been some stories circulating."

"It's a completely ludicrous idea," I said, explaining that I had not even met some of the people I was supposed to have flown to Koobi Fora. "I'm surprised it was given any credence."

"Well, Richard, we are living in rough times now. Everyone wants to win, and everyone is telling lies because nothing is certain. In politics you must always be careful whom you trust."

I agreed. We wished each other well and rang off. I sat by the phone for a minute, thinking over our conversation. We saw each other so seldom now that it was hard to know how to judge his comments. But I took his last remark as a warning. The government no longer trusted me.

CHAPTER 19

I knew that the director of the Kenya Wildlife Service had little business being so keenly interested in the new opposition political parties then developing in our country. However, these parties seemed to offer the best chance for ushering in critical changes in the way the country was governed and particularly for ending its long history of corruption. I thought they might help make the government more responsible and responsive to its citizens. I found myself torn—wanting to participate but not wanting to let the unfolding political drama distract me from my job.

I certainly intended and expected to support whoever won the next elections. Bringing about change through revolution and violence was not something I supported, and the rumors that I was using KWS in this way were completely ridiculous. Far too many other African countries, such as Ethiopia and Angola, had gone down this sad path and were now shadows of their former selves. Their economics were ruined; their people, who had endured great suffering and atrocities, had barely enough to eat. Many had fled, joining the sea of international refugees. This was not a fate I wanted for Kenya and its people.

As much as I abhorred the rumors about me, I did not set out deliberately to prove they were false. I believed that my actions on behalf of Kenya and KWS would speak for themselves.

Only three years before, when I had first taken office, KWS's rangers were regarded as a laughable "armed force" by the police and military. Now, however, we had highly trained and equipped security units. Much of the credit for the turnaround goes to Bashir, who commanded our men with a firm hand. Because of him, I never worried that KWS armed units would stray beyond their mandate to deal with poachers and security within the parks. Our men were well disciplined, well trained, well paid, and all of them were proud to wear the new uniforms that Bashir had designed. Our logo, displayed on the uniforms as well as on vehicles, stationery, and signage shows a stylized mother and calf elephant.

Appearances and discipline weren't the only improvements. KWS rangers also had far better weapons. In addition to automatic rifles, I had secured some night-vision equipment. One of the difficulties in dealing with poachers and bandits in the vast tracts of bush, such as in Tsavo, is in finding them. The terrain makes tracking difficult, and usually our patrols were a day or so behind the gangs they were trying to catch. A high-flying aircraft carrying an observer with night-vision glasses had proved enormously successful on those occasions when we needed to catch up. Even a small campfire with a few burning embers could be detected from several miles away. A position could be obtained using the satellite ground positioning aids (GPS) and a patrol, using night-vision, could move rapidly to the poacher camp under cover of complete darkness. Fairly simple, off-the-shelf modern technology was making a huge difference.

We were asked to demonstrate the new equipment to a group of senior police officers. Some targets had been set up at a shooting range; and after dark, a KWS patrol crept into range, opened fire, and withdrew. Once the floodlights were put on again, the officers inspected the targets and were impressed by the accuracy of the shooting. The KWS patrol had not been visible to those of us watching, and the demonstration won KWS new respect from the police.

Word of our new effectiveness would obviously spread, and reputation alone can act as an excellent deterrent. I hoped that when news reached the poachers, many would be fearful of entering the parks. I have always believed prevention is the best medicine. We needed to convince elephant poachers that their activities were especially high-risk. Given the decline in run-ins over the next year, it seems that they were convinced.

Later, we heard that the police officers, paramilitary units, and other officials who had witnessed our men's new skills, talked about them to others in the military forces. Everyone was amazed by what the KWS rangers could do.

The police officers' admiration pleased me. We had come a long way in our relationship, and I was glad that they no longer regarded KWS rangers or me as lightweights. Their words of approval would surely help reassure the government.

I also believed that the database we had built about elephant poachers and ivory traders would be useful to the government. It was compiled and managed by a member of our staff, a skilled computer scientist. She designed it so that every bit of information we gathered about the ivory trade and the poachers was linked and cross-linked. Everything went into the database: the name of any village raided by poachers, the location of every poacherd elephant, the name of every shopkeeper—or official—with ties to the ivory trade. When Bashir organized a field operation, he first asked for a report about the area.

"He would come to me and say, 'We're planning to do this. What do you have?' " our computer specialist explained to me. "Then I would tell him everything we knew: the names of the poachers who worked in that area and who they sold their ivory to, the number of animals killed in the past, how many operations we'd done there before and whether or not they had been successful, and, if we'd had trouble, how many of our men had been killed or wounded. That way, he was very well prepared."

We always expected that our database would lead us to someone in the top government levels. We continued to discover that most of the illegal traders were small-time shopkeepers. However, we also discovered that we could not always prosecute these individuals. They were often protected by officials, such as provincial commissioners (a position similar to that of a U.S. state governor), or cabinet ministers. These officials might assist the trader by providing a government vehicle to transport ivory, for instance. Several times our men had followed certain buyers and were readying to arrest them when suddenly the buyers switched vehicles—cars that belonged to some senior and well-connected official.

Incidents of this sort happened more frequently at the beginning of my tenure. By now, these higher officials were wary of any connection to the ivory trade. Part of this was my own doing: I staged several demonstrations of KWS's database for some of them. At these show-and-tells, someone would type in the name of a small-time trader, and, within seconds, the system would produce a list of all the people in the illegal ivory trade that trader had dealt with. That was usually enough of an eye-opener—and a warning. On one occasion, though, I accidentally almost tipped our hand. After the demonstration, a visiting commissioner asked what would happen if his name was entered. The quick-thinking person operating the system appeared to try to enter the name but caused the database to malfunction instead.

"Oh dear, something seems to be not right with the computer," she said, hitting a series of keys, while the screen flashed a SYSTEM ERROR warning and then shut down.

But the provincial commissioner had guessed correctly. Had his name been entered, the computer would have produced a lengthy file about his activities in the ivory trade, and he would have recognized a number of names. Much of the information on a database is used only to help with analysis and to predict patterns of crime. We did discover on it some well-placed wildlife wardens who were certainly working with other officials, and I simply retired them from the service. (Criminal prosecution was not effective because so many cases were compromised through bribery and inadequate prosecution.)

Our information-gathering network often turned up details of other crimes, and we always turned this material over to the police. They seemed to appreciate our help. Police Commissioner Kilonzo was so impressed with KWS's database that he asked if we could design a similar system for the police—a request I readily agreed to. He would send a small team over for training in the spring of 1993. Again I thought the attention being paid to KWS's computer system was a good thing. The database was helping Kenya, and we were getting some recognition for our hard work.

Similarly, in the summer of 1992, when KWS rangers got wind of a Somali warlord's encampment inside Kenya's borders, I thought it my duty to investigate and inform our government.

The warlord was a former officer in the Somali military who now led his own ragged band of men. He and several other warlords were fighting over the remains of a country that had disintegrated into a messy and complicated civil war. This clan was allied to clans in northern Kenya and perhaps had ties to people in our government. Nevertheless, I doubted that the Kenyan government wanted a warlord's military base ensconced on Kenyan soil.

When word of his base reached our KWS Lamu Island office, I had one of our pilots fly over the camp and take a few photographs with a handheld 35-mm camera. I then passed these to the appropriate national security agency, which quickly dealt with the problem. The warlord left the Lamu area and never returned.

Nonetheless, no matter what I did, I could not quash the rumors about my supposed subversive activities. Everyone had heard them, and even officials I considered friends seemed at times to regard me suspiciously. Had I known a way to get my hands on that rumor, I would have strangled it. But in the tense, political atmosphere that prevailed in the government in the fall of 1992, such whispered rumors and lies proved elusive enemies. As soon as I thought I had silenced one, it reappeared in a slightly different—and even more dangerous—disguise.

❖ ❖ ❖

The first multiparty elections were scheduled to take place in December 1992, and there was considerable excitement. As the date approached, politicians from the ruling KANU party appeared absolutely desperate to win. Opposition party members accused KANU of buying votes with outright cash payments, of bullying and beating up their candidates, and of planning all manner of election frauds. Of course, members of the opposition were doing the same, though less successfully. Watching the melee, I was glad that I had not entered the fray this time around. I hoped the opposition parties might join forces and support one candidate for president. That would have given them their best shot at winning, and for a time it appeared that they might adopt this strategy. However, the opposition leaders were soon bickering among themselves. KANU, which had a smoothly oiled political machine, undoubtedly helped stir up some of the trouble. But it was also clear that the opposition leaders, who hailed from different tribes, simply did not trust one another. As President Moi had warned, tribalism was going to be a factor in our democratic elections.

As the election approached, the number of tribal clashes increased. The government continued to do very little to stop them. Indeed, when anyone spoke out, they made matters worse. According to newspaper accounts, William Ntimama, in particular, made numerous and unnecessarily inflammatory remarks. He said that those Kikuyu being chased from their homes could only have expected this to happen, since they had behaved like colonialists to the Maasai. In the narrowest sense, his charge was true. As I've suggested, the colonial government and President Kenyatta had both given large tracts of Maasai country to Kikuyus for farming. Such past wrongs were not easily corrected, and Ntimama's approach—supporting those who advocated violence—would only make things worse, creating a potentially endless cycle of revenge.

Ntimama was also after KWS. He was probably serving as a mouthpiece for others who shared his views. Time and again he lashed out at me and KWS in Parliament, charging us with being more concerned about Kenya's wildlife than with its people.

Only a few months earlier, in April 1992, the World Bank had authorized the first loan payment to KWS. The signing ceremony, involving Kenya's ambassador to the United States and the bank's vice president for African affairs, had been organized and made headlines in our local papers. Sixty million dollars was, after all, a sizable sum and came at a time when nearly every other government department had been cut off from foreign aid because of corruption. I knew that many people wanted to get their hands on that money, and, as I've explained, I had tried to arrange things with the bank so that they could not. The funds were sent to Kenya's Treasury Department but could only be spent on the bank-approved projects in our Protected Areas and Wildlife Service (PAWS) plan. These projects required the director's signature, so I believed that the money was safe. Nonetheless, I was also sure that plots were afoot to try to wrest that control from me. Ntimama's attacks, beginning a mere two months after the bank's authorization, may have been a part of these, particularly since, as I've said, the Masai Mara National Reserve and the Narok County Council that controlled it were *not* on KWS's list for World Bank funds.

Ntimama and the county council had made it very clear that they wanted KWS to spend money on the Mara for new roads, vehicles, buildings, and other necessities—all of which they needed. I had been equally forthright in explaining that until the county council could demonstrate its commitment to developing a sound management policy for the Mara, it would not be getting large injections of cash from KWS's coffers. It was a stand-off, pure and simple. Ntimama used his position in Parliament to lambaste KWS.

"If KWS doesn't lock up its animals," he declared in one such attack, "then the *wananchi* [the people] will do the job for them. These marauding elephants and lions will be killed and chased back to where they belong."

"KWS doesn't care for the people of Kenya, only its elephants," he charged a few weeks later. "Do we ever hear of KWS paying money to people who've been harmed by these rogue animals? No. We know that

KWS has the money, but Dr. Leakey uses it only to help his friends—the elephants."

It was difficult to counter Ntimama's charges, as I was not a member of Parliament and therefore not present when he made these pronouncements. A large, forceful man with a flair for public speaking, Ntimama's speeches always made it into the newspapers—without any rebuttals from me or any of my supporters. Occasionally, someone would write a letter to the editor, objecting to his declarations and arguing that Kenya's wildlife needed to be protected, not hounded to death. I also occasionally tried to explain to reporters why KWS could not make payments for injuries and deaths caused by wildlife. The Kenyan government had scrapped that policy because it was too easily abused, I told them. People were now expected to apply directly to the government for any compensation they felt was due them. It was, however, no longer KWS's responsibility, as spelled out in the legislation that had created our agency.

"We do understand the problems of the people living near our parks," I said. "And we have every intention of trying to help them. As our parks become profitable, KWS will assist the communities outside our parks and reserves with schools and health centers. We'll be sharing a small portion of our revenues with them through these projects."

Indeed, in May 1992, KWS distributed $300,000 to community projects near Amboseli. Grace Lusiola, KWS's community projects leader, had identified a number of schools, clinics, and small businesses worthy of assisting. We were also helping some Maasai families establish small reserves on their land: these would take some of the pressure off Amboseli. We had even given $140,000 to group ranches near the Masai Mara to build extra classrooms, clinics, and small dams. These were our model projects. By seeing what worked there, we believed, we would learn how to develop better projects elsewhere.

However, few ever listened closely to what we were doing. They either chose to ignore the word "model" or misunderstood what it meant. Every community near a park around the country wanted a "project"—and what they regarded as their share of the parks' revenues.

It was impossible to defuse the situation. Ntimama and his allies seized on the revenue-sharing plan as another point of attack. Where were these revenues? they demanded to know. KWS now had funds but had yet to "deliver the promised 25 percent" due to the communities. KWS had failed on another promise, too: constructing fences to keep elephants away from villages. "The only fences KWS has built," our critics complained, "are to protect wealthy white ranchers."

Lost in the flurry of words was what we actually were doing. We never intended to simply hand out money, particularly to any county council members, many of whom were now insisting that we do so. That was the surest way for the funds either to be stolen or misspent. The revenue sharing would come in the form of projects, such as those we were experimenting with at Amboseli. And the fences that supposedly protected the white ranchers were, in fact, built to keep the wild game *on* these ranches and thus out of the fields of the neighboring small villagers, who were delighted by the new fences. But, as is often the case, newspapers found it more exciting to print Ntimama's colorful half-truths than the far more placid and boring truth. An effective elephant fence, after all, is not nearly as entertaining to read about as a marauding "killer Jumbo," or a barrier that seemed to favor the "white elite."

I thought that perhaps after the elections, KWS would be less of a political target, and, for a little while, I was right.

The elections were held in mid-December 1992. No one was very surprised when President Moi and the ruling KANU Party were returned to office, although with only 33 percent of the vote. The rest of the vote was divided among the opposition political parties. Had they stuck together, they might have won.

Life in Kenya quieted down after the elections. People were worn out from all the political speeches, campaigning, and shenanigans of the previous six months. Yet, oddly, the tribal clashes continued. I often puzzled over these with Meave.

"What purpose can these possibly serve now?" I asked her over dinner one evening shortly after the New Year. "The election is over. KANU has won. You'd think it would be time to call off these thugs, or whoever is behind this unrest."

"It *is* worrisome," said Meave. "It looks like people are just using these as an excuse to steal from their neighbors."

"The government should speak out and stop them. I don't understand why it doesn't."

We both shook our heads, perplexed about the real, political reason behind the clashes.

One key ingredient to a successful marriage is the patience simply to wait out the difficult times. Happily, Meave's professional life was soaring. She had made some excellent fossil discoveries and was now a sought-after speaker at universities and museums in the United States and Europe. And she was nurturing a crew of young Kenyan scientists. She spent three months every summer at Turkana, and when I visited, I came solely at her invitation.

At the end of January 1992, a few weeks after our conversation, one of KWS's antipoaching units encountered a gang in a cave on the border of the Masai Mara reserve. We had been receiving curious reports about a giraffe-poaching operation. Giraffe seemed such an unlikely target, yet our rangers were finding numerous carcasses both inside and outside the reserve. They tracked the gang to a cave and decided to move in on it the next morning. Shortly after dawn, they surrounded the cave and shouted for those inside to give themselves up. The poachers shouted back that they could not be arrested.

"We have official permission to be here!" one called out. "Go away and leave us alone."

Our rangers thought this an insolent response and once again demanded that the group surrender. Instead, the poachers launched a volley of arrows. One hit the commanding sergeant. His rangers instantly returned fire. Five poachers—all Maasai—were killed, and four others were arrested.

The scene seemed to be very confused. The Maasai continued to protest that they should be left alone and wailed over the deaths of their friends. The rangers searched the cave and to their utter bafflement found what amounted to a factory for manufacturing bows and arrows. Giraffe sinews, as one of our rangers later explained to me, make extremely strong bow strings. They had unwittingly stumbled onto a weapons center of sorts: this was where many of the bows and arrows used in the tribal clashes had been made.

Suddenly Odinga's accusations about how the KWS was training terrorists in the Masai Mara began to make some sense. No doubt the rumors he had heard referred to these "poachers" who were making weapons and perhaps even training people in their use.

But what did the poachers mean when they maintained that they had "official permission" to be in the cave? Were they referring to officials in Nairobi or to the local Narok County Council? Certainly, this entire region had been hit hard by the tribal clashes, though not one council member had spoken out against the attackers. Ntimama had reportedly even urged them on. Newspapers claimed that he advised the Kikuyu living among the Maasai to "learn to lie as low as an envelope if they want to stay here." However, he has denied ever making such a comment.

There was little I could do but report what our rangers had found. By law, all the material we confiscated that day, as well as the statements our rangers took from the gang members, had to be turned over to the local police station in Narok. All this evidence—including the bows and arrows—vanished overnight.

A few weeks later, Ntimama was once again on the attack. He demanded an explanation from the minister of Tourism and Wildlife.

"What is this Leakey doing, having his rangers shoot unarmed Masai at a meat feast? We need an investigation!"

Without the evidence, there was little the minister could say in my defense. He tried, however, arguing that these were not, in fact, "innocent *wananchi*" but poachers.

"Where is your proof?" Ntimama challenged him. "These men were doing nothing but taking some game they are entitled to. And now five are dead! That's how KWS goes about its business: it kills the villagers and protects the animals that are killing us!"

The minister declined to respond.

We had given Ntimama more ammunition to use against me and KWS. And sadly, I knew more than I cared to know about the tribal clashes. Some officials were supporting these attacks, apparently even authorizing the making of weapons for them. The clashes continued through the spring of 1993.

Ntimama, too, continued his public bashing of me and KWS. No one in the government spoke up in our defense.

After the bows and arrows incident, I once again retreated to my low-profile stance. A few months earlier, in the fall of 1992, the government had renewed my contract as director of KWS, and I had agreed to serve another three years. That would give me, I thought, time enough to build the institution I envisioned. Then I would step down.

In the meantime, there was much to do. We had several big projects in the works, from fencing and community conservation to rebuilding park roads and buildings. We were also still wrestling with the best way to share some of KWS's potential profits with communities near the parks. I had designed a new headquarters building to replace the dumpy little hovel we now used. Too often, when such public works projects get underway in Kenya, they are immediately abused. Government officials with relatives in construction find a way to see that the jobs go to their relations. Others bribe their way in to get a cut of the action. Inevitably, the money for the project is misspent. The project soon goes over budget and ends up only partially completed. That had happened numerous times under the old Wildlife Department, and I wasn't about to see it happen on my watch.

I wanted to use only independent companies, not ones run by men who had powerful connections. To ensure this, I carefully monitored the entire bidding process. More than once a contractor came to me to argue that I wasn't handling the construction properly—in other words, he had not received a bribe. I turned those people away immediately. Undoubtedly my brusque words and insistence on honesty earned me more enemies. I no longer cared. KWS was now a parastatal agency, autonomous of the government, and had the backing of the World Bank. I ran it as I saw fit—or tried to.

The Treasury Department was making it annoyingly difficult to tap the funds the World Bank had put at KWS's disposal. There were forms to fill out, the procedures were inconsistent, and officials kept insisting that that or this wasn't the way the department operated. I was in a cat-and-mouse game for the money now, and I waited to see how long the Treasury Department tried to hold out. As a last resort I would turn to the World Bank officials for assistance. In the meantime, I signed credit slips for payment. Everyone knew about KWS's fat coffers and readily gave us credit.

I seldom had any contact with President Moi or others in the higher levels of the government and simply got on with my tasks. My hope was that my lower profile would keep my enemies from worrying about me.

Then one day in mid-May I received a call from the president's office. His secretary told me that President Moi wanted to see me. I can recall nothing about this meeting. In my diary I noted only that we met and that the president was "surprisingly warm." I imagine I wrote that because several months had passed since our previous private meeting, which had been awkward and chilly. This time we must have shared a few laughs, shaken hands, and parted amicably.

That was to be my last diary entry for several months.

Two weeks later, on June 2, 1993, I left to attend a brief meeting at the KWS Training College in Naivasha, north of Nairobi in the Rift Valley. Getting there would mean either a three-hour drive or a twenty-five-minute flight and I decided at the last moment to save time and take my own aircraft. I took four members of my staff with me so that I could have some discussions on the way up.

About ten minutes out of Nairobi, the engine began rapidly to lose power. I did a quick cockpit check and changed fuel tanks, but it was soon clear that I had little engine power left. I notified the airport that I would have to make an emergency landing. Telling my passengers to expect the worst, I guided the plane toward a playing field between school buildings. The area was hilly and dotted with homes and trees. I was not especially hopeful about the outcome.

The aircraft touched down and the left wing hit a fairly large mango tree. Even if I'd seen it, I wouldn't have been able to do anything. I had no control. Later, seeing photos of the wreck, I was surprised that any of us survived; but we all did. Two were barely injured, one had a fractured shoulder and lower jaw, another had leg injuries. My head had a series of lacerations and bumps, but apart from a concussion and a few cracks, these were not critical. The greatest problem for me was my lower legs, which were mangled.

I do not remember much about the crash except that some local villagers helped to pull us from the wreckage. Someone took my rather fancy Rolex watch, but aside from that, everyone was friendly and helpful. A pickup truck took us to a nearby hospital from which, after a bit of first aid, I was transferred to Nairobi by helicopter.

I knew that Meave was at Turkana, but I desperately needed her. Fortunately Joyce had been informed of the accident and had already arranged with Phil Mathews, the KWS's chief pilot, to fly at once and bring Meave back. Hearing this was comforting, for I knew that more than anything else, my ability to cope with what was ahead would depend on Meave.

I knew I was in a bad way, but I found myself worrying more about KWS than my injuries.

"I'll need a phone," I told Joyce. "I must tell everyone I'm okay. They must keep KWS going."

"They will, Richard, they will," she said, doing her best to reassure me. "Everything is going to be all right."

I wanted to agree with her. After all, it was my job as director to keep everyone upbeat and positive. But this time I was not so sure everything would be all right.

CHAPTER 20

Like many people who have been severely injured, I don't remember a great deal about my first few hours in the hospital. There seemed to be rather a lot of nurses rushing about, and I felt thoroughly confused. Joyce reassured me that Meave was on her way back from Turkana and told me that I would have to go in for surgery fairly soon. I do remember saying that there would be no surgery until I had seen Meave: she was the one person I could really trust to make the right decision. Nobody else was making any sense.

Then, about an hour after I had been admitted and before I had received any treatment, the hustle and bustle in the emergency ward suddenly stopped. The room fell absolutely silent.

A moment later the screen around my bed was parted, and there stood President Moi.

I could not have been more surprised or confused to see him. He looked distressed and worried, and came close to my bedside.

"Richard, I am so sorry about this accident," he said, shaking his head sympathetically. "This is very bad. Very bad."

I was still in shock but I am told that initially I carried on a rather lighthearted conversation with the president. He wanted to know if there was anything he could do, and apparently I told him that we needed to stop the destruction of Kenya's forests, explaining the gravity of the situation in some detail.

President Moi listened gravely while I talked away and finally said that he would see to it that we met about this important issue as soon as I was well enough to leave the hospital. He asked if there was anything else he could do to help, adding that he would pray for me and my full recovery.

I am an atheist and for some reason, probably because of my state of shock and the drugs I had been given, I'm afraid I responded badly to the president's overture. I rudely brushed aside his offer of prayers, telling him that I did not want them. The best thing he could do, I continued, was to see to it that the former employees of KWS were not reinstated.

President Moi was greatly offended by my words. He looked shocked, as if I had slapped him in the face. He bent his head, offered a few more sympathetic words, then left with his entourage.

Joyce had remained in the room during his visit and looked at me rather wide-eyed, as if afraid I would bark at her, too.

I didn't offer any apologies for my behavior. I knew I was a mess, but I was far more worried about the mess KWS would sink into if people thought I was out of the picture.

"We can't let KWS go down the drain just because of what's happened to me," I told her. "Now I need a phone."

It was about 4:30 in the afternoon. I had been at the hospital for over two hours and kept swimming in and out of consciousness. Suddenly an attendant appeared next to the bed holding a telephone.

"Good," I said. I had him dial the number for my assistant at KWS.

"Lynnette," I said, when she answered, "tell everyone there that I am fine. They shouldn't worry about me. Tell them to carry on with their work. That's the best thing they can do now. I'm fine."

I could tell that she was trying to respond as naturally as possible, as if my injuries were minor. She would pass on my message, she said, and hung up.

A nurse stopped by to give me more painkillers. She said that they were preparing the operating room. My family had been alerted, and my mother was coming to see me. Everyone was very concerned.

There was another gap. I must have fallen asleep, and when I awoke, Meave was walking into the room with my brother Philip. Phil Mathews had flown her down from her field camp, which, she later told me, she had entrusted to our nineteen-year-old daughter, Louise. I noticed that Meave was still wearing her field clothes. She smiled faintly. Then her eyes locked onto mine. She walked straight to my side and took my hand.

If I had ever had any doubts about the depth of my love for Meave, they disappeared in that instant.

"Looks like you've given yourself a pretty good bashing this time," she said, doing her best to smile. There were tears in her eyes.

"Well, yes. I'm a bit of a wreck. But they haven't finished me off entirely. I'll be up soon."

"Yes, of course, Richard. You're strong; you'll recover soon."

She pulled a chair up close to my bed and sat down. It wasn't going to be soon, of course. She knew it and I knew it. I had a battle ahead of me, although I didn't know then how rough it would be. All that mattered at that moment was that Meave was there with me.

I had my first operation later that night. The surgeon did what he could to stabilize my legs and ankles. My ankles were crushed and badly broken, both tibias were broken, and my left femur was broken in four places between the knee and the ankle. I had received a nasty knock above my left eye, which left a deep dent in my skull, though it was nothing serious.

My transplanted kidney also worried the doctors. Kidneys do sometimes fail in trauma cases, and mine would be particularly vulnerable were I to develop a serious infection. Apparently, one was already setting into my severely broken legs. The doctors discussed their worry with Meave and suggested that I be flown to an overseas hospital with better medical facilities. They wanted me to leave as soon as possible.

I refused, despite the fear that I saw in Meave's eyes. I couldn't leave the country without first seeing to it that KWS was left in good hands. There were certain pending matters—matters that I'm not at liberty even now to discuss—that I simply could not turn away from. Instead, I asked for an office to be set up in my room so that I could telephone people and send and receive faxes.

While this was being arranged, Bashir and some senior KWS wardens came to see me. I think they were shocked by my condition, but I wasn't about to let them feel sorry for me. Again I don't recall these conversations, but I'm told that I thanked them for their visit then ordered them back to their posts.

"I don't need you here, but KWS needs you. That's the best thing you can do for me: Keep KWS working and working well."

They saluted and left, later telling me that they could not believe their eyes when they saw me.

"Anyone else would have been lying in bed moaning," said one senior warden. "But you were sitting up, talking on the telephone, asking for someone to get a fax that was coming in. We had to go back to KWS and work twice as hard just to keep up with you."

Bashir joined me again the next day, and we had a lengthy discussion about my present situation. There were no easy explanations as to why the aircraft's engine had failed, and it was unclear whether or not it had been sabotaged. Lying around in a public hospital, at any rate, was inviting further troubles. With help from Bashir and Meave, I was quickly moved to a more secure room. KWS armed guards were posted outside my door. From then on any visitors were carefully vetted and few people were allowed into my room. Phil Mathews and Bashir supervised the recovery of the wrecked plane and instigated a full inquiry. Experts from the United States joined in with the Kenya accident inspectors.

Had the crash been an assassination attempt? It wouldn't have surprised me, given how many people were keen to get their hands on KWS's money. President Moi had warned me from the beginning that there were people who wanted me out of the way. During my four years as director, I'm sure I had added others to the list. Bashir's fears deeply worried Meave. She moved into the hospital room with me and rarely left my side. I worried, too, and apparently because of my fears and the drugs I was being given, I suffered hallucinations about being attacked. I had great difficulty sleeping through the night.

Several times during those first few days, Meave urged me to stop obsessing about KWS. I needed to think about her and our family and myself. But I was pigheaded, as usual, and refused to leave the hospital until I had sorted out the last things on my list. By the fifth day, however, it was clear even to me that my chances for recovery would not be good if I stayed in Nairobi. I needed better medical care.

For many years I had been a close friend of HRH Prince Claus of the Netherlands and his family. I sought his advice. We spoke on the phone, and I asked him to use his connections to find out where I should go for the best emergency treatment. Within hours, Prince Claus offered Meave his suggestions and arranged for Dr. Christopher Colton, from the Queens Medical Center in Nottingham, England, to fly to Nairobi. Within twenty-four hours, Dr. Coulton was at my bedside.

One quick look at my injuries told him everything.

"I'm not mincing words with you, Dr. Leakey," Dr. Colton said. "You're developing a severe infection—sepsis—in your wounds. It will soon become gangrene. And it will kill you, quickly. I'm taking you to England tomorrow."

Meave and my mother were equally adamant. I had managed to take care of most of the things I had been most worried about and so I finally gave in, telling them that they were the two pushiest women I knew.

The next morning, I was strapped tightly to a stretcher and put on-board a British Airways flight to London. It was a dreadful experience. My only consolation was that the doctor allowed Meave to provide me a fairly steady supply of wine, which the cabin crew were kind enough to offer.

Ten hours later, slightly inebriated and in pain, I arrived in London. Kenya and all my troubles at KWS temporarily faded away.

❖ ❖ ❖

For most of July and August, I was a patient at London's Nottingham Hospital. Meave was with me constantly. She set up a camp bed in my hospital room and cooked all my meals herself. Her constant presence and encouragement made such an otherwise depressing experience bearable. Dr. Colton wanted desperately to save my legs, and I hoped that he could. From him I learned the full extent of my injuries and what might be done to repair them. While the left leg might be rebuilt, the nerves in the foot and the blood supply to it were severely damaged. Dr. Colton was very forthright, explaining that my left foot would be largely senseless for the rest of my life. I could not expect to have much feeling in it, and the blood supply would remain poor and cause other troubles. Given the active life I lead, this was a serious matter.

Although Dr. Colton disliked the idea, he recommended that because of these future problems my left leg be amputated eight inches below the knee. He assured me that with the aid of a prosthetic leg, I would be able to walk again. It was hard to hear this news, but I chose to focus on how very lucky I was to be alive and agreed to the amputation. The loss of a leg was nothing compared to the loss of life. Early one morning I was wheeled into surgery and my left leg was removed.

When I came to, I had the same curious sensation many amputees get—that I needed to scratch my toes, which were no longer there. The stump would heal quickly, the doctor told me, and in a few weeks I would have a new leg.

Everyone was very sympathetic about my loss, which was both kind and annoying. I wasn't dead. I would manage, I assured all my clucking visitors. Then my daughter, Anna, cheered me up in a way that only a Leakey can.

To amuse myself, I had begun writing some notes for my memoirs (which led to this book). Anna stopped by after my amputation and I told her about my book plans. As a family we are known for our sometimes morbid wit, and my dear daughter did not miss a beat.

"Your memoirs?" she said, sounding elated. "I know just what you can call it: *One Foot in the Grave.*"

I laughed long and hard for the first time in days. I also asked the surgeons to keep my leg so that we could give it a proper burial at Lake Turkana when I returned home. "It's the only part of my burial that I'll be able to attend," I joked.

My right leg seemed more salvageable, though I had lost several inches of bone just above the ankle. Dr. Colton felt that, with a bone graft, I would regrow most of this bone and over time regain the use of my foot. For several weeks, I underwent a series of operations—fourteen altogether. None of these was easy, but I endured them to save my leg. However, the surgery also left me feeling completely done in. I no longer felt capable of making decisions. Indeed, I wasn't participating anymore in the decisions about my medical condition; I now left this entirely in the hands of my physicians. Although I trusted Dr. Colton, I needed to be more actively involved.

At this stage Dr. Colton wanted to begin the first bone graft, which required removing a piece of bone from my hip and attaching it to my ankle. This would be the first step toward linking the two severed pieces of my leg. I wasn't so sure and shared my concerns with Meave. It seemed better to postpone the surgery. I wanted to go home, recuperate from all the anesthetics I had been given, and think. Dr. Colton wasn't happy about this but eventually agreed that I could return to Kenya if I traveled in a wheelchair with my leg secured with various rods and pins. After a few weeks, I would fly back to Nottingham for the surgery.

The flight home was a very different experience. No longer on a stretcher, I traveled with Meave, getting first-class assistance from everyone. Good friends of ours, Geoffrey and Jorie Kent, had generously arranged that we spend a couple of nights in one of London's best hotels to "get used to being out of hospital," and between them and British Airways we had the best possible service. Most importantly, the journey was in the right direction: I was going home.

Being confined to a wheelchair was a new experience, but I quickly learned to get about quite efficiently. The rough roads and dust were not particularly good for my injured leg. It didn't matter. The sounds and smells of Africa were like a tonic. I rapidly recovered from the many operations and began to feel happy again and in control of my own destiny. It had become increasingly difficult to think clearly about my options while under regular sedation in the hospital.

I had left KWS in the hands of Bashir and Joe Kioko, my deputy director. They had been in touch regularly with me throughout my stay in London, keeping me abreast of how KWS was faring. Everyone had worked doubly hard during my absence and the organization had run smoothly—even though it was as cash-strapped as before. The World Bank funds were in place, but various bureaucratic problems continued to make KWS's operations unnecessarily difficult.

My enemies may have thought that the plane crash had finished me off. It certainly had taken me out of the picture for three months. I wanted them to know, however, that it would take more than the loss of a leg to keep me down.

Three days after flying to Kenya, I returned to KWS. The entire staff was waiting outside as I was driven to the main entrance. They applauded heartily as I was assisted out of my Land Rover and wheeled to my office. Then I turned around and applauded them for keeping KWS going. As I clapped my hands, everyone began to smile and then to laugh, and I think for a moment they forgot that I was in a wheelchair. That was what I wanted—to be seen as myself, Richard Leakey, and not as someone deserving their pity. I know that most handicapped people feel this very strongly; and one has to both learn how to use a wheelchair and, perhaps as importantly, teach families and friends about what it is like to be in one. It's not in my nature to be dependent, but for the time being, I was. There were so many things I could not do: stand up, fetch a glass of water, open a door. Such little things, and yet I could not do them. These were humbling lessons, but they also had their positive side. Because I was dependent on others, I realized first-hand how important sympathy and empathy must have been during the early years of our evolution.

In the 1970s, our fossil-hunting team discovered the femur of an early *Homo erectus*, a human ancestor who lived about 1.8 million years ago. The leg had been broken, but the break had healed. In the East African savanna, there is only one way a human with a broken leg can survive, and that is with the assistance of others. Someone had brought this individual food and water, and protected him or her until the leg was mended. Over the years I have shared this story with many audiences and written about it. But experiencing what that human ancestor endured nearly 2 million years ago—and understanding just how truly helpless one is with one leg—gave me a deeper understanding of how critical our capacity to care for one another has been to our survival as a species. It is one of the things that makes us human.

My time in the wheelchair also opened my eyes to how difficult life is for the disabled, particularly in a developing country. I resolved someday to find a way to do whatever I possibly could for the handicapped in Kenya.

I did not have many weeks to spend at KWS. Dr. Colton wanted me back in London by early October. In the few weeks I did have, I would try to break the logjam blocking KWS's funds. I started my campaign by arranging a meeting with President Moi.

I felt very uncomfortable in my wheelchair and uneasy about visiting the president in this condition. He was kind to me, as were his officials, but being seated while tall, powerful men stand around you and talk about you was something I realized that I would never get used to. A photographer was present when we met and snapped a picture of me that was printed in *Daily Nation* the next day. It made me laugh. President Moi towered over me as if I were some kind of a supplicant. I decided I would never again meet with him while in that chair, and I was suddenly very keen to complete the medical procedures necessary to help me walk again.

Our meeting was not as productive as I had hoped. President Moi was friendly but distant, probably because of my wheelchair. Many find it extremely difficult to interact normally with physically disadvantaged people. He encouraged me to take as much time in England as I needed to regain the full use of my leg.

I did not have much success in getting his help to remove some of the obstacles blocking KWS's progress. KWS was in what seemed a strange situation. There was plenty of money available through the PAWS project, but government officials were effectively preventing us from getting it. I was not sure whether this was politically inspired or simply because I had so consistently refused to allow kickbacks and percentage commissions.

Wheelchair or no, I made several visits to Amboseli and Tsavo to meet with the wardens and rangers. These expeditions provided therapeutic preparation for the rounds of surgeries and painful procedures I would undergo when I got back to the Nottingham Hospital.

All too soon, it was time to return to England. A few days later, Dr. Colton scheduled the grafting surgery. I had given this much thought and decided that these extreme measures were in fact too extreme. Taking my destiny into my own hands, I arranged an urgent conference with Dr. Colton. He had an international reputation for repairing broken legs and arms and was confident that he could achieve a good result with my leg. But he also conceded that my artificial left leg might remain my "best" one. I would very likely have pain and stiffness in my right ankle, and suffer back pains as a result. In time, I would probably develop osteoarthrits.

That news worried me. My father suffered terribly in his sixties from arthritis in his hips. He was often in a bad temper in his later years, and I think some of that was simply because of the excruciating pain in his hips.

I did not want to end up a bitter old man in a wheelchair with a pain-racked body.

"Why can't I have two good legs?" I asked Dr. Colton.

"Well, you'll have a reasonably good leg after this one heals," he replied.

"But it won't be as good as my 'good leg?' " I asked.

"No. It'll be stiff and you will have arthritis, that is true."

"Then I want two good legs. Take this one off, too. Let's get rid of it, and I will use two prosthetic limbs instead of one."

Dr. Colton said that I should think hard about such a decision.

"I have. Meave and I have discussed it," I said, "and it's what I want."

She and I had talked about it more than once, and she knew my fears.

"It will be very bad if he has to spend much time in a wheelchair," she said.

"I just don't see the point," I continued. "Somewhere down the line, this 'bad' leg is going to get worse. It's painful now. I say, take it off."

Although Dr. Colton wanted to save that leg and could have, he ultimately did what I wished. Instead of another bone graft operation, he amputated my left leg eight inches below the knee. I was now a double amputee. Many might disagree with my choice, but for me it was the right decision, if also an excruciating one. My legs had been very much a part of my life. Some of my best experiences were on expeditions on which we had hiked for miles and miles over rugged terrain. Many fantastic fossil discoveries came at the end of long walks. I knew that all this would now be impossible.

When I regained consciousness after the second amputation, I am sure that I had not yet realized what life would be like, but I knew that others before me had done remarkably well. I was determined that if others could, I could too. My immediate need was to get out of the hospital, learn to walk, and get home to Kenya.

While the leg was healing, I was fitted for my first pair of prosthetics. As soon as was possible, Meave got me out of hospital and we went to stay with a good friend, George Bronfman, at whose home I planned to relearn to walk. I will never forget the very first time I put my full weight on the ground through the artificial limbs. I simply could not believe that it would be possible to walk. My heart sank at the thought that I had made a terrible mistake; the complete lack of any feeling below the knees was terrifying for a few moments. I was not allowed anytime to think about my misfortune—the woman who ran the rehabilitation program for amputees urged me to get moving. Remarkably, within a few hours I was "walking" between parallel bars, supporting myself partly with my hands. The session lasted three hours. I returned twice more, and at the end of the third session I was told that all I needed now was practice. I could go home to Kenya. Of course, I was using canes and my steps were very uncertain, but Meave and I celebrated my departure from the wheelchair by going to a very good restaurant in London after leaving the prosthetics center. I felt as if I had broken free. For the first time in many months, I began to think seriously about the future.

When I visited President Moi at the State House three weeks later, I wore my KWS uniform and I walked in on my new legs. Perhaps I should have waited another week. To my dismay, I lost my balance and fell prone at President Moi's feet. There I was, once again, on my knees. At least this time there were no photographers on the scene. The president and his aides were quick to help me to my feet again.

Despite my stumble, I think I surprised many people at the State House by arriving under my own steam and without any canes (I use one only when walking over rough terrain). They greeted me warmly and inquired after my health, but I found most of their remarks insincere. The investigators had found no evidence of tampering or sabotage with my plane. Nonetheless, I believed that someone had done something to it—perhaps one of my enemies here.

Yet such thoughts were dangerous. They could turn me into a complete paranoid, unable to function. It was better, I decided, to put the matter out of my mind as much as possible and focus on the here and now—and that meant putting my all once again into KWS.

I soon realized, however, that not even every ounce of my energy and desire would make KWS work. Some people in the government wanted me to fail. And that thought depressed me almost as much as the loss of my legs.

I'm not Pollyannish, but some good things did come out of my plane crash. For starters, it ended my midlife crisis. My self-doubts and self-questioning simply vanished. I'm not even sure when I realized that the queasy, sour feeling I had had off and on for the previous three years was gone; it just was no longer there. And I didn't miss it.

Meave's support throughout the entire nightmare had been unwavering. For many couples, such traumas can spell the end of a relationship. We emerged stronger and closer. I know that I could not have coped with it all without her support and encouragement.

Over the next few months, I needed Meave more than ever. During my absence, my political enemies had laid low, waiting to see whether I would live or die. Once it was clear that not only had I survived but was going right back to my job, they pounced on me with renewed fury.

As before, William Ntimama led the charge. He launched his attack on Christmas Eve 1993, when I was at Lamu with my family. A reporter from the *Daily Nation* called to ask if I wanted to respond to what he was saying.

"No," I replied. "I don't pay any attention to the newspapers while I'm on holiday."

But some members of my family were curious, and someone bought a newspaper. This time Ntimama's comments were front-page news: NTIMAMA LASHES OUT AT LEAKEY. "We have a very bitter relationship between the Maasai and KWS," he was quoted as saying. "It seems that animals have been licensed to kill and live, while the Maasai are destined to die." Dr. Leakey might be a "hero in the West," he continued, but he was denying the "basic human rights of the Maasai." He called me arrogant and dictatorial, and concluded by charging that I cared more for wildlife than for people.

The name-calling was to be expected. What I didn't expect was a companion story. PRESIDENT REVOKES KWS EXEMPTION. President Moi had taken away KWS's exemption from certain laws governing state corporations. The exemption had allowed us to recruit and pay for professional staff; without it, I would not be able to hire people from the private sector as I had planned. And without managers of this caliber, KWS's projects would falter.

KWS was already in a huge financial bind. We were still having difficulties getting access to the World Bank money, yet I had already approved numerous contracts for constructing the headquarters' building, staff housing in some parks, and road improvements in nearly all of them. The building continued apace, but the contractors weren't being paid. Some were threatening to sue. And to top it off, now came this new presidential directive.

"Whatever are you going to do, Richard?" Meave asked. "They are making it very difficult for you."

I wasn't under any illusions as to what was going on. "It's going to get much worse," I said. "Wait and see. They want that money, and they're going to turn up the heat on me. It's going to get very, very rough."

Ntimama continued to attack me in the newspapers. Nearly every day he leveled a fresh accusation at me: that I ran KWS, a public institution, as if it were my personal property; that I had millions of dollars at my disposal from the Western donors, but that I refused to pay even a penny to a family who had lost a loved one to an elephant or lion.

I would not break my holiday silence. Some readers realized what the fight was really about. One wrote in to say, "Mr. Ntimama! The problem is not 'my people, the Maasai,' it is 'Leakey's money that we cannot loot!' "

That made me laugh. The charges, however, were not a laughing matter. It worried me, too, that once again no one in the government spoke up to defend me and KWS. We'd gone from being the good guys who'd saved the elephants and the country's key industry to being heartless thugs.

Soon other government officials were jumping on Ntimama's bandwagon. They demanded that they be given their "share" of KWS's revenues. Another cabinet minister recalled the bows-and-arrows shooting incident and charged that "KWS molested innocent people whenever they were seen with bows and arrows near the parks," but did nothing when "its wildlife" destroyed peoples' crops and killed women and children.

The charges were so ridiculous that I refused to respond. It seemed to me that my boss, Katana Ngala, should be speaking up for me—

unless he intended to have me fired. I half-expected that this was what the Ntimama fusillade was leading up to. Apparently, Ntimama thought so, too. His next attack, delivered shortly after New Year's Day 1994, called for my dismissal. NTIMAMA: LEAKEY MUST GO, the newspapers proclaimed. As before, a lengthy article full of scurrilous charges followed. And once again I was silent, though I did tell reporters that I would respond in my own time. I planned a meeting with Ngala and the chairman of KWS's board. If they no longer supported me, I would take that as a sign that I had lost the government's backing and step down. In earlier days I might have turned to President Moi in a crisis of this nature, but he, too, had been silent throughout Ntimama's attacks. He appeared to have been persuaded by my enemies that I was up to no good.

The day after Ntimama called for my resignation, the leaders of twenty-five county councils demanded the same thing. They called their own press conference at which they boldly argued that the national parks in their counties should be converted into game reserves so that they could manage them—a thinly veiled effort to get their hands on the parks' tills. Fortunately, several newly elected members of Parliament from the various opposition parties also held their own press conference that same day. They voiced their strong backing for me and said that KWS's critics were simply "wishing to get their hands on [KWS's] money."

It was heartening to have these people speak up for me. The very next day, however, Ngala announced that a Probe Committee (something like the Special Prosecutor's Office in the United States) would be investigating me and KWS "for alleged financial and employment irregularities." It appeared that KWS "had violated the law and the act of Parliament under which it was formed," he said. KWS, he further explained, was now operating on a bank overdraft (which was true, since the Treasury would not release our funds), and that was against the law. The Probe Committee would also look into allegations made by Ntimama and the county councils about the mishandling of contracts and the illegal collection of funds from the public. Ngala added that his ministry considered these allegations to be very serious as they came "from the elected representatives of the people." In spite of these charges, he was not going to dismiss me. I would remain as director until the Probe Committee finished its investigation.

I had never liked Ngala. I liked him even less after reading this. The story embarrassed and humiliated me, suggesting as it did that KWS was engaged in illegal, corrupt activities—the very thing that I had spent the better part of three years fighting against.

To my great relief, President Moi finally stepped in and came to my defense the next day, ordering everyone to "stop this talk on Leakey." He was departing for a state visit to Israel and would look into all the matters upon his return, he said.

I still had not broken my silence to the press. I had many things that I wanted to say but would wait until I had met with the president.

CHAPTER **21**

Throughout the nearly month-long vilification campaign that Ntimama and his allies waged against me, my friends, family, colleagues, and even newspaper reporters kept asking one question: "Why don't you respond?" I had run into much the same situation during my years in paleoanthropology, when certain American scientists spread rumors about me at various universities and research institutions in the United States. For one thing, I have always been a firm believer that actions speak louder than words. In neither case were the rumors true, as should have been apparent to anyone willing to take a closer look. For another, I'm not interested in trying to win over people who believe malicious gossip. Rumors are generally spread for very specific reasons: to make the person saying nasty things about someone else look better or to get that person something. The American scientists would have been happy if I had never again received financing for my fossil expeditions from any American scientific organization, thus preventing me from making any more discoveries. In the case of Ntimama and his associates, the attacks were a way of trying to get the World Bank to release funds for the Mara and Narok County Council and of stopping KWS's plans to change the way the Masai Mara was managed. As I've suggested, however, Ntimama probably did not orchestrate the campaign on his own.

Somewhere in the background were others in the government who wanted me out of the way because they feared me and what I had achieved at KWS. Ntimama was simply a tool to achieve that end.

President Moi wasn't part of this equation, and I appreciated his order that the campaign against me cease. His trip to Israel was short; and when he returned four days later, he arranged a meeting with me, as promised.

Of all the meetings I had had with the president, this was the most difficult. Despite my trying not to take any of the accusations to heart, I was deeply hurt by some of the things that had been said—or, rather, that had *not* been said. Aside from the opposition MPs, hardly any official had spoken up on my behalf. Those who had written letters to the editor enthusiastically backing me and severely criticizing Ntimama were ordinary citizens.

Part of me wished that some of these brave souls had been in Parliament. Perhaps then someone would have had the guts to stand up to Ntimama and say, "What a lot of rot! Every word you've uttered is a lie. You know it and we know it. Now sit down and shut up." Ntimama had not, as some of the newspapers noted, produced any evidence to back up a single one of his allegations. And the East African representative for the World Bank, which has a policy against commenting on a country's internal political disputes, had nevertheless told reporters that KWS was managing the bank's funds properly and that the bank was satisfied with our performance.

In spite of the World Bank's comments and the lack of evidence, however, the government had now ordered a full inquiry based on Ntimama's charges. Katana Ngala agreed that this was the proper and necessary thing to do. It was as if I was in some kind of *Alice in Wonderland* world, in which all you had to do was utter something to make it so.

So, yes, I was angry and hurt when I went to see the president, and as usual, I came right to the point.

"Do you want me to resign, sir?" I asked.

"No, no, Richard. The government wants you to remain as head of KWS. But there are some irregularities that must be looked into."

"There *were* irregularities at the Wildlife Department when I took it over. You asked me to fix those. To clean it up. And I've done that. The only irregularity we have now is that we're deeply in debt because the Treasury won't release our funds."

President Moi frowned. He didn't know what irregularities were or were not involved at KWS, he continued. No one knew because I ran the organization without any government oversight. He wanted the investigation to proceed, and he wanted me to work more closely with KWS's board so that the government would know what KWS was doing. He also had heard some things about the kind of training KWS's rangers received and about KWS's intelligence department that, frankly, worried him. How did he know all this was being done for the good of Kenya?

We were clearly poles apart.

"I can't run KWS without your confidence in me and your full backing," I replied. "We agreed on that in this office when you first gave me the job. I don't believe I have your support anymore, and I certainly can no longer work with the minister of Tourism, who has publicly backed my attackers. I'm offering you my resignation."

President Moi protested again that he did not want it, but I saw no way to reconcile our positions. If he and the government no longer trusted me, as seemed to be the case, it was better to step down.

The next day I held a press conference in Nairobi's Serena Hotel. This was to be my first public response to the attacks, and the room was jammed with reporters from the Kenyan and international press. I wore my KWS uniform and walked on my new prostheses to the podium. Several of the reporters present had speculated in their articles that Ntimama's attacks and the investigation of KWS were designed to force me to resign. They were about to find out that they were right.

I had written a fairly lengthy statement. I pulled it out of a folder and began to read:

I have kept silent over the past few weeks because the priority issue here is one of national interest, not personal interest, and I did not want to take any action in my personal defense that would inhibit the ability of KWS to remain aside from, and above, what would hopefully be recognized as transparent politicking.

The overriding priority was, and is, that KWS should be able to continue its work and maintain its determined policy, principles, and targets. The implications of this policy to conservation, to the national economy through tourism, and to Kenya's international reputation, surely require no further elaboration here.

I speak now, with the knowledge of His Excellency the President, because the attacks on me . . . and KWS have been globally reported and are doing damage to the principles and national interests we represent.

Although many leaders and an extraordinary number of *wananchi* have given their views in support, clear and official *political support* . . . has not been there.

I then explained that I had met with the president the previous afternoon to discuss the attacks, particularly those coming from the minister of Tourism and Wildlife. The minister had ordered a "probe" of KWS, but I had yet to be told what this investigation would constitute.

When I asked the Minister . . . the response was, "It is none of your business." I am forced to ask, therefore, whether this is a probe or is it a smear? I have to question motive when an obvious effort to totally discredit KWS and its management is made for reasons that are not stated . . .

Many have asked why is this happening and why now? The ministers speak of arrogance, racism, and irregular management decisions. Let me address some of these . . .

It was true that there were "irregularities" at KWS, I said. Indeed, the very first was my appointment to the directorship by the president.

I was not asked if I wanted the job; I was not sacked from my other job; I was not asked to sign the Official Secrets Act, and yet, long before I became a Civil Servant or gazetted officer of the Service, I was put in charge of armed men across the country . . . We then destroyed a total of 18 tons of ivory and countless trophies including rhino horn. Although "irregular," it was certainly the best possible course of action . . . Under the rules of government, I believe it was irregular to turn me loose to raise money directly with foreign governments. To do what I did, I had many contacts with ministers and even heads of state in foreign countries. I had the explicit mandate to do so in spite of the technical irregularity of the action. We needed the funds urgently at a time when money from abroad was getting scarce. I was told to go to it and I did.

My "irregular" approach had raised $300 million dollars for Kenya's wildlife, I noted. Similarly, I pointed out that it was "irregular" for KWS to have semiautomatic weapons to deal with security problems in the parks. We had them because "it works and has proved to be a success."

Why, I demanded, were irregularities of this sort overlooked for five years; but when KWS paid "irregular" salaries (because they were higher than the Civil Service scale) to some of its managers, did it create a crisis?

I have been accused of arrogance. Is this because I have said no too many times to people who were asking for things that they should not have asked from a public corporation? Has my insistence that the wildlife-protected areas be protected from some greedy people been the reason for this charge? I suspect so . . . The attempts to "grab" the Ndere Island National Park in 1992 and the efforts by certain political figures to have 50,000 acres of Tsavo National Park degazetted were successfully resisted. Is my defense of the national heritage wrong? I am happy to say that I had the support of the President and he put a stop to these efforts.

My attackers, I told those gathered, had leveled other charges at me and KWS, both in the newspapers and in Parliament. I did not know if these were to be investigated during this "probe," I said, but I would address them nonetheless. One accuser claimed that KWS had given wildlife from National Parks to private, white ranchers. In fact, I noted, the opposite was true. A rancher had donated forty rhinos from his ranch to KWS for a breeding program.

> I would not dispute that there are some problems at KWS. But the corporation is only four years old and it has been expected to perform miracles. There are no major financial scandals . . . or scams that have defrauded the public of millions of pounds . . . It is unrealistic for me to work under a minister and permanent secretary who have so clearly demonstrated their lack of confidence in me personally . . . On the personal level, I have given the best years of my life to public service and I recently gave my legs too! I have no wish to give my life at this time, and the stress and pain of being vilified by senior politicians and others is more than I think is good for my health. Under these circumstances, I have today sent a letter to His Excellency the President offering my resignation, and until I hear his decision I am removing myself from the premises of KWS and going to my *shamba* [small farm].

I then excused myself and left.

I had already learned how to drive with my false legs (it was surprisingly easy; I simply treated them as if they were extensions of the brake and gasoline pedals) and was soon on my way out of Nairobi, heading toward the knobby green Ngong Hills and home.

My offer to resign was front-page news in all the Kenyan newspapers as well as big news overseas. Apparently, few thought I would take this step because suddenly everyone—from government officials to conservationists to Kenyan and foreign tour operators—was publicly lamenting my decision and calling on the government to find a way to make me reconsider. Representatives from Kenya's tourism industry held a press conference of their own, appealing to the president not to accept my resignation. Overseas, Britain's top seven wildlife and conservation organizations wrote a joint letter to the president asking him to retain me.

"The loss of Dr. Leakey would be real a real blow to the conservation world," a spokeswoman from the Environmental Investigation Agency told the press. "Bearing in mind Kenya's reputation as a leading light in the protection of such species as the rhino and elephant, we are appealing to President Moi to retain Dr. Leakey." And the Worldwide Fund for Nature issued a statement, saying that "we regard his [Dr. Leakey's] departure with considerable apprehension . . ."

A flood of letters supporting me swamped the local newspaper offices, too.

If I had felt slighted before submitting my resignation, I was now overwhelmed by this outpouring of support and goodwill, particularly from average citizens. It's easy when you're down and being publicly attacked, as I had been, to lose perspective. For a time it seemed that no one had recognized the changes and improvements we had brought to KWS: that only thirty elephants had been poached in all of 1993 (that many had been killed in the first month of 1989 alone); that KWS now received only 5 percent of its operating budget from our government, instead of 100 percent, as it had in 1989; that the corrupt staff was gone and our parks secure; and that Kenya, which had once been regarded as a conservation basketcase, now led the movement in Africa. We had done all this and more in four short years, a remarkable achievement for a once-beleaguered government service in a developing country. I might have led the effort, but its success was due to the hardworking men and women of KWS.

Not every letter writer or commentator praised me, of course. Intriguingly, among the conservationists, David Western, who had resented my appointment from day one, was the sole critic. His words could have come straight from the mouth of Ntimama. "Dr. Leakey's belief in the inevitability of fenced game parks," he told the *London Times*, "and in getting funding from overseas donors has meant that he has ignored the role local people can play in the conservation of wildlife. The only way it will survive is if they perceive wild animals as valuable resources to the community rather than as dangerous pests."

Neither KWS or I had ever ignored the role of the local people. I had met numerous times with county councils, villagers, and landowners as we experimented with methods to control the wildlife and sought ways for our neighbors to benefit from the wildlife and the parks. Various community projects were well underway, as were plans to share some of our revenues. Western's criticism, however, was fast becoming the accepted line to explain the attacks against me. Yet no one ever checked out whether the allegation that KWS ignored its neighbors was in fact accurate. It was an excellent example of how rumors come to be accepted as truth. All that was required was for people such as Ntimama and Western to repeat them over and over again.

My bigger complaint was with the "statistics" a *Times* reporter then used to support Western's statement. These came straight from a study Western published in 1989, although the reporter did not identify his source. (I put the word "statistics" in quotations because I tend to agree with the great American writer Mark Twain, who said, "There are lies, damned lies, and statistics." Western's "statistics" regarding Kenya's wildlife are a good example of what Mr. Twain meant.) "Only 5 per cent of wild animals live in parks run by KWS," the reporter wrote. "Another 15 per cent live in reserves, such as the Masai Mara, which are run by county councils. All the rest live on private land, mainly group ranches run as co-operatives by tribal elders."

To get these figures, it seemed to me, Western had mixed apples and oranges. It appeared that he was comparing a census study other researchers had made in 1978 of the wildlife and livestock living on Kenya's rangelands with his own estimated (and unpublished) count of wildlife living in parks and reserves in the late 1980s. There was a good ten-year gap between the two counts, yet he compared them as if they had been made at the same time. Further, it's well known that many species migrate out of the parks at certain times of the year. Western never refers to this most basic behavior of Kenya's wildlife. Nor do his references indicate whether these counts were made during the height of the outmigration or at some other time of year.

It was true that the Kenyan countryside once teemed with wildlife. When I moved to our home on the edge of the Rift Valley in 1987, eland (large antelope with long dewlaps and spiraling horns), leopards, buffalo, and gazelles roamed over our land and the surrounding hills. We even saw a small herd of elephants from time to time. By 1994, however, the elephants, eland, and buffalo were gone, the leopards were on their way out; and the gazelle had been reduced to a handful. The same was true throughout the country (outside the parks), and the reasons why were easy to find. Kenya's population had nearly doubled between 1978 and 1994. There had been a concurrent increase in agriculture, with people moving into areas such as where we lived, on land no one had farmed before. We had bought our acreage from a Maasai elder who wandered the hills with his cattle. It was wide-open then. He and other Maasai in the area had continued to sell parcels of land and soon we were surrounded by other farms—some large, some small, but nearly all of them fenced. Farms, and no doubt small-scale poaching, were finishing off our local wild animals. And this was happening all over Kenya. Besides bringing tourist dollars to Kenya, national parks were important for another reason: they were fast becoming the last safe haven for Kenya's wildlife.

Western's figures reflected what Kenya and most of East Africa had been, not what Kenya now was.

It would not have taken much effort to discover the errors in Western's percentages, yet they would be quoted unquestioningly many times over in the next few months and years, as if they'd been handed down by Moses himself.

Western, it seemed, was angling for a job.

For the next two months, I stayed out of the public eye and away from KWS. Joseph Kioko, my deputy director, was appointed acting director by the KWS Board of Directors, and he did what he could to keep things from falling apart. It was a thankless task, however, and I felt badly that he had to shoulder this burden.

The investigation was to be conducted by some government officials, all handpicked, so that they could be relied upon to refrain from reporting anything that was not consistent with the required "conclusions." All were given instructions directly from Minister Ngala. Their job was to find something I had authorized at KWS that broke the law. In other words, they were on a witch hunt and behaved like any other inquisition in other repressive countries: they called in staff members for long interrogation sessions, subjected them to repeated, sometimes meaningless questioning, and demanded every conceivable record going back to the beginning of my tenure.

I was questioned as well, but only for fifteen minutes, and was never called back. However, my closest staff was summoned into the Probe Committee's presence numerous times for what would be a grueling, demoralizing, and frightening experience. They had no idea whether the information they gave was going to be used against them. And when they gave answers that their interrogators did not like—however true those answers were—they were called back. Some were even advised that their responses were not the ones the government wanted to hear.

Such was the government's thanks for the long hours and hard work my staff had given to build up KWS. They'd made personal sacrifices, particularly in their pay, working for low government wages when they could have been in the private sector earning handsome salaries. They'd remained honest when many of the old employees were busy lining their pockets. They'd worked evenings, weekends, and holidays in times of crisis; and those in KWS's Security Department had often risked their lives. Now they were being treated like criminals. It angered me more than I can say.

I knew why the Probe Committee was hounding these people: because they could not find the evidence of the wrongdoing that they so desperately sought. Bashir handled many of their inquiries. I advised him and my personal assistant to open every file, every drawer to our inquisitors.

"Let them see everything and take what they want," I said. "We have nothing to hide."

The committee had certain topics in which it was most interested: KWS's hiring practices and the salaries it paid its staff; the expenditure of the World Bank funds; the relationship between KWS and the communities outside the parks; and possible abuses by the security unit. Supposedly, we—or more precisely, I—had broken the law or made bad management decisions in all these areas.

Once again, that old bugaboo of tribalism entered the picture. Why had we employed so many Kikuyu in "top" management positions? Why were no Kalenjin in Bashir's crack security unit? Why did my personal assistant receive a larger salary than mine? This was a curious "crime," I thought, and the reason for it was simple. I insisted on receiving the same pay as my top rangers, whose lives were on the line, until KWS became a self-supporting institution, capable of paying the wages all its employees deserved. My assistant, who ranked higher on the Civil Service pay scale than the rangers, thus received more money than I did.

There weren't a preponderance of Kikuyu managers either. But what had truly peeved the government investigators was KWS's practice of awarding every one of its managers a salary larger than the government normally paid. As I've explained, we had done that in order to attract top people from the private sector. And again, after our commercial projects began to flourish, we anticipated raising all the salaries at KWS. As for the idea that KWS did not regard the Kalenjin as "brave"—as the questioner demanded of Bashir—what can one say? There were numerous Kalenjin in various positions throughout KWS. The crack antipoaching unit they complained about was one made up largely of men from the northern desert tribes who could fight the Somalis. There weren't any men from the Kamba or Kisii tribes in that unit either. That did not make Kamba or Kisii men cowards. It just meant that KWS attempted to hire the right people for the right jobs.

The committee also insinuated that KWS had engaged in racial policies, that it had given the title of "honorary warden" to more white ranchers and businessmen than it had to black ones. In fact, these people held these very same titles when my predecessors, Perez Olindo and Daniel Sindiyo, ran the Wildlife Department. The honorary wardens owned some of the largest ranches in Kenya and had sizable populations of wildlife on their lands. As a result they often faced the same kind of trouble with poachers KWS did. Their affiliation first with the Wildlife Department—and then with KWS—allowed them to arrest these criminals and turn them over to us or to the police. This saved KWS and the police, which were always short-handed in those more remote regions where these ranchers lived, the trouble and expense of providing law enforcement outside the parks. It was a good policy, and I'm sure it saved Kenya's wildlife. Had there been more indigenous Kenyans with large land holdings and big wildlife populations, we would have gladly added them to the list.

The idea that any of these charges actually constituted crimes—particularly when compared with those committed by numerous individuals in the old Wildlife Department, which was not investigated by any probe committee—was laughable.

Far more serious was their investigation of KWS's Security Department. They demanded a list of all our firearms, and I was thankful that Bashir and his staff had kept meticulous records. On occasion we had added the firearms and ammunition of the poachers we arrested to our own stock, as we were always short of weaponry. Bashir had notified the police whenever we did this, and the two records jibed. Again, the committee pored over our files, looking for the smallest error, but failed to find a single problem.

They seemed to think that we had a far better arsenal than was in fact the case. I gathered they expected to find rocket launchers, machine guns, hand grenades—in short, the kind of weaponry that only Kenya's military is permitted. When I learned they had asked to see our "drone plane," a special robotic spy plane, my heart sank. Clearly, someone had fed them the same rumors that had been whispered about me to the president: I was building my own army and preparing to stage a coup.

Their belief that KWS had a spy plane stemmed from my effort to alert the government to the illegal camp of the Somali warlord at Lamu. Instead of being regarded as a patriotic move, it was seen as another example of "my" superior forces. The officer investigating this matter explained that they wanted the drone plane and the secret camera that had been used to take the pictures of the warlord's camp.

"But," the warden they were querying protested, "there was no spy plane or secret camera. I flew in a KWS Cessna. I opened the window of my plane, leaned out, and snapped the pictures with a standard 35-mm camera. Here's the camera." He handed them a small, battered, everyday-looking camera.

The officer looked baffled by the warden's reply. He asked again to be shown the drone plane.

"There isn't one. There never was. But you're free to continue to look for it," the warden said.

The committee also believed that KWS's computerized database, with its store of information on ivory traders and poachers, would contain evidence of a larger, nefarious plot. They mercilessly grilled the staff member who ran this department, in part because of her university records. Fifteen years before working for KWS, she had taken a course titled "Artificial Intelligence," which is, naturally, a field in computer science that involves designing "smart" computers. To our interrogators, however, the word "intelligence" suggested some covert, illegal activity. They were determined that the course was about spying and badgered her repeatedly to confess the truth until she had the bright idea of bringing in her college textbooks. The dull texts with their pages of equations and flowcharts put an end to their questioning.

The six-week-long ordeal ruined KWS. My staff's morale sank. The hearty spirit they had brought to their jobs evaporated. Every project was suspended while the investigators looked for evidence to substantiate the "irregularities" KWS had supposedly committed.

In mid-March 1994, shortly before the government released the Probe Committee's findings, President Moi issued a statement. He was not accepting my letter of resignation. He ordered me back to KWS.

I obeyed and returned the next morning to a round of applause and broad smiles at KWS headquarters. I warned my staff, however, that we had not yet seen the end of our problems.

"It's not over," I told my personal assistant, who had not stopped smiling since I entered my office. She wanted to believe that now that the government had carried out this little exercise it would leave us alone. But I had seen how the government had destroyed other people in its service and knew that something more was in store for us.

"You'll see," I said. "They don't want us to succeed."

Two weeks later, the president issued another directive. He had read the Probe Committee's findings, and based on them he ordered KWS to make two major changes. First, KWS would no longer be responsible for the security of the country's parks. The Commissioner of Police would take over the role of directing the antipoaching units and assuring our tourists' security. Second, based on studies of Kenya's wildlife that showed that 75 percent of the animals lived outside the parks, KWS was now to share 75 percent of its revenues with the communities outside the parks' boundaries. That left only 25 percent for running the parks. (He made no mention of David Western, but I knew he was the source of these faulty percentages.)

The president ordered other changes as well, but these were the most significant. In short order the government had reopened our parks to banditry and stopped the PAWS project, the policy that we had developed and the World Bank had approved and for which it had given us the $143 million loan. KWS was finished.

As soon as I read the president's order, I sat down and wrote my resignation.

I began by briefly discussing the events of the last few months and the allegations made against me and KWS and then concluded:

Sadly . . . I cannot see how I can perform my duties adequately as newly defined, as I am now convinced that I am not the person to carry out these new directives with any hope of success. The KWS dream of a self-financing, efficient, and effective, publicly owned, but independent conservation authority does not seem viable . . . Perhaps the original ideas were right but the timing wrong. Posterity will decide. I, together with many others in Kenya and abroad, will have to wait and see how the Kenya Wildlife Service fares in the future. I wish it well. I have submitted my resignation to His Excellency the President with immediate effect.

I read my resignation to a press conference on March 23, 1994. The room was quiet, aside from the clicking of cameras. A few reporters called out questions, but I waved them off. I would have plenty of time for them later.

I then drove back to headquarters, where KWS's brand-new office building stood, a shiny new monument to all our dreams. It was about a week away from being finished. I had designed it and had looked forward to moving in. Now someone else would sit in my office.

My staff had already heard the news. The corridors were packed with people. As I entered, they begged me to tell them that they had heard wrong, that I wasn't leaving.

"No, it's true, I'm afraid. I have resigned."

Several people, including some of my hardened, top wardens, broke down at this news. I found myself in the awkward position of having to console them.

"KWS will continue," I said. "You are all still here, and you have much to do. Keep up the good work." I know how hollow my words most have sounded.

I had already removed the most important files from my office and, as I prefer to work in a Spartan setting, little remained for me to gather up. I quickly packed my briefcase. Then I called the staff and gave a short speech, emphasizing how much I had enjoyed working with them all, and how thankful I was for all that they had done for KWS and for Kenya.

It was over. I drove out of the parking lot to the peacefulness of my home.

ment, and neglect of the communities around the parks. In an effort to prove my many misdeeds, Ngala released the Probe Committee's report to the government-supported newspaper, the *Kenya Times*, which published sections of it over the course of a week. The report was not given to the other newspapers largely free of government censorship, and consequently they had to rely on what was printed in the *Times*. Not every reporter can be led by the nose, however, and though the other papers had no direct access to the report, they tried to give their readers a better assessment of what it contained and meant. One enterprising fellow at the weekly magazine, *The Economic Review*, even managed to obtain a copy and after summarizing its contents noted that it read "very much like the 'smear' job Leakey had . . . feared."

The *Kenya Times* reports did depress me, although I tried to keep the comments they printed in perspective.

What a paradox, I wrote in my diary after several government spokesmen accused me of racism—and then used several racist epithets against me. *I am accused of racism and this then brings out the real racists. At present I feel cheated and almost ashamed of being Kenyan and of having promoted this country so strongly* [overseas]. *It is extraordinary to be treated as a criminal or worse after having done all I* [have] *done.*

Despite the government's efforts, not every reader of the *Kenya Times* was persuaded that I had done anything wrong. Many wrote in to object to the attacks against me and to thank me for building a government institution like KWS, as well as for helping to save Kenya's wildlife. Unfortunately, at that time, citizens who spoke out against the government's policies often found themselves at risk of getting arrested or harassed. For them to put themselves at danger on my behalf meant more to me than I can say. Their comments reassured me that there were Kenyans who wanted a responsible, honest government, and who were willing to stand up and say so. Others, of course, took a more opportunistic view and used my downfall to further themselves. My brother Philip was among them. He told the press that my criticism of the government in my resignation letter amounted to "treason" and defended those who were attacking me. Philip is a lifelong member of the government KANU Party, and I can only think that he said such things in part to distance himself from me and to curry favor with party leaders. Needless to say, he and I spoke very little during this time.

I had far more regard for Dominic Odipo, an editorial writer for the *Standard* who wrote a column in which he called my departure "a disaster" and the charges against me "preposterous." He noted that none of my accusers had charged me with having "misappropriated . . . one shilling out of the millions he [Dr. Leakey] raised . . . The departure of Dr. Leakey will remind us that somewhere in the innards of our public service there are still some honourable men who cannot be bent by the lure of financial reward or other material benefits . . . Shame on all those who through narrow-minded self-interest have driven away perhaps this country's most upright public servant."

Shortly after my resignation, some reporters asked me whether I intended to leave Kenya. I laughed. "No. I'm not leaving Kenya, dead or alive." I loved my country far too much to ever contemplate leaving. Although I didn't immediately see a way to bring about the kind of reforms at the national level that we'd put in place at KWS, I still had faith that it could happen. Kenya could have a government free of corruption, one that worked for the good of the people. I knew what we'd achieved at KWS, and reading Odipo's column reassured me that we'd been on the right track. Our work had not gone unnoticed.

I would weather the attacks. I was far more worried about the fate of KWS, its hard-working employees, and Kenya's wildlife. I had thrown myself into my job, into rebuilding that department, and I feared that all we had done over the previous four years would quickly be undone. I'm an optimist by nature, and I did everything I could to support David Western as the new director. I telephoned him, congratulated him on his appointment, and offered to meet with him to discuss the transition. I told the press that the president could not have picked a better man. I even wrote that in my diary. But I also wrote that I worried that Western wouldn't have the necessary backbone to stand up to politicians anxious to get their hands on KWS's money or to grab some of the parks' lands.

Although a man of personal integrity, Western had no experience managing a large government organization or public institutions—for which management experience would be critical. He was stepping into a position in which three thousand people reported to him, and the plots—both internal and external—to pilfer KWS's coffers were as plentiful as those in a James Bond movie. From the outset he promised to do more for the communities around the parks, to have a less confrontational style with the government than I supposedly had, and not to run KWS as if it was "his." According to the Probe Committee, I had committed the grievous sin of directing KWS as if it belonged to me personally. I never took this as a criticism. Any CEO worth his (or her) salt runs his company as if it is the sole purpose of his existence and therefore worries about all levels of its operations. A good leader needs to know the entire staff and their functions and to be able to communicate as easily with the lower ranks as with the directors. In any organization employing armed men who would kill and be killed as part of their job, strong bonds were essential. I could see that Western had a long way to go, and I confess I felt uncertain of his chances.

I didn't want to see KWS fail. I had far too much at stake there and many good friends who continued to work for it. Several, such as Bashir, Joyce, Lynnette Anyonge (my personal assistant), and Jim Else had initially announced that they would resign as a show of support for me. I advised them against it. Their action, while admirable and moving, would not have helped either KWS or themselves. They would need time to find other jobs, and Western would need their support and knowledge about how KWS worked. I hoped he would avail himself of it.

Sadly, I have been told that he did not. He brought his own set of people into the organization, and he and they had their own ideas about running it, although understandable this did not excuse him for the rudeness he displayed toward some people who had worked for me, particularly Lynnette. That she used her position to find a new one with the U.S. AID project attached to KWS speaks volumes about her capabilities and dedication to the department.

The hardest thing for me was knowing that by leaving KWS, I was condemning all the carefully thought-through plans we had made. The so-called PAWS project was a compendium of integrated ideas that would have helped develop wildlife management throughout Kenya. A great deal of thought and time had been devoted to how best to use the World Bank and other donor funds to create a self-sustaining conservation agency that would focus its main effort on the protected areas. New buildings, new roads, new bridges, staff housing, training, and equipment—all these were to be implemented over time. The core of this idea was to enhance the national parks so that KWS could increase its revenue base and therefore be better able to provide long-term conservation services in other areas of Kenya. This had been "my" dream, and with my departure, the new director would develop his own vision for KWS. Once it was clear that Western would make radical changes to the PAWS policies, the funding from international donors, I was convinced, should have been frozen. If you borrow money from a bank to build a home and instead buy an airplane, the bank will call in its money. The many ideas that Western had for wildlife conservation may indeed have been fine, but they were very different from the plans and strategy I had laid out and received funds for.

I talked to the World Bank's East African representative, Agi Kiss, about this and other problems. It seemed to me that now was the time to stop the money before it caused undue harm. "We're in a situation that is exactly like the one I criticized the bank for at the beginning of my tenure," I told Kiss. "And as I said then, large sums of money have large effects. They can be bad or good; but if there is no plan, if the spending is not done in a responsible way, the effects will be bad. They won't be neutral. They will cause real harm."

I reminded her of the problems the World Bank's money had caused in the Masai Mara in the 1970s, the housing and water projects that had been started and left unfinished, causing environmental damage and an unsightly mess. And all because the bank had given the government money but had not held the government responsible for how it was spent. Was the bank going to repeat its error? I asked. This time, of course, the sum was far higher and that meant any errors would be that much larger.

Kiss argued that it was not the bank's position to interfere in a government's internal policies. I argued right back that by giving the $130 million it was already interfering.

The Kenyan government had broken the contract with the World Bank in other ways. As part of the agreement, the government was committed to repairing the roads that led to the national parks. Most of them were still in dreadful condition. They turned a trip to our parks into something of an endurance test and certainly left a bad impression on our visitors. In the past this wasn't a problem, for if tourists wanted to see big game in Africa they had little choice but to travel to East Africa. However, in the post-apartheid era, tourists could visit South Africa just as easily. There they would find the highways smoothly paved. Improving our highways had been another part of the overall PAWS plan to help KWS turn a profit, yet the government had done nothing to repair a single road. That was another reason to stop or at least postpone the funding.

"The bank can force the government's hands," I told Kiss. "If it doesn't improve the roads by a certain date, then withhold the money. The bank should hold the government accountable."

After all, I added, the bank had already done this. Only the year before, when the government authorized the excision of 55,000 square acres in Tsavo, the bank had made it clear that were the acreage not restored to the park, the money would not be forthcoming. The bank was in the strong position here, I said. It should insist that the government abide by the PAWS plan and stop the money if it didn't.

To her credit, Kiss wrote a report, saying that the bank should reconsider funding KWS, as the original project was no longer being followed and the government had reneged on its agreement. Unfortunately, her superiors overruled her. The bank decided not to stop its aid. Doing so would have meant someone would have to acknowledge that the project was a failure. Such an "admission" could ruin someone's career. Far be it from me to tell the bank how to reward its employees, but I would rather have employees who present honest assessments, as Kiss had done, than those only interested in appearances. It's because of these sorts of internal, career-building decisions that so many of the World Bank's projects have failed and why the bank is regarded as contributing to rather than solving the problems of developing countries.

The World Bank's decision was bad news indeed for KWS. How ironic it all was that I had negotiated an agreement with the bank that would force the government to act responsibly, and now the bank had decided to ignore the contract. It was behaving as irresponsibly as my own government. The money would not be stopped, and no one would be held accountable for how it would be spent.

I knew then that KWS was doomed, and I feared that corruption at lower levels and poaching could well plague it again. The hardest part was being relegated to the sidelines. There was nothing I could do but watch, or so I initially thought.

Once I had come to terms with the situation and my apparent inability to do anything more than irritate Western and his staff, I decided to try my hand at being a consultant. I opened an office in town and hired a small staff. Slowly I began to feel that I was not "on the shelf" for the rest of my life, and yet I also found that I really had no heart for giving other people advice. As a result, my efforts to make a living as a consultant were generally a complete failure. I did, however, join the efforts of some friends to start a new opposition political party.

I had remained in touch with President Moi after leaving KWS, and though we were not in regular communication, I could and did call him on the phone about a number of issues. In one instance, I arranged to meet him privately. I wanted to brief him on some information that I had come across, information that, though incomplete, indicated that some disgruntled people were planning to remove President Moi from power by unconstitutional means. We reviewed what I knew over an early morning cup of tea. He had information of his own that seemed to corroborate what I had. In spite of our differences over KWS, we reestablished a sense of trust, even warmth, between us. The president must have acted quickly, for the threat of which we had spoken was soon dealt with.

Being on the outside led me to realize how many people were fed up with the government and its corrupt practices. During the last few years, since the country's move toward democracy and multiparties, they had become increasingly outspoken. One was a lawyer and member of Parliament named Paul Muite. He was on the attack in Parliament, hounding government officials engaged in one scandal or another, usually involving stealing large sums from taxpayers. Another was Robert Shaw, a businessman who wrote a weekly column about economics for the *Nation*. He used his column as a soap box to investigate and excoriate many of the same individuals, and to divulge the details of their activities. They had formed a small group of like-minded people who met occasionally to discuss reforms for Kenya. Of course, Muite and Shaw were watched closely by the government, which soon let it be known that it was going to ban their group. I had spoken to both men occasionally in the past, and one day Shaw called to suggest that the three of us meet for breakfast.

We had a leisurely meeting and talked about the many issues facing Kenya. We were all fathers, and our conversation often came back to this common ground: we wanted a safe Kenya, one that would let our children succeed and live a good life; a Kenya free of police brutality and repression, where ideas could be exchanged without fear, officials weren't always opening their hands to accept bribes, and the cost of everyday goods, such as medicine, was affordable for our poor. Muite and Shaw invited me to join their group. They thought that people respected me, and that if I spoke out on these issues the government was more likely to listen.

"I doubt that," I said, chuckling. "I don't think the government is listening to anything I say at the moment. I'm on their black list."

Besides, I added, speaking out on behalf of a small group of people would not accomplish very much.

"You know the government's about to ban your group. Why don't you take the next step and form a political party?" I asked.

Both men laughed at this. The same idea had been in the back of their minds, but they weren't sure that I would be interested.

"Well, I *am* interested. Very interested. I think we could make a difference."

In the 1992 election—Kenya's first with multiple political parties—the ruling KANU Party had won, as I've noted, only 30 percent of the vote. I believed that if we formed a party whose primary goal was to keep all the opposition parties united, we might very well defeat KANU in the 1997 elections. We had three years to work toward this goal, time enough to engineer a possible upset.

Muite and Shaw agreed, and a few days later, on June 20, 1994, I joined with their colleagues to announce a new political party: Safina, a Kiswahili word meaning "ark." We chose the name as a sign of our desire to bring all Kenyans from all parties on board. Using a Kiswahili word also had a special significance. While it is the official language of Kenya, Kiswahili was originally a language of the coastal peoples, many of whom are practicing Muslims. The government had often been hostile to these citizens, and of course they, in turn, felt as if they weren't really a part of the country. Safina would invite them—and Kenyans of all colors and faiths—to be part of the change that we hoped to bring to our country.

The government was neither pleased nor amused by our announcement. The president and his cabinet seemed to think that I had joined this party simply to outrage or embarrass them and unleashed a barrage of attacks. These made the ones I had suffered while at KWS seem like gentle jibes. I was now a "racist, traitor, foreigner, colonial, and atheist" who embraced radical terrorists. The charges were so outlandish that one newspaper began using the term "leakeyed" for "vilified." Once again, numerous citizens wrote letters to the newspapers to defend me. And once again, others used the moment to feather their own caps. Many white citizens were particularly worried that my prominent political stance would provide a reason for the government to deprive them of their land or businesses, and several telephoned me to beg me to disband Safina. I had little patience with their worries. If they would join in the efforts to change the government, I countered, perhaps they wouldn't have to live in fear of it. I had even less patience with these people after my brother Philip led a group of eighty-seven white Kenyans (a group that later came to be called, derisively, "Club 88") to the State House to pledge their allegiance to the president and government.

The government's attacks were designed to take me down a notch in the public eye. Ironically, they seemed to have the opposite effect. People who had never noticed me before now stopped me on the street to tell me how proud they were of me and of all I had done and was trying to do for Kenya. As I drove home at night, others shouted, cheered, and waved the little V for victory sign we had adopted at Safina. Many of these people would have joined Safina if they could have. The government, however, would not allow us to register as a legitimate political party. Incredibly, although Kenya was now a multiparty state, one party—the ruling party—continued to dictate which parties could be registered and which could not. And until Safina was legally registered, we could not hold political rallies or campaigns. We could not even have meetings of more than nine people.

These were dangerous times, as I learned on one especially memorable occasion. I had gone to Nakuru with several of my political colleagues, and while waiting outside the local courthouse was set upon by a mob of hired thugs with whips and clubs. I struggled back to my car, having received a good number of blows, and managed to drive off, though all the windows and the windshield were smashed. I was lucky to have gotten away with my life. That there was official involvement in this thuggery was later established in court. The whole event made me reflect on how deeply I really wanted to be a politician.

Several times after I joined Safina, reporters and others asked me whether I planned to run for president. Nothing was further from my mind. I was interested in helping get someone who represented all of the opposition parties into the highest office, and I hoped that I could act as an adviser to that person. We needed to reform Kenya's constitution, to eliminate the section that gave the president and the ruling party inordinate power. I wanted to be part of the team that would bring about that reform, and I still wanted to tackle the massive problem of straightening out the Civil Service. I didn't need to be president to accomplish these tasks.

Nonetheless, none of the name calling or physical attacks deterred me or my fellow Safina members. The government continued to prevent us from registering, relenting only after being pressured by influential Kenyans and foreign diplomats. We became an official party eleven days before the official closing date for naming candidates. Two short months later, in December 1997, the election was held. We came close—within inches, I think—of achieving our primary goal of holding all the opposition parties together. Sadly, the leaders of these parties were again more suspicious of each other than of KANU, and at the last minute our carefully crafted coalition fell apart. KANU and President Moi were again reelected by a slim margin. But the opposition parties held their own, keeping most of their seats in Parliament. Safina managed to win five parliamentary seats, which pleased us enormously. I myself had not contested any seat, but I was nominated anyway and ended up becoming a member of Parliament—an unexpected role I decided to accept and use, at least for a time.

After I lost my legs, I made a vow that someday I would find a way to help other disabled Kenyans. I had not realized until I was in a wheelchair just how difficult life can be for the disabled, particularly in a developing country in which there are no wheelchair ramps or any amenities to assist them. I was a fortunate legless man. Through friends' donations I was able to afford a pair of expensive, high-tech artificial legs. This was not the case of the average disabled Kenyan, who is confined to a wheelchair or forced to make do with crutches. To make a point of how difficult such a life can be, I had my staff wheel me into Parliament on the day I took my oath of office. Because of the numerous obstacles, they had to practically carry me and my chair into Parliament.

I created a huge scene, which was just what I wanted. For one of the first times in Kenya's history, the plight of the disabled made the front page of our newspapers. I spoke regularly in Parliament on the subject, insisting that more should be done to help provide our handicapped citizens with jobs and support.

I saw President Moi briefly that day, too. We had not seen each other since discussing the Civil Service issue four years earlier. From my wheelchair, I caught his eye and said, "Hello, Mr. President."

I can't say that he looked happy to see me. After all, I had tried to bring about the end of his rule. The president was as gracious as ever, however, and returned my greeting—although it was the iciest "hello" I had ever received from him.

Kenya's Parliament is modeled on the British system. Members are recognized by a speaker, who controls the proceedings. The Parliament I was inaugurated into was designed to do little more than rubber-stamp the policies of the State House. As Kenya had been a one-party state for so many years, the Parliament had essentially become a forum for debating government decisions and had no real authority to influence government by bringing forward new legislation. Many of these debates centered on reforming the Constitution and on enacting a bill that would give Parliament more power to affect national policy and development. I enjoyed those debates and working on this bill. We could also question the ministers about their decisions and about how they were running the government. We all knew that they weren't telling us the truth. There was little we could do about it, other than jeer and heckle—and that I found frustrating.

Still, my position as a member of Parliament gave me a platform for working for Kenya, something I had sorely missed doing. I used it not only to argue for reform and better services for the disabled, but to improve Kenya's commitment to science and science education, and to encourage foreign investment and industry. And I used it to meet with and debate some of my former antagonists, such as William Ntimama. Ultimately, I used my position to renew my contacts with President Moi.

❖ ❖ ❖

I knew from my previous dealing with David Western that he would have entirely different approaches to mine, but the future of Kenya's wildlife, and in particular the fate of KWS, remained a major distraction to me. I was very concerned that poaching appeared to be on the rise, and, even more worrisome, that KWS was clearly facing serious financial strains. Without funds, antipoaching policies would be ineffective, and before long the evidence was there for all to see. Western gave greater priority to spending money on projects outside of the national parks; the idea was to create buffer zones for wildlife and to encourage conservation among pastoral communities. As a part of the fiftieth anniversary celebration of Kenya's national parks, Western promoted a "Parks Beyond Parks," a catchy way of describing the new policy. While I agreed that friendly relations with communities near the protected areas were and are essential, I also felt that the full implication of "Parks Beyond Parks" was to give over the parks themselves to communities and that such a move would be disastrous. These communities were experiencing enormous poverty. This debate continues to rage. There remains a clear divide between those who favor strict preservation of our national parks and those who believe that a national park will never survive unless local peoples can exploit its resources through consumptive utilization of animals (for meat and trophies).

There was also evidence that KWS was building up a huge financial debt. During the years after I had left, published accounts showed that expenditures had far exceeded revenues. The dwindling resources meant cutting back on the air patrol's aircraft and equipment for field ranger units, both so essential to preventing poaching. The World Bank PAWS project had raised expectations among the KWS staff; and when it became clear that new roads were being allowed to deteriorate and projects were being left uncompleted, staff morale sank even further.

By late 1997, I heard a growing number of complaints from wardens and other members of the KWS staff. Most of them were actually frightened to contact me, as Western had forbade them to do so. Several told me that he had announced he would fire anyone who came to see me. Even without their input, it was clear that the department had fallen on hard times. A series of investigative articles in the weekly newspaper the *People* reported on the mess KWS had become. Most of the World Bank and donor money had been misspent, the reporters wrote, and KWS was now bankrupt, even though its director continued to draw one of the largest government salaries in the entire country. Furthermore, because the previous loan had been so badly managed, no additional aid would be coming. *At least*, I thought to myself as I read this, *the bank has come to its senses.* But the damage had been done. The entire PAWS project had been tossed aside, and the effort to make KWS a self-sustaining business had come to one thing: bankruptcy.

A few days later, the telephone rang. It was my old friend and mentor, Charles Njonjo. Could we meet for lunch? he asked. I always have time for Charles and happily agreed. We would dine at his home, where we could be assured of privacy.

Over lunch Charles divulged that the president had asked him to become the new chairman of KWS's board of directors. This was excellent news. It meant that President Moi was also concerned about the future of KWS. It also meant that Charles's public service career was about to be rehabilitated. On an even higher level, his reinstatement into government would ease tension between the Kikuyu and Kalenjin tribe. Charles was one of the elder Kikuyu statesmen, and many of his fellows had been angry at the way he had been treated. I thought the president's choice was brilliant.

Charles was pleased, too. He was a great lover of wildlife and as unhappy as anyone to see the disarray at KWS. We talked at length over lunch about what had gone wrong and how it could best be sorted out. For the first time since leaving KWS, I slept easily. At last, the parks and elephants had a new defender.

Over the next few weeks other changes came about, largely due to Charles's engineering. He arranged for me to meet quietly and discreetly with President Moi. I do not want to elaborate on the details of this meeting. Suffice it to say that I apologized for my rude reply to his offer to pray for me following my accident, and that we were able to patch up our other problems and misunderstandings. A few days later, again through Charles, the president asked if I would reassume the office of KWS director. I was faced with a difficult choice. My earlier experience at KWS and my frustration at what had happened during the subsequent five years weighed heavily. I thought it over for a day or two, then said yes.

I would have to leave my seat in Parliament—one cannot be both the head of a government agency and an MP—but I made it known that I was not resigning from my membership in an opposition party. A person should be able to belong to any party and yet serve their government, I told reporters who asked me how this was possible. I didn't find it difficult to leave Parliament behind. We had just enacted the bill giving MPs more legislative powers, and the constitutional reform process was well underway. I was ready for something new. Even if it meant going back to sort out a mess.

Meave was a bit incredulous that I would step into the "lion's den again," as she put it, although after we talked she was fully supportive. Like all of us who love Kenya's parks and wildlife, she was unhappy to see them in such a state of collapse and bravely willing to once again let her husband tackle the problem.

I returned to KWS in May 1998. It was one of my proudest moments. The entire headquarters staff turned out to greet me. They stood on the balconies, staircases, and lawn, and applauded as I stepped out of my Land Rover. I waved a hello and then told them in Kiswahili how glad I was to be back.

"You should know," I announced, "that I have not eaten *ugali* to get here." That's a Kiswahili phrase which means that you've accepted a bribe. And of course everyone laughed at this colloquialism.

"We have work to do, and I'm here to help do it. We have the parks and animals and elephants—and Kenya—to work for. Let's join together and get the job done."

I turned and walked into the new building I had designed and built four years ago, and took my seat in the director's office.

❖ ❖ ❖

I remained as director of KWS for one year. The department was bur-
dened with numerous problems, including a huge deficit. Within that
one year we put it back on track and ended with a surplus. I'll never
know whether PAWS would have succeeded or not. It is impossible to
turn back the clock. But I do believe that had there been proper fiscal
management after I left in 1994, and had the PAWS project been ad-
hered to, KWS would have become a successful government enterprise.

David Western had chosen to emphasize projects outside of the national parks. Most of these projects turned out to involve little more
than handing out sums of money to the local councils, ignoring the
larger issue of the problems between the parks and communities; and
when the money stopped, the problems remained.

I chose to put KWS back on a "parks first" footing. It may not be
the most popular approach in conservation circles today; however, I
continue to maintain that national parks serve a fundamental and necessary purpose. Kenya created its first national park more than fifty years
ago for a specific reason: to save and protect its wildlife. It was a wise
and sensible solution to the problem of losing its flora and fauna. I don't
think anyone has come up with a better solution. National parks—
whether here, or in India, or in the United States—are still the best way
we know of to protect species and to save them from extinction.

By the end of my first year back at KWS I had become quite involved
in other areas of Kenya's national life. President Moi invited me to help
put together an initiative that would help restore Kenya's economy. This
led to renewed contacts with donor countries and with organizations
such as the World Bank. By the middle of June 1999, I agreed to accept
a new task. I would head an informal "reform team," and to do so I
would take up the position of permanent secretary to the president,
secretary to the cabinet, and head of Kenya's Public Service. This of
course meant stepping down as director of KWS, which I did on July
23, 1999. I was replaced by Mr. Nehemiah Rotich.

I led the so-called "Reform Team" for a period of twenty-one months, stepping down at the end of March 2001. My term as one of the very senior officials in the government of Kenya was certainly challenging and it has left me with a very different appreciation of the difficulties that face Africa's nations. The conservation of wildlife remains important within my own priorities but there are enormously complex socioeconomic and political obstacles to be overcome. At the end of the day, transparency in public affairs and the delivery of measurable results in government programs is crucial. In many respects, the story told in this book is not very different from a good many others as yet untold. This is neither the time nor place but a strong government with adequate resources offers the best chance for elephants and other wildlife inside as well as outside the parks. How well we succeed will be a different story; perhaps it will be a different book.

The elephants and their families—mothers, aunts, and playful babies—seem far away now. They are not, however, forgotten. Every step my colleagues and I take to help Kenya become more democratic and prosperous also helps save the elephants. Responsible government—government that listens to and respects the needs of the people—offers the only way for our elephants, our wildlife, our parks, and our country to endure.

INDEX